Disgust in Early Modern English Literature

What is the role of disgust or revulsion in early modern English literature? How did early modern English subjects experience revulsion and how did writers represent it in poetry, plays, and prose? What does it mean when literature instructs, delights, and disgusts? This collection of essays looks at the treatment of disgust in texts by Spenser, Shakespeare, Donne, Jonson, Herrick, and others to demonstrate how disgust, perhaps more than other affects, gives us a more complex understanding of early modern culture.

Dealing with descriptions of coagulated eye drainage, stinky leeks, and blood-filled fleas, among other sensational things, the essays focus on three kinds of disgusting encounters: sexual, cultural, and textual. Early modern English writers used disgust to explore sexual mores, describe encounters with foreign cultures, and manipulate their readers' responses. The essays in this collection show how writers deployed disgust to draw, and sometimes to upset, the boundaries that had previously defined acceptable and unacceptable behaviors, people, and literatures. Together they present the compelling argument that a critical understanding of early modern cultural perspectives requires careful attention to disgust.

Natalie K. Eschenbaum is Associate Professor and Chair of English at the University of Wisconsin-La Crosse, USA.

Barbara Correll is Associate Professor of English at Cornell University, USA.

Disgust in Early Modern English Literature

Edited by Natalie K. Eschenbaum
and Barbara Correll

Routledge
Taylor & Francis Group

LONDON AND NEW YORK

First published 2016
by Routledge
2 Park Square, Milton Park, Abingdon, Oxon OX14 4RN

and by Routledge
711 Third Avenue, New York, NY 10017

Routledge is an imprint of the Taylor & Francis Group, an informa business

British Library Cataloguing in Publication Data
A catalogue record for this book is available from the British Library

Library of Congress Cataloging-in-Publication Data
A catalog record for this book has been requested

ISBN: 9781472440044 (hbk)
ISBN: 9781315577579 (ebk)

Typeset in Times New Roman
by Apex CoVantage, LLC

Contents

vi *Contents*

Figures

Contributors

Georgia E. Brown is author of *Redefining Elizabethan Literature* (Cambridge University Press, 2004), which focuses on aesthetics and shame in late sixteenth-century English poetry. She edited the volume on Thomas Nashe for The University Wits Series (Ashgate, 2011) and has published articles on Queen Elizabeth I, Marlowe, Spenser, Shakespeare, Renaissance embroidery, early modern Ottoman culture and collage, as well as on disgust in John Marston's drama.

Barbara Correll is Associate Professor of English at Cornell University. She is the author of *The End of Conduct: Grobianus and the Renaissance Text of the Subject* (Cornell University Press, 1996) and has published essays on Erasmus, Donne, Shakespeare, Webster, and film. She is currently completing a book on early modern amatory and economic discourses, *Chiasmatics: Love, Money, and Economies in Shakespeare and Donne.*

Natalie K. Eschenbaum is Associate Professor and Chair of English at the University of Wisconsin-La Crosse. Her essay "Robert Herrick and the Five (or Six) Senses" was published in *The Senses in Early Modern England (1558– 1642): Representations, Configurations, Experiences*, edited by Simon Smith, Jacqueline Watson, and Amy Kenny (Manchester University Press, 2015). She has also published on Herrick in *Notes & Queries*.

Galena Hashhozheva holds a postdoctoral fellowship and teaches Renaissance literature in the English Department at Ludwig-Maximilians-Universität, Munich. She has recently published on "The Mousetrap: Hamlet's Courtly Spectacle and Its Jurisdictions" in *Zeitsprünge* (Summer 2013), on "The Christian Defense against Classical Skepticism in Spenser's Legend of Holiness" in *English Literary Renaissance* (May 2014), and on "Starving against Gold: Spenser's Mammon Canto in *Timon of Athens*" in the online journal of the German Shakespeare Society (2014).

Colleen E. Kennedy holds a PhD in English from the Ohio State University and is a Visiting Assistant Professor at Shippensburg University. Her essay "'Do

You Smell a Fault?' Deodorizing King Lear" appears in *Appositions* (2010) and "Performing and Perfuming on the Early Modern Stage: A Study of William Lower's *The Phaenix in Her Flames*" in *Early English Studies* (2011). She is a regular contributor to *The Recipes Project*, the Theatrical Review editor at *Early Modern Studies Journal*, and erstwhile editor at *The Shakespeare Standard*.

Emily L. King is Assistant Professor of English at Louisiana State University, Baton Rouge. Her latest work includes an article on regenerative flesh in the early modern imaginary for *Postmedieval* (2013) and a chapter on eroticized violence, gender, and spectatorship in *Titus Andronicus* in *Titus Out of Joint*, edited by Liberty Stanavage and Paxton Hehmeyer (Cambridge Scholars Publishing, 2012). Her current book project, "Civil Vengeance: Rethinking the Literature of Revenge in Early Modern England," theorizes anew the manner in which retaliation informs identify formation, interpersonal relationships, and the construction of the social body.

Laura Kolb is Assistant Professor of English at Baruch College, the City University of New York. She is currently at work on a book exploring the role of rhetoric and performance in early modern economic life. Her work has been published in *The Sidney Journal*, *The Shakespeare Newsletter*, and *The Forum for Modern Language Studies*.

Marcela Kostihová is Associate Dean and Professor of English at Hamline University. She has researched changing structures of identity formation in Central Eastern Europe represented in literature, theater, and film. She is the author of *Shakespeare in Transition: Political Appropriations in the Post-communist Czech Republic* (Palgrave Macmillan, 2010). Her second book is a textbook teaching teens to apply critical theory to the works of Stephenie Meyer.

Dan Mills has a PhD in English from Georgia State University where he wrote his dissertation on early modern utopian literature. His other research interests include critical theory, appropriations of Shakespeare, and print culture. He has published articles in *Pedagogy*, *Cahiers Élisabéthains*, and *In-Between: Essays and Studies in Literary Criticism*, and has articles in edited collections on critical theory and early modern literature and Western encounters with the East.

Ineke Murakami is Associate Professor of English at the State University of New York, Albany. She is the author of *Moral Play and Counterpublics: Transformations in Moral Drama 1465–1599* (Routledge, 2011) and has published in *Studies in English Literature*, *Religion & Literature*, and the *Journal for Early Modern Cultural Studies*. Her current monograph explores the ways scripted and unscripted performances from court to street constitute, test, and reconfigure the contours of political community in seventeenth-century England.

Gitanjali Shahani is Associate Professor of English at San Francisco State University. Her edited volume *Emissaries in the Early Modern World: Mediation, Transmission, Traffic, 1550–1700* (with Brinda Charry) was published by Ashgate in 2009. She has published essays on the early modern East India trade, on women's writing from the early modern archive, and on Shakespeare in Hindi cinema. She is currently editing a volume on food and literature for Cambridge University Press and completing a book manuscript on the early modern spice trade.

Acknowledgments

The idea for this book was born during some excited chatter following a Renaissance Society of America panel on disgust in 2012. Our first thanks go to the audience members whose interest encouraged us to continue this work, and to the panelists who became contributors and stuck with the project over the years. We also thank those who gave the authors of the "Sexual Encounters" chapters feedback at a special session of the Modern Language Association in 2014. In addition, the extensive comments we received from three anonymous press readers helped to make this a more cohesive and an all-around smarter collection. The contributors have delighted us with their varied readings of disgust, and we are grateful for the opportunity to work with them.

We received financial support from the University of Wisconsin-La Crosse College of Liberal Arts Dean's Office, and from Cornell University's Department of English. Thanks also to Sara Hilliger (University of Wisconsin-La Crosse) for her research assistance. And thanks to Jonathan Reinhardt (Cornell University) for his careful copyediting and indexing work.

Natalie K. Eschenbaum also would like to thank her family (Ted, Sylvia, and Zenon) for being an eager audience for disgusting discussions (admittedly, the two preschoolers were an easy sell).

Introduction

Natalie K. Eschenbaum and Barbara Correll

The Aversive Affect

The word "disgust" enters the English language from the French in the late six-teenth and early seventeenth centuries. Yet, early modern English literature offers numerous examples of what we would now call the disgusting, and it includes descriptive terms – loathsome, loathly, qualmish, beastly, vile – as a lexicon that seems to anticipate the introduction of the word "disgust." Early modern writers' relationships to disgust – particularly the canonical Shakespeare's – are complex, under-scrutinized in early modern scholarship, and, as this collection will show, worthy of close critical attention. In *The Anatomy of Disgust*, William Ian Miller notes that "Shakespeare does not use the word disgust. Yet his tragedies are incomprehensible without a very strong notion of it," and other contemporary studies of that aversive affect turn to him for examples of disgusting behaviors and disgusted reactions.[1] In a recent study of the aesthetics of aversion, Carolyn Korsmeyer points to the disgusting actions in "*King Lear*, whose character Gloucester, suffers his eyes gouged out ('Out, vile jelly!'), and *Titus Andronicus*, whose character Queen Tamora is made to eat the bodies of her two sons."[2] Rachel Herz sees Shakespeare as "an experimental psychologist way ahead of his time," and she points to Lady Macbeth who "tries to alleviate her guilty conscience about the murder of King Duncan with a bit of hand-washing."[3]

The scholarship on disgust covers a range of levels and comes from several camps: topical and analytic studies, some appealing to a broad audience (Miller, Herz); others more deeply invested in questions of history and philosophy (Menninghaus, Kolnai); theoretical studies and their critics, some of which are interested in political, ethical, and legal questions (Nussbaum, Kelly); and an important and admittedly heterogeneous group who represent or debate theory's current "turn to affect," some of whom are marked by a reaction to post-structuralism's "death of the subject" and privileging of language over feeling or the body.[4] The last mentioned shows affect theory and its interest in disgust enjoying a robust contemporary life, one that is enlivened by debate and controversy. Key examples of affect theory are Silvan Tomkins, Gilles Deleuze, Brian Massumi, and Eve Kosofsky Sedgwick, but they are joined by more recent contributors such as Rei Terada, Sianne Ngai, Sara Ahmed, and Lauren Berlant.[5]

In a lengthy critique and review essay, Ruth Leys provides a very good bibliography of affect theory, reviews its positions and representatives, and locates points for questioning its validity and consequences. She notes affect theory's robust reaction to post-structuralism, but also sees affect theorists' "indifference to ideology and the social"; above all, she questions the claim by such theorists "that action and behavior are held to be determined by affective dispositions that are independent of consciousness and the mind's control."[6] She describes what she calls a "Basic Emotions Paradigm" shared by analytic theorists (Tomkins) that categorizes affects in six to nine categories of emotion and holds them to be pre-cognitive, physiologically hard-wired, separable, and autonomous (Massumi). Leys, whose critique has not gone unchallenged, also critiques the attempt of such theorists to valorize scientific, physiological, even neural connections between affects and human beings.

It seems important, even essential, to acknowledge the work of affect theorists such as those named above, not least because of their usefulness for those raising questions about affects like disgust and early modern texts. In effect, some contributors to this collection address, knowingly or tacitly, the prominent place of disgust in affect theory. Insofar as the essays look at disgust in historical texts and historicize disgust, however, *Disgust in Early Modern English Literature* also tacitly critiques a priori assumptions about affect as autonomous and "what eludes form, cognition and meaning."[7] The interest here is in close cultural and literary reading in which contemporary affect theory, among other conceptual and interdisciplinary tools, might prove to be helpful, if not determining.

As for topical and analytic work, recent studies addressing disgust come from the fields of psychology, philosophy, and law.[8] References they make to Shakespeare's works and characters might say more about his canonical status than anything else, as he remains, at least in the West, the cultural literary icon for scholars and a general audience. But though many of these studies are interested in the psychological (therapy for obsessive compulsive disorder), political (recognition that conservative voters have a lower disgust threshold), and business (disgust does not sell products) ramifications of disgust, their interest in Shakespearean characters who show repulsion raises issues less related to the bard's popularity: Shakespeare was writing at an important moment in the history of this aversive emotion and, as contributors to this volume note, a distinctive lexicon signaled the introduction of the word that came to identify it.[9]

Miller turns to a familiar scene in *Hamlet* for a Shakespearean example of disgust that may be either questionable or paradigmatic, an ambiguous situation in which, perhaps, "disgust without the word disgust is not quite the same."[10] In Act V, Hamlet holds the skull of Yorick, remembers the jester in his younger days, and says, "how abhorred in my imagination it is. My gorge rises at it" (5.1.180–81).[11] Sniffing the skull, he exclaims, "And smelt so? Pah!" and puts it down (5.1.194).[12] What draws Hamlet to smell something that has nauseated him, and why does Shakespeare have him do this? What does the action reveal about disgust in this historical moment?

This volume of essays explores such questions about early modern disgust. Does Hamlet here provide "evidence of the culturally conditioned higher disgust thresholds of an earlier time"?[13] Were early moderns comparatively less disgusted than us because they bathed less, witnessed more death, and were inured to the smells and sights of decay, infestation, and putrefaction? Or are we witnessing an example of "broad vulgar comedy," or the Bakhtinian, life-affirming grotesque?[14] Hamlet's expression of disgust is related to death and the fecund cycle of life, which one could argue is a major theme of the play and characteristic of disgust in general.[15] Julia Kristeva defines abjection through death: "The corpse, seen without God and outside of science, is the utmost of abjection. It is death infecting life. Abject."[16] But Hamlet not only rejects death's infection; he invites it by raising the skull to his nose *after* he has expressed disgust. As Kristeva argues, subjects are both repelled by and drawn to horrors and their power to break down boundaries of the Symbolic Order.[17] What this iconic scene seems to reveal about the composition of disgust and a writer's struggle with it is a certain, perhaps even constitutive element of attraction. As one of our contributors notes, quoting Cicero, *omnibus in rebus voluptatibus maximis fastidium finitimum est* (the greatest pleasures reside closely with disgust).[18]

Most recent studies of disgust pay little attention to the history or the etymology of this aversive emotion.[19] Benedict Robinson's "Disgust c. 1600" is a recent exception that begins with a similar claim: "What no one seems to have noticed is that in one sense, at least, the years on either side of 1600 actually invented disgust."[20] Winfried Menninghaus' *Disgust: Theory and History of a Strong Sensation* is another important exception that offers a comparative (English, French, German) linguistic perspective on disgust. Acknowledging the difficulties of producing a complete history of disgust (including an element of self-censorship), he notes ancient literary examples but limits his philosophical study to "the most important theoretical approaches to disgust taken during the past 250 years" and makes the eighteenth century (Kant) his starting point.[21] Noting that "the words *dégoût*, disgust, and *Ekel* first come into general usage in the sixteenth and seventeenth century," he begins with eighteenth-century philosophy because it is there, he claims, that disgust "attains to 'a life of its own,' becoming worthy of consideration for the sake of its own (anti)aesthetic and moral qualities."[22] Miller, whose interest is more literary, reads medieval texts to make a similar claim: the "social organization of disgust as it related to bodily substances was mostly subsumed into the moral and social economy of shame and honor, but we can begin to discern it taking on a life of its own."[23] He argues that subjects before the Renaissance experienced disgust before the word was current, and he finds evidence of disgust in medieval Icelandic sagas "enmeshed with the politics of shame."[24] Disgust, for him, does not really take on "a life of its own" until the sixteenth and seventeenth centuries.[25] To get some critical perspective on what it is about early modern culture that produced more focused interest in disgust, even as a new English word appeared to name it, *Hamlet*, once again, may offer a clue.

"No work in the English literary canon has been so closely identified with the beginning of the modern age as *Hamlet*," according to Margreta de Grazia.[26] Hamlet is modern because he "draws attention to what is putatively going on inside him" and thus demonstrates "psychological depth and complexity."[27] In textual evidence of Hamlet's interiority, disgust plays an especially important role. As we move into the early *modern* era, Miller argues, "Shame, as before, remains public and organizes relations among the respectable," where disgust "works to support shame in public settings but . . . has a more private and secret life, working in darker places."[28] For Miller, disgust becomes an internal emotion that controls social behavior, clearly placing him in debt to Norbert Elias' position that the civilizing process was marked by the internalization of disgust.[29] Disgust, then, is intimately linked to the development of the early modern subject. Hamlet's expression of disgust in regard to Yorick's skull may better mark his modernity than his pondering of human existence.

The psychological aspect of disgust can be understood, in part, by its etymology and definition. *Disgust* comes from the French, *desgoust* (modern *dégoût*), which in turn comes from the Latin *dis-* and *gustus* ("distaste") and refers to the physical sense of taste.[30] In his study of taste and private life in Renaissance France, Jean-Louis Flandrin states that because the word was linked specifically to the consumption of food, "people for a long time remained conscious of the fact that to use the word taste in other than a culinary sense was to use a metaphor."[31] In England, however, according to the *OED*, *taste* acquired a secondary, more psychological meaning as early as the fourteenth century: that of "mental perception of quality; judgement, discriminative faculty."[32] It was not until the seventeenth century that *taste* came into use to describe aesthetic appreciation: "The sense of what is appropriate, harmonious, or beautiful; *esp.* discernment and appreciation of the beautiful in nature or art; *spec.* the faculty of perceiving and enjoying what is excellent in art, literature, and the like."[33] By the end of the seventeenth century, in both England and France, "good taste became a primary social virtue" and "taste affected what a man was, what he felt about the world."[34] To be civilized and modern, then, meant demonstrating good taste.

Miller wonders if it is "a coincidence that the word disgust appears roughly contemporaneously with the expansion of the meaning of the word taste to name a newly recognized general capacity of refinement, a discernment of style."[35] This volume answers "probably not," and this is why a study of the literature written in this period is crucial to understanding disgust, early modern culture, and the aesthetic project of literature in general. It is possible, hypothetically, that disgust becomes more present and powerful in early modern English literature because writers were instrumentalizing the disgusting and using it to explore the boundaries of good taste.

The first recorded use of the word *disgust* was in John Florio's *VVorlde of Words* in 1598. It was used to define the Italian "*disparére*" as "a disopinion, a diuersitie in conceit. Also a disgust or vnkindnes. Also not to seeme."[36] For Randle Cotgrave, in his 1611 *Dictionarie of the French and English tongues*, disgust becomes more visceral: "*Desappetit:* . . . a queasinesse, or disgust of the stomacke" and "*Desaimer.* . . . to fall into dislike, or disgust of."[37] The *OED* defines disgust as "Strong repugnance, aversion, or repulsion excited by that which is loathsome or offensive, as a foul smell, disagreeable person or action, disappointed ambition, etc.; profound instinctive dislike or dissatisfaction."[38] Disgust is now seen as an emotion common to, though differentiated among, all cultures, but there is disagreement among affect theorists, such as Massumi and Tomkins, and cultural historians about whether it is innate or culturally acquired.[39] If it is "built up from education and habit," as Korsmeyer and others argue, then examining the things, people, and ideas that disgust will reveal much about a culture or, for the early modern period, early modern culture.[40] As this volume demonstrates, studying disgust in the literature of the period reveals another view, perhaps more raw and real, of what it meant to be an early modern subject.

Because the term "disgust" was introduced in this period, and because the emotion seems connected to emerging ideas of modernity, it may be tempting to focus on the congruencies between early modern and contemporary feelings of disgust. We might also argue that disgust is universal and transhistorical. But, as the editors of *Reading the Early Modern Passions* stress, "Scholars interested in reading emotions transhistorically need to question the match between their own normative scripts for emotion and those of the culture whose affects they explore."[41] It is crucial to look back, as many of the essays in this collection do, to the practices and philosophies that informed early modern writers' expressions or representations of aversion.

Aversion is central to the conduct books that were available in Europe in the sixteenth century. Although subject to criticism, Norbert Elias' *Über den Prozeß der Zivilisation* (*The Civilizing Process*) provides a fascinating and useful survey of how civil values were gradually internalized by way of social conduct rules.[42] For Elias, Erasmus' *De civilitate morum puerilium* (*On civility in boys*, 1530) marks a pivotal moment in the civilizing process:

> Did the thresholds of embarrassment and shame advance at the time of Erasmus? Does his treatise contain indications that the frontiers of sensibility and the reserve which people expected of each other were increasing? There are good reasons for supposing so. The humanists' works on manners form a kind of bridge between those of the Middle Ages and modern times.[43]

Elias provides numerous examples of behaviors that gradually became disgusting, from removing food from one's mouth and dropping it on the floor, to blowing one's nose on one's sleeve, to farting at the dinner table.[44] He explains that "habits were condemned more and more as such, not in regard to others. In this way, socially undesirable impulses or inclinations became more radically suppressed. They became associated with embarrassment, fear, shame or guilt, even when one is alone."[45] In concert with the rise of good taste, disgust and shame worked together to make early moderns conscious of and disgusted by their own manners and bodily processes, even when nobody was around to witness them. Renaissance conduct books made disgust a second nature.

If Renaissance conduct books explicitly advised against disgusting behavior, a popular subgenre sought to accomplish the same by doing exactly the opposite and in the process revealed the key to conduct teaching. In *The End of Conduct*, Barbara Correll looks at Friedrich Dedekind's *Grobianus et Grobiana*, an "ironic-didactic poem . . . composed of reverse precepts that systematically rec-ommend the most disgusting behavior – indecency – as the way to teach decent behavior."[46] Like other conduct literature, works in the *Grobianus* tradition pro-duced "visceral disgust and revulsion in a way that contribute[d] to the control of the body by a newly cultivated mind."[47] This new mind, Correll argues, cor-responded to a specifically masculine identity, constructed in opposition to others; the disgusting (grobian) behaviors of animals, peasants, foreigners, and women were those a courtier or male class aspirant needed to avoid.[48] A text like *Grobi-anus et Grobiana* helps to explain how Otherness could be linked to disgust in this period, and how disgust might have been deployed, even in literature whose primary goal was not the teaching of conduct.

To date, Correll's is the only book-length study focused on disgust in early modern literature.[49] For the last two decades, though, study of other passions and emotions in early modern literature has been varied and rich.[50] Gail Kern Pas-ter's work on the bodily humors, passions, and shame is most relevant to the project of this volume. In *The Body Embarrassed*, Paster argues that an under-standing of humoralism can help us to make better sense of Elias' conduct books and Bakhtin's grotesque.[51] Humoralism also gives us a vivid picture of the bodily fluids and vapors that civility would deem necessary to control:

> All parts of the humoral body were capable of containing fumes and smoky 'fuligigous' vapors that could rise from the guts to the cranium, winds that roared and rumbled, sharp and vehement gripings, belchings, gross and clammy crudities, fluids that putrefied and stank, or burning up, became 'adust,' seed that sent up poisoned vapors to the brain.[52]

The passions, or the emotions – including shame and disgust – were also under-stood through humoralism. Like humors themselves, "the passions actually *were* liquid forces of nature, because, in this cosmology, the stuff of the outside world and the stuff of the body were composed of the same elemental materials."[53] Sig-nificantly, leading up to the early modern period, Galenic physiology was general knowledge, whether people were learned in medicine or not; frequent references to it in literature of the period are not surprising.[54] Indeed, humoral theory might help to explain why disgust – the concept and the word – came into its own in the sixteenth and seventeenth centuries. Humoralism maintained a close relationship between subjects and their bodies; that which is familiar is less likely to disgust. As the new sciences challenged humoral theory, that relationship was compro-mised, and passions and bodies became alienable. Separated from their human connection, bodily fluids were less familiar, more likely to disgust.

Early modern theories of emotion were certainly informed by humoralism, but the passions were defined through religion and philosophy. As the editors of *Reading the Early Modern Passions* explain, early modern writers were faced with "competing taxonomies of passions: a range of ancient categories were avail-able, and these vie for dominance not only with each other but with the Christian classifications in early modern passions discourse."[55] One influential work most pertinent to a study of disgust is Thomas Aquinas' *Summa Theologiae*, Pars Prima Secundae, Q. 22–48 (c. 1265–1274), which Thomas Wright's *The Passions of the Mind in General* (1601) takes as its starting point. Aquinas identifies eleven passions and divides them into the concupiscible (love, hatred, desire, aversion, joy, sadness) and the irascible (hope, despair, daring, fear, anger).[56] According to Aquinas, concupiscible passions are driven by the senses that either draw us to things that are suitable or repel us from things that are not; irascible passions begin and end in the concupiscible passions, but are met with some difficulty along the way.[57] Aversion is the Thomistic passion most closely aligned with disgust, its contrary being desire. Aquinas believed in the "superiority of good to evil" and this hierarchy structures his description of the concupiscible passions.[58] Desire is prior to and stronger than aversion, the idea being that we are naturally inclined toward what is good, while aversion protects us from evil: "Thus hate, aversion, and pain are repulsions of evil. Within the realm of 'sensible good and evil considered absolutely,' there can be no repulsion from good or attraction to evil."[59] As if to emphasize his point, Aquinas does not dedicate any of his organizational questions to aversion, although he addresses at least one to each of the other concupiscible passions.[60] If even Aquinas skirted the question of disgust, it is perhaps not surprising that scholars did the same for the next 725 years (and perhaps continue to today). Disgusting things are to be avoided. Disgusting things repulse.

In contradiction to Aquinas' ideas on natural inclination, however, early modern literature is replete with disgusting scenes, images, people, and ideas. Why would early modern writers include repulsive characters, images, and ideas if their primary goals were to delight and to entertain? Perhaps disgust is also delightful and entertaining. A return to *Hamlet* suggests how the early moderns in effect challenged the Thomistic view of aversion. Even though Yorick's skull makes Hamlet's gorge rise, he does not turn away from it but brings it close enough to smell and to gag. Hamlet's reaction suggests that disgust and desire are not binary opposites in competition but related affects. What desire, then, is at work in Hamlet's attraction to Yorick's skull?

These questions and observations could look to a Bakhtinian reading of the grotesque. Great pleasure comes from transgressively embracing what should be avoided. But, as Bakhtin argues, the grotesque is usually over the top: "In the sphere of imagery cosmic fear (as any other fear) is defeated by laughter. Therefore dung and urine, as comic matter that can be interpreted bodily, play an important part in these images. They appear in hyperbolic quantities and cosmic dimensions."[61] The texts examined in this volume may contain disgusting images that are exaggerated to the point of the grotesque, but many lack such hyperbolic embellishment. And, according to Menninghaus, even desirable things that are exaggerated become disgusting: "like a sweet that is all too sweet, the beautiful is in danger – from the first and by its very nature – of turning out to be *in itself* something disgusting."[62] Surfeit, whether of grossness or of beauty, is not the only thing that demonstrates the connection between disgust and desire.

In *Savoring Disgust*, Korsmeyer argues that disgust, in and of itself, exerts "a paradoxical magnetism": "aesthetic disgust is a response that, no matter how unpleasant, can rivet attention to the point where one may be said to *savor* the feeling."[63] She disputes Kant's famous assertion that art cannot transform something disgusting into something desirable, arguing that "there are many ways that disgust converts from pure aversion to paradoxical attraction while retaining its trademark visceral shock."[64] Literature in particular holds this transformative power. Kristeva describes the power of horrific literature as cathartic rather than desirable or pleasurable: "One does not know it, one does not desire it, one joys in it [*on enjouit*]. Violently and painfully. A passion."[65] But Korsmeyer believes that more than catharsis is at work in the transformation because crafted "eloquence [can convert] onerous subject matter into beauty."[66] Disgusting things "become beautiful not just because the rendering is deft or poetic but also because they capture in a breathtaking manner something terrible that we may recognize as true."[67] As Hamlet seems to understand, beauty, or something desirable, may reside in the disgusting; as this volume demonstrates, writers in early modern England exploited, scrutinized, and embraced this attractive and aversive emotion.

Disgusting encounters

With this rich historical, philosophical, and theoretical background in mind, *Disgust in Early Modern English Literature* seeks to interrogate and understand the complexities of disgust in early modern English literature. Hypothesizing that emotions are culturally conditioned reactions to real or imagined encounters with things or ideas, the chapters address three kinds of disgusting encounters: sexual, cultural, and textual. The authors explore how early modern English writers used this aversive emotion to explore sexual behaviors, to describe encounters with foreign cultures, and to manipulate their readers' responses. These themes tell us a lot about disgust in this period – it was intimately connected to sexuality and "Otherness," and it became a rhetorical technique writers employed to certain effect – but they also reveal how interest in disgust is something shared by a number of kinds of literary scholarship. This volume's authors approach disgust through sexuality studies, post-colonialism, and the history of reading practices, but they also are informed by feminism, the history of emotions, sensation studies, food studies, and aesthetics. Disgust is pervasive and various fields of literary and cultural study profit from its study.

The first four essays (King, Correll, Eschenbaum, and Kostihová) focus on *Sexual Encounters*. Aquinas defined desire and aversion as opposing passions, but much early modern literature invites us to experience both at the same time. Through scenes of love and lust, early modern writers challenge a Thomistic view of emotion. Today, Miller argues, the "connection between disgust and the sexual comes as less of a surprise; the knowledge of such a connection, after all, lies at the core of much of the Freudian enterprise as well as of the traditions of ascetic, Stoic, Christian, and other anti-sexual discourses."[68] Some believe love and sexual desire lower the thresholds of disgust; the same viscous bodily fluids that disgust when oozing from a stranger lose this ability when they ooze from a loved or desired one. Recent research claims that desire and disgust are neurologically linked, because both emotions activate the insula cortex of the brain in a similar way.[69] Herz explains that even though the genital response to a picture of a "tub of vomit, or naked bodies sensually entwined" can vary, the insula cortex does not recognize a difference.[70]

Early modern writers anticipate the modern notion that, as Herz puts it, "lust and disgust . . . are neurologically in bed together."[71] In Chapter 1, "Dirty Jokes: Disgust, Desire, and the Pornographic Narrative in Thomas Nashe's *The Unfortunate Traveller*," Emily L. King describes a scene from Pietro Aretino's *Ragionamenti* that is dripping with sexual secretions and metaphors. The scene begins with the threat of gang rape and ends with an episode of diarrhea that disgusts and, disturbingly, invites laughter. King finds that Nashe's comic mode differs drastically from Aretino's when Jack Wilton describes the rape of Heraclide, violated on the corpse of her husband. If Aretino's comedy is conservative, Nashe's is radical in drawing readers into the disgusting rather than shielding them from it. King challenges critics who have traced the scenes of disgusting, violent sexuality ("sexual scatology") in Nashe solely back to Aretino; she sees a more complicated genealogy. King's chapter also raises concerns that link many of the chapters in this volume: literature that disgusts frequently has a reception history of critical disgust; working with disgusting things or events (like rape) can still feel disgusting, no matter the critical purpose; it is easy to presume universalized responses to affects, but disgust *always* denies this possibility.

In their essays about attractive aversion, Barbara Correll and Natalie Eschenbaum consider specific instances of desire that also disgust. Correll's instance is the blush, an emotive expression that crosses shame and desire. In "Guyon's Blush: Shame, Disgust, and Desire in *The Faerie Queene*, Book 2," Correll explains how Spenser's representation of the blush challenges orthodox notions of temperance. As a visual representation of the struggle between desire and shame, the blush structures Book 2, and leads to disgust in Guyon's passionate and horrific attack of the Bower of Bliss. It suggests the role of disgust in Spenser's relationship to his own art: the destruction of the Bower could be read as a response to Spenser's own desire to write pornographic poetry. Such a claim connects Correll's argument to King's in fascinating ways, as does her suggestion that Guyon's blush offers a critical perspective on current affect theory in unsettling assumptions and calling for a pluralized view of emotion. The instance of desirable disgust that Eschenbaum explores is less poetic than a blush. In "Desiring Disgust in Robert Herrick's Epigrams," Eschenbaum looks at Herrick's depiction of a woman licking her husband's coagulated eye drainage. Eschenbaum surveys the early critical disgust that Herrick received – people were, quite literally, repulsed by his verse – as well as more recent scholarship that claims Herrick's disgusting epigrams critique base commoners.[72] Herrick's commoners might have failed the "civilizing process" (Norbert Elias' phrase) encouraged by conduct books, but Eschenbaum finds that he is working through a more complex understanding of disgust. Like Christian displays of abject adoration, the wife's action is "sweet" because it reveals loving devotion. In Herrick's imaginary, things, people, and actions – whether secular or religious – are not inherently disgusting. The aversive affect is relative, specific to the individual experiencing it, and inseparable from erotic desire. According to Eschenbaum, Herrick employs disgust in order to upset the very affect it is supposed to elicit.

In the final chapter of Part I, "Discerning (Dis)Taste: Delineating Sexual Mores in Shakespeare's *Venus and Adonis*," Marcela Kostihová also addresses the relative nature of disgust, but she contends that Shakespeare uses disgust to challenge normative boundaries of sexuality. Like King, Kostihová is interested in the ways in which disgust and desire cross when Venus rhapsodizes about and smears herself with Adonis' bodily secretions. And, like Correll, Kostihová is interested in shame as an emotive expression linked to both disgust and desire. She argues that Shakespeare makes Venus a vile commoner, rather than a desirable goddess, and that he connects heterosexual practices with vulgar and repulsive actions. In contrast, Adonis' putatively homosexual encounter with the boar is cultured and shrouded in private refinement. Considering the poem's connection to Elias' civilizing process and focusing on the powers of disgust, Kostihová advances a strongly stated argument: Adonis' death does not teach the dangers of homosexual encounters, as other scholars have claimed; rather, it shows how cultured homo-eroticism transcends disgusting and bestial heteronormativity.

Kostihová and Eschenbaum both discuss the complex pressures of disgust on the civilizing process, and Kostihová complicates this further with her treatment of normativity. The issue of foreignness or alien encounter, and the possibility that such otherness may react in or intensify disgust, is explored in greater depth in Part II of this volume, with three essays (Hashhozheva, Shahani, and Kennedy) that focus on *Cultural Encounters* and explore literary expressions of disgust for foreigners. Like the essays on *Sexual Encounters*, these three are interested in the competing emotions of desire and disgust, but in the sense of Otherness being both fascinating and nauseating.

There is a long history of studying the link between disgust and Otherness. Miller traces this link to Darwin who describes an encounter in Tierra del Fuego when "a native touched with his finger some cold preserved meat which I was eating at our bivouac, and plainly showed utter disgust at its softness; whilst I felt utter disgust at my food being touched by a naked savage."[73] Darwin's description demonstrates how disgust is a visceral reaction to strangeness, a universal emotion in which all people are disgusted by what is unfamiliar. Benedict Robinson observes that even the verb "disgust" was used in ambiguously multi-directional ways in travelogues around 1600: "Is the danger that English travelers will be disgusted by foreign nations, or that they will disgust foreign nations? The answer seems to be both. . . . To be disgusted by strange customs is to disgust those whose customs they are, as well as to overlook the ways we might ourselves be disgusting to others."[74] In *Purity and Danger*, Mary Douglas explains that pollutants are constructs of culture that simply vary in kind: "Our ideas of dirt . . . express symbolic systems and . . . the difference between pollution behaviour in one part of the world and another is only a matter of detail."[75] More recently, in *From Disgust to Humanity*, Martha Nussbaum considers the ways in which disgust can be instrumentalized to justify social and legal discrimination of gays and lesbians.[76] In its social and political settings and applications disgust was, and still is, a powerful, often devastating means of separating "us" from "them."

The first two chapters in the *Cultural Encounters* section cover quite a bit of territory and time in their exploration of various Others. In "Indecorous Customs, Rhetorical Decorum, and the Reception of Herodotean Ethnography from Henri Estienne to Edmund Spenser," Galena Hashhozheva focuses on sixteenth-century travel writing about French Catholics, Caribbean natives, and the Irish. Gitanjali Shahani's "Food, Filth, and the Foreign: Disgust in the Seventeenth-Century Travelogue" situates its discussion in the Cape of Good Hope and then in the Mughal Court and Ottoman Empire. Both chapters are concerned with how disgust functions as a generic marker of ethnography.

Hashhozheva reveals how Herodotus influenced the ethnographic writing of Henri Estienne, Michel de Montaigne, Barnabe Rich, and Edmund Spenser. When faced with the unseemly customs of Others, those with a more Herodotean bent acknowledge and affirm cultural diversity. Hashhozheva describes how Estienne mocks the customs of Catholic devotion, including the Eucharist – a custom Eschenbaum and Mills also examine. Hashhozheva explains that this mockery is something Herodotus, the proto-cultural relativist, would deplore. Hashhozheva concludes her chapter with a focused look at Spenser's *A View of the Present State of Ireland* to discover a text that both delights and disgusts, because it both gestures toward Herodotean cultural relativism and exploits it for its own colonial, political, and literary purposes.

In her chapter, Shahani notices that disgust is employed in nearly all seventeenth-century travelogues at the same moment: in observing and describing food preparation. She argues that the tone shifts drastically from objective observation to visceral disgust, and that it happens so consistently in this genre of writing that disgust might be read as a generic marker rather than an emotive reaction. Shahani looks at the ethnographic descriptions of the intermingling of food and filth – entrails seasoned with dung – of the African Hottentots as well as the hyper-civilized and excessive food rituals of Ottoman Court Sultans. Shahani also touches on the *Sexual Encounters* section of this volume when she examines the ways in which pleasure and disgust cross when travelogue writers muse about what women do with cucumbers at the Ottoman Court.

Shahani and Hashhozheva show that disgust became a defining feature of the genre of the travelogue, no matter the destination, well before Darwin. The fact that the gustatory rituals of these Others become the focus of foreign disgust might predict Darwin's focus on the same, but it also reflects the close connection of the word disgust with its etymological root in the seventeenth century. Early uses of this new word frequently have to do with gustatory rituals and the physical sense of taste. In "'Qualmish at the Smell of Leek': Overcoming Disgust and Creating the Nation-State in *Henry V*," Colleen E. Kennedy also is interested in the role of the senses in disgust, but she focuses on smell. She argues that, in Shakespeare's history play, Fluellen's stinky Welsh leek shows Pistol's disgust with him to be more repulsive than the vegetable itself. Pistol needs to overcome his own disgust – he needs to assimilate to the Other – in order for Britain to be unified. Previous scholars have commented that the play tries to depict a unified England and Wales with uncertain success; Kennedy complicates these readings by considering how disgust, aimed at certain odors, is a sociological and sensate aspect of the unification process.[77] She reads early modern herbals, gardening, and receipt books, alongside recent work on the senses and disgust, to claim that the young Henry V learns how a garden needs vegetation *and* manure to thrive, thereby upsetting the boundaries of attraction and aversion.

The essays in this volume are interested in the entwined affects of desire and disgust in early modern literature. They consider why a writer might employ disgust in a literary text that aims, officially, to teach and delight. The final section, *Textual Encounters*, includes essays (Murakami, Kolb, and Mills) that directly address the ways in which early modern writers use disgust to craft their texts and their readers' reactions. The early moderns knew the power of the passions. In *The Passions of the Mind in General* (1601), for instance, Thomas Wright explains how orators should use Aquinas' eleven passions to improve their skills of rhetoric.[78] Because of its aversive nature, disgust is a tricky passion to employ. Its use must be purposeful and controlled. One aim might be to educate readers in good taste, making literature a kind of conduct book. The imaginary offers a space to test and evaluate revulsions. If readers are repulsed by certain images or ideas, it means they have good taste and can direct their disgust "toward the unrefined who are able to indulge and not experience disgust."[79] Another purpose, however, might be to exploit the aesthetic possibilities of disgust. Korsmeyer explains, "often with art, the disgusting remains disgusting but also attains aesthetic virtues, becoming interesting, comic, curious, dreadful, titillating, tragic, uncanny. Some of these appreciative experiences are exceedingly difficult to tolerate. Others achieve a weird poignancy and even beauty."[80] Roland Barthes said writing makes the disgusting disgust less ("When written, shit does not smell"), but the essays in this volume show how textualizing disgust might intensify visceral, embodied reactions.[81] For example, in Eschenbaum's chapter, when Herrick transforms a man's foot sweat problem into words – when he describes Pimpe's sweat oozing and bubbling out of his shoes like lathering soap – readers are perhaps more disgusted than they would be if they encountered the image in real life. The simile intensifies the disgust, but it also is what creates the simultaneous aesthetic and comic delight Korsmeyer describes. Similarly, in her chapter Shahani explains how visceral disgust becomes a generic marker of ethnographic writing. Written shit might not smell, but when shit becomes something people taste or eat, ethnographic writers do not filter disgust from their otherwise objective writing.

Readers may or may not be physically affected by textualized disgust, but disgust is not solely an embodied response, as this volume demonstrates. Early modern English writers use disgust to test and mark boundaries of taste. The *Textual Encounters* section includes two essays on Ben Jonson, the seventeenth-century master of disgust and definer of taste. In "'The Fairing of Good Counsel': Allegory, Disgust, and Discretion in Jonson's *Bartholomew Fair*," Ineke Murakami shows how Jonson uses disgust for both its pedagogical and aesthetic values. She argues that Jonson constructs complex, indecorous allegories – such as the one that transforms Ursula from a bear to a fat pig to the grease that lubricates wagon wheels – to provoke laughter while teaching the good taste and judgment required by London's ubiquitous market culture. Murakami demonstrates that allegory, generically, evokes disgust in order to get the audience to regulate their own discretion. Murakami's discussion aligns compellingly with Shahani's here; both argue that disgust is used as a particular generic marker. By reading *Bartholomew Fair* together with psychoanalytic studies of the boundary functions of disgust, Murakami adds to the ongoing discussion in Jonson studies regarding his ambivalence toward print and popular theater markets. She suggestively concludes that Jonson's play cautions readers to attend to the visceral repulsion that disgust triggers: we should not be too quick to tolerate the behaviors of those we deem uncivilized or disgusting.

Suppression of disgusting feelings can be dangerous, too, as the *Cultural Encounters* chapters revealed. In "Jonson's Old Age: The Force of Disgust," Laura Kolb sees Jonson using disgust itself as an allegory for textual relations. She focuses on grotesque, aging bodies in *Volpone* and "My Picture Left in Scotland" to argue that, for Jonson, disgust is a rhetorical force. Because disgust is so affecting, Jonson uses it to control his texts and their receptions. In his textual production, disgust resembles desire, both psychologically and aesthetically; for example, when Jonson relishes the pleasures of copious language in his descriptions of Mosca's disgusting face and Celia's desirable beauty. Kolb reads the links between disgust, desire, and textuality across Jonson's career, from the sickly bodies in *Volpone* to the author's own aging body in "My Picture Left in Scotland." She finds that Jonson ends his career by creating textual monuments to two competing aspects of the poet-speaker: his status as mere, dying matter and his poetic skill.

In the final *Textual Encounters* chapter, "'Rankly digested, doth those things out-spue': John Donne, Bodily Fluids, and the Metaphysical Abject," Dan Mills considers how disgust becomes the defining feature of the metaphysical style. If, as Kolb argues, Jonson was preoccupied with his aging body, Donne is preoccupied with death. But Donne's morbidity, Mills contends, leads Donne to acknowledge the body in all its gorgeous and gross detail. He reads Donne's early works, his *Satyres* and *Elegies*, as manifestations of Julia Kristeva's abject: something that must be cast out. He sees Donne creating a disgusted poetic persona that is influenced by his biographical background and his own aesthetic designs. Donne's physical repulsion at aspects of his conversion from Catholicism is manifested in vile, excremental imagery. Mills argues that Donne was also influenced by the tradition of Renaissance rhetoric, but made a conscious break from the rhetorical Christian grand style through the juxtaposition of emotional content and imagery of ugliness and disgust. Mills employs the theories of Kristeva, Lacan, Bakhtin, and others to explore Donne's apparent purpose in critiquing Renaissance rhetorical theory and in revolting his readers. In the eighteenth century, Samuel Johnson famously described Donne's hyperbole as "enormous and disgusting"; Mills here examines what it means to describe a style of writing, and not just its content, as "disgusting."[82]

Taken together, the essays in this volume demonstrate what can be gained from considering the vile underbelly of early modern English literature. In the literature, we encounter "disgust" being defined and redefined through a varied, descriptive lexicon, from its etymological roots in vile food stuffs, to the policing of sexual and interpersonal encounters, to the judgments of repulsive styles of thinking and writing. If, as Herz maintains, "disgust reveals the fundamental concerns that underlie our existence," then study of this emotion offers essential insights into early modern culture, as well as a genealogy of modern disgust.[83] The volume begins to address these issues, even as it reveals that the repulsive features of literature are also some of the most attractive.

Notes

1 Miller, *Anatomy*, 163.
2 Korsmeyer, *Savoring*, 92.
3 Herz, *That's Disgusting*, 193. In a 2006 study, cited by Drake Bennett in *The Dallas Morning News* (August 27, 2010), psychologists Chen-Bo Zhong and Katie Lijenquist called what they observed as "an unconscious link between immorality and actual dirt and infection" the "Macbeth effect."
4 Miller, *Anatomy*; Herz, *That's Disgusting*; Menninghaus, *Disgust*; Kolnai, "Der Ekel; Nussbaum, *Disgust to Humanity*; Kelly, *Yuck!*
5 Tomkins, *Shame and Its Sisters*; Deleuze and Guattari, *A Thousand Plateaus*; and Massumi, Parables for the Virtual. Other major works include Sedgwick, *Touching Feeling*; Ngai, *Ugly Feelings*; Clough and Halley, *Affective Turn*; Terada, *Feeling in Theory*; Ahmed, *Cultural Politics*; Nussbaum, *Hiding*; Gregg and Seigworth, *Affect Theory Reader*; and Berlant, *Cruel Optimism*.
6 Leys, "Turn," 439.
7 Leys, "Turn," 450. Responses to Leys came from Adam Frank and Elizabeth A. Wilson, "Critical Response I: Like-Minded," and Charles Altieri, "Critical Response II: Affect, Intentionality, and Cognition: A Response to Ruth Leys," and provoked a final defense, "Critical Response III: Facts and Moods: Reply to My Critics," *Critical Inquiry* 38, no. 4 (2012), 870–81.
8 See, for instance, Miller, *Anatomy*; Susan Miller, *Disgust*; Nussbaum, *Hiding* and *From Disgust*; Kelly, *Yuck!*; Korsmeyer, *Savoring*; McGinn, *Meaning*; Herz, *That's Disgusting*.
9 Herz explores the effects of disgust on obsessive-compulsive disorder and on advertising. Nussbaum focuses on the legal and political ramifications of disgust and shame for such cases as homophobic defenses and shaming punitive practices.
10 Miller, *Anatomy*, 164, 166.
11 Shakespeare, *Hamlet*.
12 Shakespeare, *Hamlet*.
13 Miller, *Anatomy*, 166.
14 Miller, *Anatomy*, 166.
15 Repulsion is central to many important scenes and speeches in *Hamlet* and usually centers on things being rotten or overabundant – too dead or too alive. Hamlet says the world grows "things rank and gross in nature" (1.2.126); Marcello famously proclaims, "Something is rotten in the state of Denmark" (1.5.90); after the Mousetrap performance Hamlet speaks of the "time of night, / When churchyards yawn and hell itself breathes out / Contagion to this world" (3.3.379–81); Claudius describes his "offence" as "rank" (3.3.36); and Hamlet chides his mother for her putative incest: "Nay, but to live / In the rank sweat of an enseamed bed, / Stew'd in corruption" (3.4.91–3). Adelman famously links Hamlet's revulsion to fantasies of the maternal in *Suffocating Mothers*.

16 Kristeva, *Powers*, 4.

17 Kristeva, *Powers*, 9.

18 Cicero, *De Oratore*, III.xxv.100. The translation of the Latin is Correll's.

19 Even a recent *BBC News* piece reminds us that *disgust* "was not a word at . . . [Shake-speare's] disposal – it only entered the English language towards the end of his life. He instead wrote of 'gorge rising'. Same emotion. Different phraseology." Lane, "Disgust."

20 Robinson, "Disgust c. 1600," 553. Robinson declares that the "one sense" in which disgust was invented around 1600 was rhetorical or literary: "Disgust had to be made, or made intelligible, by means of a literary process that first distinguished it from loathing by dis-figuring it and then gave it character and meaning by embedding it in narrative," 575.

21 Menninghaus, *Disgust*, 3.

22 Menninghaus, *Disgust*, 3–4.

23 Miller, *Anatomy*, 154.

24 Miller, *Anatomy*, 147.

25 Miller, *Anatomy*, 162. It seems important to acknowledge Menninghaus' critique of Miller (20–24) for his insularity (for Menninghaus, "ignorance") in reproducing arguments of long-published German scholarship without having read it (Kolnai, "Der Ekel") and claiming originality for his ideas. Menninghaus adamantly "refrains from writing a history of the – widely undocumented – 'reality' of disgust" (3), where Miller embraces the transhistorical, perhaps at the risk of appearing more anecdotal than rigorous. Nonetheless, Menninghaus praises the last three chapters of Miller's book for their discussion of disgust and contempt, and their social role in modern democracy.

26 De Grazia, "*Hamlet*," 355. For sustained humanist claims of *Hamlet*'s supposed modern psychology, see both Bloom and Bate.

27 De Grazia, "*Hamlet*," 355.

28 Miller, *Anatomy*, 162.

29 Herz emphasizes the subjective aspects of disgust: "What is disgusting, or not, is in the mind of the beholder." *That's Disgusting*, 6.

30 Research in psychology confirms the etymological link between *taste* and *disgust*; cf. Paul Rozin, who discovered that "our response to bitter taste is the sensory origin of the emotion of disgust, and all our other disgusts are built upon it." Herz, *That's Disgusting*, 30.

31 Flandrin, "Distinction," 299.

32 *Oxford English Dictionary*, 2nd ed., 1989 (online version, June 2012), s.v. "taste."

33 *OED*, "taste."

34 Flandrin, "Distinction," 307.

35 Miller, *Anatomy*, 168–9.

36 Florio, *A VVorld*, 108.

37 Cotgrave, *Dictionarie*.

38 *OED*, "disgust."

39 Massumi, *Parables*, 28, argues that affect is "irreducibly bodily and autonomic." Tomkins (and followers), according to Leys, "interpret the affects as non-intentional, bodily reactions . . . only contingently related to object in the world." Leys, "Turn," 437.

40 Korsmeyer, *Savoring*, 6.

41 Paster, Rowe, and Floyd-Wilson, "Introduction," 11.

42 Elias, *Prozeß*. Miller notes, "Medievalists resent the caricatured picture of a vulgar uninhibited childlike medieval people that Elias takes as his starting point, and medievalists can prove it to be a partial and flawed account." But Miller also concedes that Elias' work "still manage[s] to offer a truth about the larger picture that would not have been achievable if all of the particulars were right." *Anatomy*, 170.

43 Elias, *Prozeß*, 60–61.

44 Correll reminds us that the medieval period Elias describes "was not an age of crude habits but rather one in which habits came increasingly to be perceived as crude and

shameful, was not an age of boorishness but one which produced a standard which created – and used – boorishness." "Politics of Civility," 641.

45 Elias, *Prozeß*, 127.
46 Correll, *End*, 9.
47 Correll, *End*, 33.
48 Correll, *End*, 9.
49 Important articles and unpublished dissertations focused on disgust in literature of the
    early modern period include Greenblatt, Schoenfeldt, Douglas-Fairhurst, and Hardy.
50 To name just a few of these important studies: Paster, *Body Embarrassed*; Paster,
    Rowe, and Floyd-Wilson, *Reading*; Paster, *Humoring*; Gross, *Secret History*; and
    Smith, *Key*. In response to growing interest in this area, Queen Mary, University of
    London, established The Queen Mary Centre for the History of the Emotions in 2008.
    The center's blog tracks the numerous current conferences and publications in the
    history of emotions. Accessed December 22, 2014. http://emotionsblog.history.qmul.
    ac.uk/?p=23.
51 Paster, *Body Embarrassed*, 16.
52 Paster, *Body Embarrassed*, 11.
53 Paster, *Humoring*, 4.
54 Paster, *Body Embarrassed*, 8.
55 Paster, Rowe, and Floyd-Wilson, "Introduction," 2.
56 Cicero's classification of just four passions (fear, desire, distress, and pleasure) was
    also popular in the period. Paster, Rowe, and Floyd-Wilson, "Introduction," 2.
57 Miner, *Thomas Aquinas*, 53–5.
58 Miner, *Thomas Aquinas*, 27.
59 Miner, *Thomas Aquinas*, 55.
60 Miner, *Thomas Aquinas*, 27.
61 Bakhtin, *Rabelais*, 305, 336.
62 Menninghaus, *Disgust*, 7.
63 Korsmeyer, *Savoring*, 3.
64 Korsmeyer, *Savoring*, 11.
65 Kristeva, *Powers*, 9.
66 Korsmeyer, *Savoring*, 175.
67 Korsmeyer, *Savoring*, 175. For Kristeva, horror and the abject offer an opening onto or
    a kind of access to the otherwise inaccessible (Lacanian) Real.
68 Miller, *Anatomy*, xi.
69 Herz, *That's Disgusting*, 159.
70 Herz, *That's Disgusting*, 160.
71 Herz, *That's Disgusting*, 159.
72 Coiro remarks that the "targets of Herrick's wit are all poor (or nouveau riche), unedu-
    cated members of the lower class." *Robert Herrick*, 156. Schoenfeldt suggests that
    Herrick "pretend[s] that he is temporarily superior to the flesh he inhabits and shares
    with the lower-class figures his mocks." "Art," 150.
73 Qtd. in Miller, *Anatomy*, 1.
74 Robinson, "Disgust," 559.
75 Douglas, *Purity and Danger*, 36.
76 Nussbaum writes strongly against "projection-reactions" in spurious disgust defenses –
    for example, reducing a murder charge to manslaughter when the victim is homosex-
    ual – and she includes William Ian Miller among those whose work would lend support
    to pro-disgust arguments. *Hiding*, 75–87. See also Cahill, "Abortion and Disgust," on
    the legal consequences of linking abortion to disgust.
77 See, for instance, Parker, "Uncertain," and Outland, "Eat."
78 Wright, *Passions*, vii.
79 Miller, *Anatomy*, 169.

80　Korsmeyer, *Savoring*, 58.
81　Barthes, *Sade, Fourier, Loyola* (Paris: Editions du Seuil, 1971), 140; translation in Laporte, *The History of Shit*, 10. Thanks to an anonymous press reader for suggesting this connection.
82　Johnson, "Abraham Cowley," 17.
83　Herz, *That's Disgusting*, xii.

References

Adelman, Janet. *Suffocating Mothers: Fantasies of Maternal Origin in Shakespeare's Plays, "Hamlet" to "The Tempest."* New York: Routledge, 1992.
Ahmed, Sara. *The Cultural Politics of Emotion.* New York: Routledge, 2004.
Aquinas, Thomas. *Summa Theologiae.* Translated by Alfred J. Freddoso. University of Notre Dame. Last modified March 1, 2013. Accessed December 20, 2014. http://www3.nd.edu/~afreddos/summa-translation/TOC.htm.
Bakhtin, Mikhail. *Rabelais and His World.* Translated by Hélène Iswolsky. Bloomington: Indiana University Press, 1984.
Bate, Jonathan. *The Genius of Shakespeare.* London: Picador, 1997.
Bennett, Drake. "The Surprising Moral Force of Disgust." *The Dallas Morning News,* August 27, 2010. Accessed July 20, 2013. http://www.dallasnews.com/opinion/sunday-commentary/20100827-Drake-Bennett-The-surprising-moral-3508.ece.
Berlant, Lauren. *Cruel Optimism.* Durham, NC: Duke University Press, 2011.
Bloom, Harold. *Shakespeare: The Invention of the Human.* New York: Riverhead, 1998.
Cahill, Courtney Megan. "Abortion and Disgust." *Harvard Civil Rights-Civil Liberties Law Review* 48, no. 2 (Summer 2013): 409–57.
Cicero, Marcus Tullius. *De Oratore Book III.* In *Cicero IV.* Translated by H. Rackham, 2–185. Loeb Classical Library 349. Cambridge, MA: Harvard University Press, 1942.
Clough, Patricia Ticineto, and Jean Halley, eds. *The Affective Turn: Theorizing the Social.* Durham, NC: Duke University Press, 2007.
Coiro, Ann Baynes. *Robert Herrick's* Hesperides *and the Epigram Book Tradition.* Baltimore: Johns Hopkins University Press, 1988.
Correll, Barbara. *The End of Conduct:* Grobianus *and the Renaissance Text of the Subject.* Ithaca: Cornell University Press, 1996.
———. "The Politics of Civility in Renaissance Texts: Grobiana in *Grobianus.*" *Exemplaria: Journal of Theory in Medieval and Renaissance Studies* 2, no. 2 (October 1990): 627–58.
Cotgrave, Randle. *A dictionarie of the French and English tongues. Compiled by Randle Cotgrave.* London: Adam Islip, 1611.
de Grazia, Margreta. "*Hamlet* before Its Time." *Modern Language Quarterly* 62, no. 4 (December 2001): 355–75.
Deleuze, Gilles, and Felix Guattari. *A Thousand Plateaus.* Minneapolis: University of Minnesota Press, 1987.
Douglas, Mary. *Purity and Danger: An Analysis of the Concepts of Pollution and Taboo.* London: Routledge, 1966.
Douglas-Fairhurst, Robert. "Tragedy and Disgust." In *Tragedy in Transition,* edited by Catherine Silverstone and Sarah Annes Browne, 58–77. Malden, MA: Blackwell, 2007.
Elias, Norbert. *Über den Prozeß der Zivilisation.* Basel: Verlag Haus zum Falken, 1939. Translated by Edmund Jephcott as *The Civilizing Process,* edited by Eric Dunning, Johan Goudsblom, and Stephen Mennell. Rev. ed. Malden, MA: Blackwell, 2000.

Flandrin, Jean-Louis. "Distinction through Taste." In *A History of Private Life: Passions of the Renaissance*, translated by Arthur Goldhammer, edited by Roger Chartier, 265–307. Cambridge, MA: Belknap Press, 1989.

Florio, John. *A VVorld of words, or Most copious, and exact dictionarie in Italian and English, collected by Iohn Florio*. London: Arnold Hatfield for Edw. Blount, 1598.

Greenblatt, Stephen. "Filthy Rites." *Daedalus* 111, no. 3 (Summer 1982): 1–16.

Gregg, Melissa, and Gregory J. Seigworth, eds. *The Affect Theory Reader*. Durham, NC: Duke University Press, 2010.

Gross, Daniel. *The Secret History of Emotion: From Aristotle's Rhetoric to Modern Brain Science*. Chicago: Chicago University Press, 2007.

Hardy, Nat Wayne. "Anatomy or Pestilence: The Satiric Disgust of Plague in Early Modern London." PhD diss., University of Alberta, 2001.

Herz, Rachel. *That's Disgusting: Unraveling the Mysteries of Repulsion*. New York: Norton, 2012.

Johnson, Samuel. "Abraham Cowley." In *Lives of the English Poets*. Everyman's Library 704. London: Dent & Sons, 1925.

Kelly, Daniel. *Yuck! The Nature and More Significance of Disgust*. Cambridge, MA: MIT Press, 2011.

Kolnai, Aurel. "Der Ekel." In *Jahrbuch für Philosophie und phänomenologische Forschung*, vol. 10, edited by Edmund Husserl. Halle an der Saale: Max Niemeyer, 1929. Edited and translated by Barry Smith and Carolyn Korsmeyer as *On Disgust* (Chicago: Open Court, 2004).

Korsmeyer, Carolyn. *Savoring Disgust: The Foul and the Fair in Aesthetics*. New York: Oxford University Press, 2011.

Kristeva, Julia. *Powers of Horror: An Essay on Abjection*. Translated by Leon S. Roudiez. New York: Columbia University Press, 1982.

Lane, Megan. "Disgust: How did the Word Change so Completely?" *BBC News Magazine*, November 16, 2011. Accessed July 20, 2013. http://www.bbc.co.uk/news/magazine-15619543.

Laporte, Dominique. *The History of Shit*. Translated by Nadia Benabid and Rodolphe el-Khoury. Cambridge, MA: MIT Press, 2002.

Leys, Ruth. "The Turn to Affect: A Critique." *Critical Inquiry* 37, no. 3 (Spring 2011): 434–72.

McGinn, Colin. *The Meaning of Disgust*. New York: Oxford University Press, 2011.

Massumi, Brian. Parables for the Virtual. Durham, NC: Duke University Press, 2002.

Menninghaus, Winfried. *Disgust: Theory and History of a Strong Sensation*. Translated by Howard Eiland and Joel Golb. Albany: SUNY Press, 2003.

Miller, Susan. *Disgust: The Gatekeeper Emotion*. New York: Routledge, 2004.

Miller, William Ian. *The Anatomy of Disgust*. Cambridge, MA: Harvard University Press, 1997.

Miner, Robert. *Thomas Aquinas on the Passions: A Study of* Summa Theologiae *1a2ae 22–48*. New York: Cambridge University Press, 2009.

Ngai, Sianne. *Ugly Feelings*. Cambridge, MA: Harvard University Press, 2007.

Nussbaum, Martha. *From Disgust to Humanity: Sexual Orientation and Constitutional Law*. New York: Oxford University Press, 2010.

———. *Hiding from Humanity: Disgust, Shame, and the Law*. Princeton: Princeton University Press, 2006.

Outland, Allison M. "'Eat a Leek': Welsh Corrections, English Conditions, and British Cultural Communion." In *This England, That Shakespeare: New Angles on Englishness and the Bard*, edited by Willy Maley and Margaret Tudeau-Clayton, 87–103. Farnham: Ashgate, 2010.

Parker, Patricia. "Uncertain Unions: Welsh Leeks in *Henry V.*" In *British Identities and English Renaissance Literature*, edited by David K. Baker and Willy Maley, 81–100. Cambridge: Cambridge University Press, 2002.

Paster, Gail Kern. *The Body Embarrassed: Drama and the Disciplines of Shame in Early Modern England*. Ithaca: Cornell University Press, 1993.

———. *Humoring the Body: Emotions and the Shakespearean Stage*. Chicago: Chicago University Press, 2004.

———, Katherine Rowe, and Mary Floyd-Wilson. "Introduction: Reading the Early Modern Passions." In *Reading the Early Modern Passions: Essays in the Cultural History of Emotion*, edited by Gail Kern Paster, Katherine Rowe, and Mary Floyd-Wilson, 1–20. Philadelphia: Pennsylvania University Press, 2004.

———, Katherine Rowe, and Mary Floyd-Wilson, eds. *Reading the Early Modern Passions: Essays in the Cultural History of Emotion*. Philadelphia: Pennsylvania University Press, 2004.

Robinson, Benedict. "Disgust c. 1600." *English Literary History* 81, no. 2 (Summer 2014): 553–83.

Schoenfeldt, Michael. "The Art of Disgust: Civility and the Social Body in *Hesperides.*" *George Herbert Journal* 14 (Fall 1990–Spring 1991): 127–54.

Sedgwick, Eve Kosofsky. *Touching Feeling: Affect, Pedagogy, Performativity*. Durham, NC: Duke University Press, 2003.

Shakespeare, William. *Hamlet*. The Arden Shakespeare, Second Series. Edited by Harold Jenkins. Walton-on-Thames: Thomas Nelson, 1982.

Smith, Bruce. *The Key of Green: Passion and Perception in Renaissance Culture*. Chicago: Chicago University Press, 2008.

Terada, Rei. *Feeling in Theory: Emotion after the "Death of the Subject."* Cambridge, MA: Harvard University Press, 2001.

Tomkins, Silvan. *Shame and Its Sisters: A Silvan Tomkins Reader*. Edited by Eve Kosofsky Sedgwick and Adam Frank. Durham, NC: Duke University Press, 1995.

Wright, Thomas. *The Passions of the Mind in General* (1601). Edited by William Webster Newbold. The Renaissance Imagination 15. New York: Garland, 1986.

Part I
Sexual encounters

1   Dirty jokes

Disgust, desire, and the pornographic narrative in Thomas Nashe's *The Unfortunate Traveller*

Emily L. King

Disgust is a peculiar beast. It refuses to present itself as a reliable object of study. It cannot be observed from a safe distance. It will not be met on your own terms. Instead, disgust revolts you in an encounter that almost always feels like an attack. Sianne Ngai observes that this "ugly feeling par excellence" is no vague, amorphous affect, but rather one characterized by the "vehement rejection or *exclusion* of its object."[1] In its emphasis on exclusion, Ngai's discussion of disgust recalls Julia Kristeva's abject. Disgust emerges as the affective response to an encounter with the abject. The connection between disgust and the abject does not end there. As with the abject, there is no universal object of disgust, for that affect depends on a host of variables that include cultural norms, ideological structures, and personal preferences.

That revulsion is not the sole constituent of disgust complicates matters further, for "the disgusting itself has the power to allure," and social taboo only augments its strange appeal.[2] Desire keeps company with revulsion, creating an uncomfortable, even unthinkable blend. Building on the work of Kant and William Ian Miller, Ngai concludes of the amalgam, "What makes the object abhorrent is precisely its outrageous claim for desirability. The disgusting seems to say, 'You want me,' imposing itself on the subject as something to be mingled with and perhaps even enjoyed."[3] That which evokes disgust possesses a magnetism at once convincing and coercive. Excessive consumption of an otherwise utterly desirable object may generate disgust too.[4] What was so attractive the night before can metamorphose into a strange and violent loathing the following morning.[5]

Thanks to the chameleon qualities of disgust, even its theorization offers ample difficulty, as the very attempt to make sense of this unwieldy monster is simultaneously an attempt to domesticate it. For instance, when I label something "disgusting," I channel the overwhelming affects produced by an encounter – fear, loathing, revulsion, rage – into language. I am not left speechless and shaking, but rather am able to categorize that experience and its attendant affects. To name the disgusting is to know it, and it – whatever *it* is – cedes much of its power to overwhelm. Moreover, the term "disgusting" can encode and hold steady ideological frameworks and values. This, too, is domesticated disgust.

With these limitations in mind, I investigate critical reading practices produced in the engagement with disgusting texts in the following pages. What kinds of knowledge – or knowledge gaps – are generated by this affect? What might critical disgust forestall in academic discourse? To initiate a conversation in response to these questions, I examine the literary lineage that pegs Italian pornographer Pietro Aretino as the degenerate father of Elizabethan erotic writing and approach this lineage as a case study of critical disgust. For Elizabethans, Italian satirist and pornographer Pietro Aretino emerged as a "mythic figure of exotic transgression – known by rumor and innuendo, more talked about than read."[6] That mythos has endured for centuries, as Aretino has come to represent all that smacks of scandal within the early modern English imaginary.[7] Identifying a vein of "violently sexualized discourse" in Elizabethan erotic writing – writing that includes the work of John Marston, Thomas Middleton, and Thomas Nashe – Lynda Boose pins the blame squarely on Aretino for this trend. Strikingly, though, Boose offers no evidence from Aretino's writing to substantiate these claims.[8] Despite this notable omission, her landmark work charting out a derivative relationship between Aretino and Elizabethan erotic writing continues to be echoed by recent critics, including Ian Moulton and Andrew S. Keener.[9]

To call into question the presumed influence of Aretino on English erotic writing, I look at two texts: Aretino's *Ragionamenti*, published in London in 1584, and Thomas Nashe's *The Unfortunate Traveller*, published there ten years later, an unwieldy picaresque novel that makes use of travel and romance genres, and in which Aretino himself makes a posthumous appearance.[10] To distinguish the work of Aretino and that of the English Aretine, I attend to the comic modes underpinning analogous scenes of rape in each text.[11] Comedy emerges to me as a most unlikely, even unwelcome, lens through which to view rape in literature. But, as Rick Bowers reminds us, "laughter is not always pleasant . . . [and] comedy is not always safe."[12] To pursue that perilous line of inquiry, I make use of Alenka Zupančič's foundational work on comedy to demonstrate how Aretino's text is aligned with conventional comedy, which is governed by substitutive logic, while the work of Nashe is aligned with radical comedy, which is governed by the logic of surplus.[13] This comparison suggests how, if the violent turn in Elizabethan pornography derives from Aretino at all, it is a child turned changeling.

Disgust comes into play through my investigation of pornographic descriptions of rape. Beyond the gross violation and attendant trauma of sexual violence explicit or implicit in the depiction of these moments, what also seems disgusting is the possibility of deriving pleasure from another's suffering and, perhaps more unthinkable, deriving amusement. Even as I make that assertion, though, I recognize that the classification is purely subjective. Treating representations of rape as static objects heralds the specter of the disgusting as well. Rather than focusing my efforts solely on the condemnation of rape or delegitimizing the literary works in which these moments are included, I take them seriously. I deem these episodes worthy of study. That, too, feels disgusting. Given the affective baggage such a project can bring with it, it is little wonder that this work has been largely avoided.

In troubling the assumed lineage of Elizabethan erotic writing, I will not supply an alternative history or origin story to account for its more violent, misogynistic turns. After all, the search for an origin is an attempt to locate and to quarantine disgusting material, to allocate blame to some while exonerating others. Such a move might well characterize most critical reading practices that engage with disgusting texts. Instead, my project illumines more broadly the problems that disgust poses to critical reading practices: namely, that this affect distorts interpretations of literary texts and that the blind spots that originate from such reading practices can persist for centuries. If we may deduce anything from these "disgusting" early modern texts, it is that their inclusion of seemingly disgusting sexuality suggests an early modern culture that was beginning to normalize the uncomfortable mingling of desire and disgust. Surely, then, we need critical reading practices that are adequate to the task of encountering disgust or, barring that, scholars who remain aware of the effect of critical disgust on interpretative practices.

Dirty books

To what does early modern pornography refer? Notable critics, among them David Frantz, Ian Moulton, Bette Talvacchia, and Sarah Toulalan, have wrestled with this question, and nearly all agree that pornography, early modern or otherwise, resists definitive boundaries.[14] As for the historical specificity of early modern pornography, some scholars argue that the term is an anachronism; others point to its existence in early modern culture.[15] For those who come to the latter conclusion, like Sarah Toulalan, early modern pornography emerges as distinct in several ways. Early modern pornography solicited laughter in its construction of narrative, for instance treating laughter not as an obstacle to orgasm but as an outburst that resembled and, perhaps, aided climax.[16] The disgusting discharges of the body, rather than being fodder for fetish or other pornographic subcategories, were part and parcel of the early modern erotic. In humoral theory, insofar as bodily secretions are substitutive, blood could represent both semen and breast milk; these excretions are not dirty, but rather integral to the maintenance of good health.[17] Yet, it is not simply the solicitation of laughter or a subscription to humoral theory that distinguishes early modern pornography from its twenty-first century analogues. In the later decades of the sixteenth century, a trend emerged in erotic writing that was characterized by the "hostile, malcontented potential aggressions of the violently sexualized discourse," a trend in which eruptions of grisly violence are grafted onto erotic episodes.[18] Boose first identifies the trend in Elizabethan writing and reads it as the implicit target of the 1599 Bishops' Ban, which, she contends, was inspired by the "pornographic pleasures of Aretino."[19]

Throughout sixteenth-century Europe, however, Aretino was regarded as more than a peddler of the salacious. He was one of the best-known writers in Europe.[20] As the notorious "scourge of princes," Aretino was both satirist and pornographer, often deploying sexually explicit writing as the means by which he ridiculed those in power.[21] But it was his reputation as pornographer that exceeded him posthumously. "In the word 'Aretine,'" as Moulton observes, "Elizabethans coined an

adjective that powerfully linked troubling notions of foreignness, erotic disorder, authorial power, and social mobility."[22] To complicate Aretino's reputation
further, a range of works that he did not author nevertheless became associated
with him.[23] His early work included the composition of sixteen obscene sonnets
(*I Sonnetti Lussuriosi*) to accompany Giulio Romano's *I Modi* (1527), a collection of sexual pictures. *Ragionamenti*, of which *The Secret Life of Wives* is a part,
features bawdy dialogues and tales exchanged between an experienced courtesan
(Nanna), her confidante (Antonia), and her daughter (Pippa). Originally published
in Venice in 1534, *Ragionamenti* arrived in London in 1584 through the efforts of
John Wolfe, Gabriel Harvey's publisher. But *Ragionamenti*'s notoriety preceded
its London debut as the entirety of Aretino's works – and not simply the salacious ones – had been placed on the Catholic Church's Index of Prohibited Books
decades prior in 1569, three years following his death. While this ban stemmed
from political intrigue rather than moral fastidiousness, that act nevertheless stig-
matized Aretino and his work in Italy and abroad, a stigma that, I would argue,
continues today. On account of its disgusting misogyny – perceived or otherwise – Aretino's erotic work is often summarily dismissed.[24] But *Ragionamenti*
presents different voices, perspectives, and even rather liberal condemnations of
the material realities in which Italian courtesans find themselves. This is a text
sufficiently complicated and contradictory to merit sustained consideration.

One way to combat the critical blind spots that arise from such dismissals is
to examine *Ragionamenti* along the fault lines of desire, violence, and comedy.
Zupančič offers a valuable theoretical framework for comedy in *The Odd One
In*. Defining comedy as a process "in constant motion," Zupančič argues that this
fundamental feature makes comedy "so difficult to pin down with concepts and
definitions . . . [for these] definitions as materials [are then] submitted to further
comic treatment, turned upside down, or inside out."[25] While Zupančič's comedy
is predicated on ceaseless movement, it is by no means linear. She explains: "The
field of comedy is essentially the field in which the answer precedes the question,
satisfaction precedes the demand. Not only do we (or the comic characters) not
get what we haven't asked for, *on top of it* (and not instead of it) we get something
we haven't even asked for at all."[26] Whereas conventional comedy makes use of
substitution or metaphor in which one term is exchanged for another and jokes
conclude with a sense of satisfaction, Zupančič's comedy – *radical* comedy – is
predicated on excess. Jokes don't end and satisfaction is perpetually deferred.

In the following episode, one of the most troubling in *Ragionamenti* due to its
ambiguous treatment of sexual violence, I argue that Aretino's use of conventional
comedy supplants the horror of the *trentuno*, a gang rape typically reserved for
Italian courtesans, and reroutes the narrative through female voices and desires.[27]
From the very outset this story is governed by substitutive logic, beginning as it
does with a married woman who trades beds with a virginal peasant, the intended
target of this so-called "game." By tricking the male participants, the married
woman experiences the long-denied pleasures of sex. As Antonia, one of the nar-
rators, quips, "Blessed are the women who can satisfy their desires."[28] Here, Antonia recycles a line from the Gospel of Matthew only to substitute terms to form

a new beatitude. Even her use of "satisfy" in the English translation might be understood through substitutive logic. Satisfy, in the original Latin (*satisfacere*), is a portmanteau comprising *satis* (enough) and *facere* (to do). There is neither debt nor excess, but rather just enough. Such a reading holds steady in the original Italian insofar as *cavare* means to mine, to hollow out, to draw out, and even to obtain. The reflexive use of the verb (*cavarsi*) in the 1584 text suggests, then, "to get oneself." In other words, Aretino's sentence translates most literally to "Blessed are those who know how to draw out their cravings from themselves." Even desire, that yearning for something supplemental, something more, can be met in oneself.

Despite the potentially graphic nature of these sexual encounters, Aretino embeds them in euphemism. Vaginal penetration, for instance, is described alternately as "seal[ing] her letter" or "putting his pike in the fish-pond" while the aroused male participants are described as "greedy . . . monk[s] rushing to get" their "broth."[29] This is not to suggest that the euphemisms fail to convey their messages. As Toulalan argues of English erotic writing, metaphor "reveals and provides many different ways of talking about sexual matters. The indirectness of the language, the exaggerated and prevalent use of sexual innuendo and double entendre, are both part of the comedy and part of the sex."[30] But metaphors, instantiating comedy in the gaps they create between what they attempt to describe and what they actually say, are governed by a substitutive, rather than excessive, logic. The terms themselves are merely exchanged.

Such an endless exchange, however, can prove maddening. Losing her patience with the ambiguity of metaphor, Antonia tells Nanna:

> Speak plainly and say 'fuck,' 'prick,' 'cunt,' and 'ass' if you want anyone except the scholars of the University of Rome to understand you. You with your 'rope in the ring,' . . . your 'parsnip,' your 'little monkey,' your 'this,' your 'that,' your 'him' and your 'her,' your 'apples,' 'leaves of the missal,' 'fact,' '*verbigratia*,' 'job,' 'affair,' 'big news,' 'handle,' 'arrow,' 'carrot,' 'root,' and all the shit there is – why don't you say it straight out and stop going about on tiptoes?[31]

But even Antonia's castigation of circumlocution celebrates the rhetorical brilliance of innuendo, and the substantial list of phallic synonyms suggests that all signs point to the penis. Every signifier, even the innocuous "this," is subsumed under sexual innuendo.

Furthermore, even what seems to be surplus is merely metaphor in disguise. The following descriptions, reminiscent of schoolyard jests regarding excretion, are predicated on substitutive logic as well. For instance, when one of the men first penetrates the mistress of the house, he simultaneously passes gas: "He let off three claps of thunder without lightning; she broke out into a cold sweat at the smell, and said to herself, 'These thirty-oners are so rude!'"[32] But it's not simply the men that seem disgusting. Bodies and their by-products are described in vertiginous detail. The combination of semen and vaginal secretions is referred to as "joy-juice" (in which the mistress is "contentedly up to her thighs"), and attempted penetration is described as "swim[ming] in that sea of nut-oil without so much as a dried marrow for a lifebelt."[33] This excess of body fluids makes her "whistle and bagpipes . . . as gluey and slimey as a slug's lair" such that one participant requests that the mistress sniff his "caper-bush" or pubic hair instead of engaging in penetrative intercourse.[34] Nevertheless, the excess is delivered by metaphor, not simile, and these colorful euphemisms are never clarified by Aretino's text.

At the conclusion of this romp, the excess metamorphoses into lack, but not through the usual path of metaphor. Thanks to the sheer volume of bodily fluids, the mistress excuses herself to make an emergency visit to the toilet. Curiously, her urgent visit signals a violent episode of diarrhea: "But she could no longer keep her meal in, and had to rush to the loo, where she loosened her innards and, in the same way that a well-fed abbot unloads the soup from his belly, released into the earthly limbo twenty-seven unborn souls."[35] Miraculously, this blend of "joy-juice" and "nut-oil" produces "twenty-seven unborn souls" in the span of mere sentences.[36] Here, Aretino conflates gluttony with miscarriage, and in a rare use of simile, sexual incontinence is made (more) visible through the gastronomic incontinence of the now familiar figure of the monk. This conclusion in which the mistress unceremoniously deposits the remnants of her wild night in the toilet stems, certainly, from excess, but results, conclusively, in evacuation.

It is not just that Aretino deals in metaphor, the marker of traditional modes of comedy. The overall structure of his tale sidesteps altogether the excess described by Zupančič in favor of deficiency, or lack. To move the narrative along – an impulse that in and of itself betrays a desire for economy – Aretino writes: "Anyway, I won't keep you up all night telling you about every single fellow – they all gave it to her in every style, every way, every fashion, every manner and every kind imaginable."[37] Gesturing toward the infinite potentiality of this romp, Aretino repeats the adjective "every" (*tutte* in the Italian), creating the opposite of the intended effect. Indeed, whatever kinds of sex a reader might imagine, the possibilities have always already been explored. We have not a surplus of description, but a dearth. Finally, we might consider that the heroine receives not thirty-one men as the tradition demands, but only twenty-seven.[38] We have not innovation, but exhaustion.

Through the deployment of traditional comedy, one that is predicated on substitution and, when necessary, privileges lack over excess, Aretino dissipates the brutality of what would be an otherwise shocking episode of sexual violence. The comedy inverts the situation such that the initial would-be target of the gang rape, the "pretty country wench," is furious with her mistress for stealing all the fun.[39] But it is not simply that conventional comedy domesticates sexual violence. Comedy renders the abhorrent and disgusting laughable and amusing. As readers, we can snicker safely at the absurd scenario, for no characters are harmed by the neutralized violence. Indeed, this comic mode shields readers and characters from the disgusting. It functions as a protective screen from which we might court the disgusting without being forced to reel from the consequences of a genuine encounter. Any enjoyment stems, then, from our imaginary proximity to, but ultimately safe position from, the disgusting.

Radical comedy

In contrast to Aretino's minimalism, Thomas Nashe's *The Unfortunate Traveller* offers copious incoherence. As C.S. Lewis famously remarked of this text, "If asked what Nashe 'says,' we should have to say, 'Nothing.'"[40] Subsequent scholars have interpreted the unwieldiness of *The Unfortunate Traveller* as indicative of generic innovation,[41] a satire of Neoplatonic ideals,[42] and even a revision of Renaissance skepticism.[43] Still others have linked the issue of genre to Nashe's graphic representations of violence that occur throughout the text. Though Agnes Latham surmises, "Nashe found in exaggerated scenes of blood and sudden death an endless source of fun,"[44] that violence, far from gratuitous according to other scholars, is part and parcel of the generic revisions Nashe accomplishes in *The Unfortunate Traveller*.[45]

Disgust and desire collide most explicitly in the descriptions of rape in this text. Whereas Aretino domesticates rape through traditional modes of comedy, Nashe offers no such mitigation. Radical, too, is Nashe's unflinching narration of sexual assault. Despite the theatricality demanded of early modern rape victims – insofar as victims were expected to perform a particular narrative in order to prove their status as victims[46] – sexual assault was never performed or represented directly on the early modern stage.[47] Its performance takes place only at the margins. It is significant, then, that through its graphic portrayal of sexual assault *The Unfortunate Traveller* accomplishes what early modern English theater was unable to achieve.

When the notorious Esdras of Granado, a *bandito* who serves as an assassin for the Pope, attacks the vulnerable household in which narrator Jack Wilton is staying, two women are assaulted: Heraclide, the mistress of the house, and Diamante, Wilton's beloved.[48] The text focuses exclusively on Heraclide, whom Esdras of Granado assaults physically and sexually while pinning her down atop the corpse of her recently deceased husband. An impotent Wilton watches through a keyhole:

> Backward he dragged her, even as a man backward would pluck a tree down by the twigs, and then, like a traitor that is drawn to execution on a hurdle, he traileth her up and down the chamber by those tender untwisted braids, and setting his barbarous foot on her bare snowy breast, bad her yield or have her wind stamped out.[49]

To depict the violence inflicted on Heraclide, an explicit, straightforward narrative is insufficient. Nashe augments his chronicle with both figurative language and explicit descriptions. In particular, the use of simile, as opposed to metaphor, affords a supplemental, rather than substitutive, logic. Moreover, these examples of supplemental logic prove contradictory. When Nashe describes how Heraclide is pulled around her room by her hair, he likens her to a traitor brought forcibly to the site of execution. Such a comparison creates dissonance insofar as Heraclide functions as both victim and "traitor." To compare her to a traitor who in some way deserves state-sponsored execution is to thoroughly undermine her status as victim. To further complicate the excess of figurative and explicit description, Nashe aestheticizes, even sexualizes the violence as he embeds Petrarchan conceits – "bare snowy breast," "lily lawn-skinned neck," "ivory throat," and "tender untwisted braids" – into the episode.[50] Even as Nashe fixes his readers' attention to the traumatic violence visited on Heraclide's body, he unfailingly reminds us that this is a beautiful body being violated, and that perhaps even the violation itself is a thing of beauty.

But Nashe's readers are not innocent witnesses. They, too, are involved in the construction of this violent narrative:

> Dismissing her hair from his fingers and pinioning her elbows therewithal, she struggled, she wrested, but all was in vain. So struggling and so resisting, her jewels did sweat, signifying there was poison coming towards her. On the hard boards he threw her, and used his knee as an iron ram to beat open the two-leaved gate of her chastity. Her husband's dead body he made a pillow to his abomination. Conjecture the rest, my words stick fast in the mire and are clean tired; would I had never undertook this tragical tale.[51]

If Jack Wilton's engagement with this episode concluded at "abomination," the assessments of Mihoko Suzuki and Steven Mentz – that the passage marks the limit to Nashe's narrative power – would be most convincing.[52] But Wilton's stop is a false one, and "Conjecture the rest" emerges as a stranger, far more disingenuous imperative. Nashe takes great pains to detail the sexual violence enacted against Heraclide, and very little is left for us to conjecture. Nashe commands his readers to stand in as voyeurs when Wilton becomes too "tired," thus coercing us to participate in the construction of the narrative. We are permitted neither passivity nor protection from the disgusting. Furthermore, the text presupposes that we would desire to know more through the supplementary logic of this phrase – indeed, that there is always *more* to know.

The Unfortunate Traveller emblematizes the movement that Zupančič associates with radical comedy.[53] Everything, even the tragic figure of Heraclide who is aligned with Lucrece and Philomela, is fodder for the comic machine, and the joke just keeps *going*. Immediately following the rape of Heraclide, Nashe makes reference to ill-fitting analogues in classical history. When Heraclide gazes on her husband's corpse, for instance, Wilton observes how "she bewailed as Cephalus when he had killed Procris unwittingly, or Oedipus when ignorantly he had slain his father and known his mother incestuously."[54] Insofar as the text aligns Heraclide with figures who have unintentionally committed murder, patricide, and incest, she appears implicated by her proximity to them.[55] One might also make sense of this digression as a reference to Heraclide's belief – rather than that of the text, or of the narrator – in her own culpability. Present, finally, is the possibility that the text refuses to choose between these options in favor of clever complication, contradiction, and indecipherable insult.

As Jack Wilton chronicles the aftermath of the crime, his initial tone is one of mourning. He attempts to wrest a particular affect from his readers and direct their appropriately sorrowful countenances:

> Let not your sorrow die, you that have read the proem and narration of this elegiacal history. Show you have quick wits in sharp conceit of compassion. . . . This woman, this matron, this forsaken Heraclide, having buried fourteen children in five days, whose eyes she howlingly closed and caught many wrinkles with funeral kisses, besides having her husband within a day after laid forth as a comfortless corpse, a carrionly block.[56]

But what appears darkly amusing here is the command, "Let not your sorrow die," when only lines later Nashe will goad his readers into doing the opposite. Swerving away from the rhetoric of high tragedy, the tone radically shifts, urging an encounter with cruel comedy. Forced into a burlesque of a Lucrece-like suicide, Heraclide proclaims in her final speech, "Point, pierce, edge, enwiden, I patiently afford thee a sheath. Spur forth my soul to mount post to heaven. Jesu, forgive me; Jesu receive me!"[57] Insofar as Heraclide is made to fetishize the phallic qualities of the sword, insofar as "vagina" itself derives from the Latin word for "sheath," insofar as her religiosity gestures toward an orgasmic frenzy, Heraclide's graphic rape is indeed taken lightly by the text. Such lightness is made more explicit as Wilton observes wryly, "So, *thoroughly stabbed*, fell [Heraclide] down and knocked her head against her husband's body".[58] The lightness with which this "little death" is received deflates utterly Wilton's prior insistence on sympathy for Heraclide. In fact, the narrative's radical comedy emerges as yet another instance of violence against her.

Nevertheless, this witticism is hardly enough for Wilton, as the burlesque degenerates into downright farce. As Heraclide's corpse falls to the ground, its downward motion revives her "dead" husband, and he "awakens" with a start. The attendant puns are so explicit that they barely merit mention. As for Wilton, Heraclide's husband mistakes him for the rapist, and Wilton is consequently imprisoned to await execution. Wilton is saved at the last moment, only to be reunited later with Diamante, the courtesan whom he calls his wife. In contrast to the unfortunate Heraclide, Diamante seems thoroughly untouched by her sexual trauma and is located after Wilton falls through a cellar door only to spy her kissing a young apprentice in bed above him. As the text vacillates between these two extreme approaches to sexual assault, we might conclude that the blitheness with which Diamante brushes off her sexual assault undercuts further the tragic performance of Heraclide.

Through the lens of comedy, the genealogical connections between Nashe and Aretino are revealed as tenuous, and their salient difference comes to the fore. Because scholars have read this literary genealogy backwards, attempting to account for the turn in Elizabethan writing by connecting it back to Aretino, they have fit these texts to a Procrustean bed, an imposed historical narrative that distorts. For Aretino, conservative comedy operates as a screen, a buffer for both characters and readers, and domesticates sexual violence and all that might evoke disgust. As puerile jokes abound in *Ragionamenti*, no one character is the target of laughter, and readers are invited to laugh at the curiously insistent corporeal body, a body that is at once disgusting and ungovernable. And though this disgusting body might implicate readers – we have bodies, too – it does not threaten us. The substitutive humor courts laughter and relieves anxiety. Conservative comedy, with its predictable punch lines, neutralizes the potential threat of disgust.

Radical comedy, in contrast, is no laughing matter, supplementing the disgusting rather than screening against it. *The Unfortunate Traveller* coerces readers into an uncomfortable proximity to the disgusting when, for instance, its narrative demands readers to "conjecture the rest" after reading the vertiginous details of Heraclide's rape. Then, with as much pathos as the text mustered earlier, it ironizes the very sympathies elicited from readers by refashioning those affects into comic targets. But unwitting readers are not the only targets, for the comedy turns on Heraclide, too, and engages in further violence by undermining her status as victim. Finally, there is the persistent matter of the comic surplus itself, the excess that cannot be neutralized and serves as that which keeps the comic machine going. We might make sense of this surplus in *The Unfortunate Traveller* as a mode of revenge: in this pornographic episode, it's a surplus that makes us sick, a desire that metamorphoses into disgust, perhaps by giving us exactly what we thought we never wanted. And more.

One word more: A coda

In a 1988 theater review of Brian Cox's *Titus Andronicus*, a production that emphasized the violent sexual, bodily, and psychic harm enacted on Lavinia, theater critic Jack Tinker wrote: "The production . . . is possessed of a timely moral force. Who can look on Sonia Ritter's quivering Lavinia, her tongue, hands and chastity ripped from her, and not know pity?"[59] The presumption of a universalized response remains at odds, however, with disgust's complexity. In the framing of Tinker's rhetorical question, he cites not Lavinia as that which evokes pity, but "Sonia Ritter's quivering Lavinia." The structure of Tinker's question reveals that the audience's response is solicited less by Lavinia, the details of her trauma, or even the matter of rape more generally, but rather by the virtuosic performance of Sonia Ritter. Indeed, it's precisely the particularities of this performance that according to Tinker ensure a universal audience affect. And though Tinker asserts, albeit tacitly, that no one could find the disgusting amusing and pleasurable, some people do. A reasonable person cannot conclude from the insidious presence of rape in the United States and around the globe that all people find sexual violence disgusting.

But my motivation for analyzing this example is not to dissuade anyone from finding sexual violence repugnant but rather to detail the symptoms of encountering texts that provoke disgust, whether one is a theater or a literary critic. In the deployment of his rhetorical question, Tinker directs the affect of his readers. At the risk of belaboring a prior claim, I would suggest that, insofar as an audience's affect merits direction, such a move reveals the fictiveness of and anxiety surrounding the very notion of a universalized response to the disgusting. And in directing affect *toward* some end, it is also simultaneously directing one *away* from something else. In this case, audience members are urged toward pity elicited by a specific performance of victimhood; all other affective possibilities (e.g., grief, empathy, anxiety, terror, retributive fury) are shut down. Even those who might feel otherwise are themselves jettisoned according to the logic of this question. For Tinker, the ability to pity the traumatized Lavinia becomes the mark of the human. Conversely, the inability to know pity would produce not a *who* but a *what*. Indeed, as Tinker expels those who would "not know pity," he produces the very disgust he encounters in this production of *Titus Andronicus*. That is, he engages in the violent repulsion, distancing, and condemnation that characterize an encounter with the disgusting. Who could blame him? It is all too tempting, after all, to perform righteous indignation as the means by which we maintain our control over this troublesome emotion. Perhaps, then, the best we can do as literary critics is to relinquish the impulse to master our disgust, to recognize that mastering this overwhelming affect is an impossible project, and to admit the possibility that the force of the disgusting derives, in part, from a modicum of desire.[60]

Notes

1 Ngai, *Ugly Feelings*, 334, 22.
2 Miller, *Anatomy*, 111. Ngai, *Ugly Feelings*, 333. Julia Kristeva writes, "What is *abject*, on the contrary, the jettisoned object, is radically excluded and draws me toward the place where meaning collapses." Identity formation occurs, then, through the primal repression of the maternal body (i.e., the body of the Other). While the subject craves this body, that craving is ultimately prohibited, or abjected. Kristeva, *Powers*, 2.
3 Ngai, *Ugly Feelings*, 335.
4 Ngai, *Ugly Feelings*, 352.
5 Elsewhere Ngai writes of this phenomenon: "Art crams itself with what has been officially deemed desirable to a point at which it crosses a line from being disgusted to being *disgusting*." Ngai, *Ugly Feelings*, 353.
6 Moulton, *Before Pornography*, 119.
7 In recent decades, scholars have evinced interest in Aretino. Notable works include Ian Moulton's *Before Pornography*, as well as Raymond Waddington's *Aretino's Satyr* and *Pietro Aretino*. However, this interest has not yet generated a reevaluation of Aretino's influence on Elizabethan erotic writing.
8 Boose, "1599," 195, writes:

> No doubt because late Elizabethan culture recognized its own image in what it denounced as an invasion of literary filth from Italy, Aretino was not only well known by the 1590s – he was infamous. So much so that David McPherson has argued that the deluge of works in the 1590s depicting Italian diabolism owes its impetus more to England's contact with Aretino than with Machiavelli. Within a decade of Aretino's arrival, writers such as Thomas Nashe and John Marston suddenly began experimenting with a type of literature that cannot be defined generically as either the Elizabethan bawdy or the Ovidian sensual. . . . This new type of literature, *Metamorphosis* included, bears the graphic stamp of Aretino.

However, Boose offers no evidence for the assumed connection between Aretino, Nashe, and Marston. She does not, for instance, examine Aretino's work to demonstrate the proximity between his texts and theirs. Most problematically, she takes Aretino's historical proximity as proof of a causal, or influential, relationship to English writers.

9 Moulton, *Before Pornography*, 158–93; Keener, "Robert Tofte," 506–32.
10 For a nuanced portrait of the relationship between Nashe and Aretino in terms of literary authority, see Brown, *Redefining*, 98–9.
11 Diminishing the salient differences between the work of Nashe and Aretino, Rhodes argues for their stylistic similarity. See *Elizabethan Grotesque*, 26–36.
12 Bowers, *Radical Comedy*, 4.
13 Zupančič, *Odd One In*, 7–8, 140–47.
14 Frantz, *Festum Voluptatis*; Moulton, *Before Pornography*; Talvacchia, *Taking Positions*; Toulalan, *Imagining Sex*.
15 "It makes no more sense," Moulton muses, "to speak of sixteenth-century English pornography than it does to speak of sixteenth-century English haiku. Neither of these genres existed in that culture, though that did not stop people from writing about sex or writing short striking poems." Moulton, *Before Pornography*, 15.
16 Toulalan, *Imagining Sex*, 34.
17 Toulalan argues that "while today scatological humor carries overtones of dirt and disgust, the positive associations of excretion and purging with health in Renaissance medicine suggests that this may not have been a response shared by an early modern audience." Toulalan, *Imagining Sex*, 199. Though Toulalan's claim reminds us of the problems of theorizing disgust across vast historical periods, it is also complicated by other texts that, like Ben Jonson's *Bartholomew Fair*, deploy satiric depictions of the incontinent body to generate laughter.
18 Boose, "1599," 193.
19 Boose, "1599," 197.
20 Moulton, *Before Pornography*, 119. See also Waddington, *Aretino's Satyr*, 94–5.
21 Waddington makes note of the false etymology that derived "satire" from "satyr," an error that persisted through the sixteenth century. Consequently, the intertwined satire/satyr suggested the marriage of truthfulness and sexuality that was integral to satire. See Waddington, *Aretino's Satyr*, 94–5.
22 Moulton, *Before Pornography*, 120.
23 Lorenzo Veniero, for example, authored *Puttana errante* (Errant Whore) and *La Trentuna di Zaffetta* (The Gang Rape of Zaffetta), which were posthumously associated with Aretino. As Moulton observes, the latter poem chronicles the actual sexual assault of Venetian courtesan Angela Zaffetta, whom Aretino celebrated in his personal letters. Moulton, *Before Pornography*, 150.
24 Boose, "1599"; Celia Daileader, "Back Door Sex," 312–13. For a more expansive discussion of Aretino's reception, see Waddington, *Aretino's Satyr*, xvii–xxv.
25 Zupančič, *Odd One In*, 3.
26 Zupančič, *Odd One In*, 132.
27 Although early modern scholars appear in agreement regarding the definition of *trentuno* as a punishment against courtesans, there is little indication of how they arrived at this consensus. Even as I have not located primary sources that attest to the *trentuno*'s prevalence in sixteenth-century Italy, such a gap in the archive is of little surprise. Lorenzo Veniero's *Il Trentuno della Zaffetta* (1531) appears as the earliest instance of the term in Italian literature, and the poem depicts the historical rape of Angela Zaffetta, a Venetian courtesan with whom Aretino corresponded. See Ferguson, *Honest Courtesan*, 37–8; Moulton, *Before Pornography*, 150; Quaintance, "Deforming," 200–201.
28 Aretino, *Wives*, 42. The excerpts in Italian are taken from Aretino's *Ragionamenti*.
29 Aretino, *Wives*, 40.
30 Toulalan, *Imagining Sex*, 212–13.

31   Aretino, *Dialogues*, 43–4.

32   Aretino, *Wives*, 40–41.

33   Aretino, *Wives*, 41.

34   Aretino, *Wives*, 41.

35   Aretino, *Wives*, 42.

36   Aretino, *Wives*, 41–2.

37   Aretino, *Wives*, 41.

38   Recalling her own experiences with the *trentuno*, Nanna remarks: "It just goes on for too long. I admit that if it lasted just half the time, it would be a real blast." Aretino, *Wives*, 42.

39   Aretino, *Wives*, 42.

40   Lewis, *English Literature*, 416.

41   Andersen, "Anti-Puritanism"; Gohlke, "Wits Wantonness."

42   See, for instance, Jones, "Anti-Petrarchan Satire."

43   Mentz, "Heroine," 339.

44   Latham, "Satire," 87.

45   Suzuki, "Signiorie." See also Keefer, "Violence."

46   The legal responsibilities for early modern victims of sexual assault were twofold: they must make verbal complaints and offer physical proof. Inherent to these two tasks is the theatrical means by which women assume the narrative of rape and fit themselves within it in order to be taken seriously. Analyzing early modern rape legislation that ranges from the 1187 Glanvill treatise to *The Lawes Resolutions of Womens Rights* (1632), Solga concludes that these statutes "encourage women to body forth the implicit theatricality of – *the performance of innocence* implied by – the scripts in the earlier treatises" and rape is a " 'rehearsal' that, for public purposes, is an original, an event that can be witnessed and therefore subsequently may be prosecuted." Solga, *Invisible Acts*, 38–9.

47   Solga, *Invisible Acts*, 30; Catty, *Writing Rape*, 108.

48   Referred to throughout the text as "the courtesan whom I call my wife," Diamante is introduced to readers through allusions to the Wife of Bath and Alison of *The Miller's Tale*. Mentz, "Heroine," 354.

49   Nashe, *Unfortunate Traveller*, 336.

50   Nashe, *Unfortunate Traveller*, 336.

51   Nashe, *Unfortunate Traveller*, 336.

52   Of this moment and the Anabaptist execution, Suzuki argues, "Nashe's art, which attempts to imitate actuality that is ruled by such violence, can lead only to silence." Suzuki, "Signiorie," 363–9. See also Mentz, "Heroine," 351.

53   This comic movement speaks to the phenomenon Walter J. Ong observes when he writes that Nashe "tries out his reader in every role he can think of." Ong argues that the text's scattershot approach demonstrates Elizabethan anxieties about the move from a chirographic to print culture. Ong, *Interfaces*, 71. Though Mentz, for instance, has observed Nashe's comedy, he contains its unwieldiness by explaining that this unthinkable conclusion is the "essence of romance." Mentz, "Heroine," 353. In other words, this comedy is domesticated in favor of its neat categorization within the genre of romance.

54   Nashe, *Unfortunate Traveller*, 337.

55   Mentz, "Heroine," 352.

56   Nashe, *Unfortunate Traveller*, 336–7.

57   Nashe, *Unfortunate Traveller*, 339.

58   Nashe, *Unfortunate Traveller*, 339; emphasis mine.

59   Tinker, "Review," 902, quoted in Solga, *Invisible Acts*, 55.

60   Many thanks to Natalie Eschenbaum, Barbara Correll, and Diego Millan for their generous assistance with this essay.

References

Andersen, Jennifer L. "Anti-Puritanism, Anti-Popery, and Gallows Rhetoric in Thomas Nashe's *The Unfortunate Traveller.*" *Sixteenth Century Journal* 35, no. 1 (2004): 43–63.

Aretino, Pietro. *Aretino's Dialogues.* Translated by Raymond Rosenthal. New York: Marsilio, 1994.

———. *Ragionamenti.* London: John Wolfe, 1584.

———. *The Secret Life of Wives.* Translated by Andrew Brown. London: Hesperus, 2006.

Boose, Lynda. "The 1599 Bishops' Ban, Elizabethan Pornography, and the Sexualization of the Jacobean Stage." In *Enclosure Acts: Sexuality, Property, and Culture in Early Modern England,* edited by Richard Burt and John Michael Archer, 185–200. Ithaca: Cornell University Press, 1994.

Bowers, Rick. *Radical Comedy in Early Modern England.* Farnham: Ashgate, 2008.

Brown, Georgia. *Redefining Elizabethan Literature.* Cambridge: Cambridge University Press, 2004.

Catty, Jocelyn. *Writing Rape, Writing Women in Early Modern England: Unbridled Speech.* Basingstoke: Macmillan, 1999.

Daileader, Celia R. "Back Door Sex: Renaissance Gynosodomy, Aretino, and the Exotic." *English Literary History* 69, no. 2 (Summer 2002): 303–34.

Ferguson, Margaret F. *The Honest Courtesan: Veronica Franco, Citizen and Writer in Sixteenth-Century Venice.* Chicago: University of Chicago Press, 1992.

Frantz, David. *Festum Voluptatis: A Study of Renaissance Erotica.* Columbus: Ohio State University Press, 1989.

Gohlke, Madelon S. "Wits Wantonness: *The Unfortunate Traveller* as Picaresque." *Studies in Philology* 73, no. 4 (Winter 1976): 397–413.

Jones, Dorothy. "An Example of Anti-Petrarchan Satire in Nashe's *The Unfortunate Traveller.*" *Yearbook of English Studies* 1 (1971): 48–54.

Keefer, Michael. "Violence and Extremity: Nashe's *Unfortunate Traveller* as an Anatomy of Abjection." In *Critical Approaches to Elizabethan Prose Fiction, 1520–1640,* edited by Donald Beecher, 183–218. Ottawa: Dovehouse, 1998.

Keener, Andrew S. "Robert Tofte's *Of Mariage and Wiuing* and the Bishops' Ban of 1599." *Studies in Philology* 110, no. 3 (Summer 2013): 506–32.

Kristeva, Julia. *Powers of Horror: An Essay on Abjection.* Translated by Leon S. Roudiez. New York: Columbia University Press, 1982.

Latham, Agnes. "Satire on Literary Themes and Modes in Nashe's *Unfortunate Traveller.*" *English Studies* 1 (1948): 85–100.

Lewis, Clive Staples. *English Literature in the Sixteenth Century: Excluding Drama.* Oxford: Clarendon Press, 1954.

Mentz, Steven R. "The Heroine as Courtesan: Dishonesty, Romance, and the Sense of an Ending in *The Unfortunate Traveller.*" *Studies in Philology* 98, no. 3 (Summer 2001): 339–58.

Miller, William Ian. *The Anatomy of Disgust.* Cambridge, MA: Harvard University Press, 1997.

Moulton, Ian Frederick. *Before Pornography: Erotic Writing in Early Modern England.* Oxford: Oxford University Press, 2005.

Nashe, Thomas. "The Unfortunate Traveller." In *The Unfortunate Traveller and Other Works.* Edited by J.B. Steane, 251–370. Harmondsworth: Penguin, 1972.

Ngai, Sianne. *Ugly Feelings.* Cambridge, MA: Harvard University Press, 2007.

Ong, Walter J. *Interfaces of the Word: Studies in the Evolution of Consciousness and Culture.* Ithaca: Cornell University Press, 1977.

Quaintance, Courtney. "Defaming the Courtesan: Satire and Invective in Sixteenth-Century Italy." In *The Courtesan's Arts: Cross-Cultural Perspectives*, edited by Martha Feldman and Bonnie Gordon, 199–208. Oxford: Oxford University Press, 2006.

Rhodes, Neil. *Elizabethan Grotesque*. London: Routledge, 1980.

Solga, Kim. *Violence Against Women in Early Modern Performance: Invisible Acts*. Basingstoke: Palgrave Macmillan, 2009.

Suzuki, Mihoko. "'Signiorie Ouer the Pages': The Crisis of Authority in Nashe's *The Unfortunate Traveller*." *Studies in Philology* 81, no. 3 (Summer 1984): 348–71.

Talvacchia, Bette. *Taking Positions: On the Erotic in Renaissance Culture*. Princeton: Princeton University Press, 1999.

Tinker, Jack. "Review of *Titus Andronicus*, by William Shakespeare," *Theatre Record*, July 1–14, 1988, p. 902 (Reprint from *The Daily Mail*, July 20, 1988).

Toulalan, Sarah. *Imagining Sex: Pornography and Bodies in Seventeenth-Century England*. Oxford: Oxford University Press, 2007.

Waddington, Raymond B. *Aretino's Satyr: Sexuality, Satire, and Self-Projection in Sixteenth-Century Literature and Art*. Toronto: University of Toronto Press, 2004.

———. *Pietro Aretino: Subverting the System in Renaissance Italy*. Farnham: Ashgate, 2014.

Zupančič, Alenka. *The Odd One In: On Comedy*. Cambridge, MA: MIT Press, 2008.

2 Guyon's blush

Shame, disgust, and desire in *The Faerie Queene*, Book 2

Barbara Correll

Omnibus in rebus voluptatibus maximis fastidium finitimum est. (The greatest pleasures reside closely with disgust.)

—*Cicero*, De Oratore

Without positive affect, there can be no shame: only a scene that offers you enjoyment or engages your interest can make you blush. Similarly, only something you thought might delight or satisfy can disgust.

—*Eve Sedgwick and Adam Frank,* "Shame in the Cybernetic Fold"

This essay takes on, yet again for Spenser criticism, what Stephen Greenblatt has called "the great crux of Renaissance literature": Guyon's violent destruction of the Bower of Bliss, that curious, troubling, notoriously intemperate final statement on temperance in canto 12 of Book 2 in *The Faerie Queene*.[1] But it approaches that crux through another: Guyon's blush in canto 9. In looking into the workings of the blush in *The Faerie Queene*, and its relationship to temperance and wrath, I am also concerned with three interlinked areas: first, Spenser's relationship to contemporary affect theory; then, Spenser's relationship to the blush as confessor and less than competent adjudicator of boundaries and desire; and finally, when located in the Bower, the possible connections of the blush to Spenserian problems of selfhood and writing.

In Guyon's blush and his actions in the Bower, Spenser presents what could be called an affect constellation, one that, besides offering openings into the complexities of the epic, in effect challenges more systematic and systematizing notions of affects: the claims, most notably, of William Ian Miller, Silvan Tomkins, and others that there are a specific number of core affects, that affects such as shame and disgust are discrete and separable, and that the blush is the signifier of shame.[2] Whatever one could imagine Spenser's reaction to major theoretical positions in contemporary affect theory might be, his representation and positioning of the blush and its role in Book 2 of *The Faerie Queene* speak to such theoretical material in that they offer a more pluralizing view of emotion as less territorially fixed, more mobile and thus, I would suggest, more critically enabling for reading both affects and Spenser.[3] In a text marked by narrative and generic errancy, where allegorical anchoring and meaning are so often undone by the textual turns and digressions that Spenser criticism has long noted and so productively mined since at least the early and ongoing scholarship of Harry Berger, it comes as no surprise to encounter meandering affects, like shame, desire, and disgust, that cross or refuse the boundaries that some might set for them.[4] Examining the workings of the blush and the role of Guyon in Book 2, I argue that this part of *The Faerie Queene* is more an essay on than an allegory of temperance, and that it is, more importantly, one in which moral and allegorical schemes are less than successfully achieved.[5] Through the blush and the complex affect constellation it presents, Spenser links shame, desire, and disgust in an affective continuum that leads the text and its readers to the place of its critical intensification and complex critical articulation in Guyon's destruction of the Bower of Bliss. My interest, then, is to follow that meandering path to the Bower and think not only about what Spenser contributes to affect theory but also about both the experience of selfhood and the critically fruitful difficulties of Spenser's writing project.

Affect theorists like Tomkins and Miller link the blush to shame and see a clear distinction between shame and disgust; even in noting their similarities and confusions, they bring the two affects together only, analytically, to re-separate them. Miller is especially emphatic and does not hesitate to generalize or to use consensus rhetoric: "In disgust we wish to have the offensive thing disappear by the removal of either ourselves or it; in shame we simply want to disappear."[6] He uses social or territorial metaphors when he compares disgust to other affects: "Disgust . . . is distinguishable from its kin and neighbors, even though they get involved with boundary disputes every now and then and share some common ground. The others have their unique styles and feels; disgust has its own."[7] He makes equivocating and relativizing claims as well: "to the extent that shame can be understood as disgust with oneself, the physical sensations of shame and disgust are indistinguishable," although he repeats the claim of distinction, linking shame to "conscience" or the ethical, linking disgust to the senses or the visceral.[8]

Tomkins's views on affect are more nuanced than Miller's, more flexible and thoughtful in his extensive writing as a practicing psychologist and therapist.[9] Famously and eloquently promoted by Eve Sedgwick for the alternative his work offers to post-structuralism and what she calls "paranoid reading," defended for his "scientism," Tomkins identifies eight – and sometimes nine – primary affects, or primary drives, that compose what he calls an "affect system."[10] He sets out to standardize the terminology of affect and emphasizes facial responses and external or bodily signs of emotion. Observing shame in 7-month-old babies, Tomkins sees shame as pre-cognitive and pre-social, hard-wired to the species even before social prohibitions or shaming practices are introduced.[11] Again, as with Miller, Tomkins first distinguishes between disgust and shame in his eight-item taxonomy of affects and their physical or facial characteristics – "6. Shame-Humiliation: eyes down, head down; 7. Contempt-Disgust: sneer, upper lip up" – then weakens the distinction in further discussion: "While the affect of shame-humiliation encompasses shyness, shame and guilt, it is distinct from the affect of disgust-contempt. In its dynamic aspects, however, shame is often intimately related to and easily confused with contempt . . . [and] it is sometimes not possible to separate them."[12] But Tomkins singles out the blush as central to his claim that it is the face, not language, that constitutes the subject: "Blushing of the face in shame is a consequence of . . . heightened self- and face-consciousness . . . The face is the most common locus of blushing because the face is the chief organ of general communication of speech and of affect alike. The self lives where it exposes itself."[13] And shame, for Tomkins, is the affect of subject formation.

Where so much affect theory gestures toward bringing affects together in similarity, even as it re-states what it ultimately insists is their distinctiveness, Sedgwick and Frank tend to acknowledge, as they do in my epigraph, an affective layering of emotions that at least weakens or compromises conventional boundaries and foregrounds pleasure rather than aversion: "Shame is characterized by its failure ever to renounce its object cathexis, its relation to the desire for pleasure as well as the need to avoid pain."[14] Other theorists of the emotions are even less interested in systems. Winfried Menninghaus, in *Disgust: Theory and History of a Strong Sensation*, takes account of the relationship between disgust and the beautiful in classical aesthetic theory.[15] In *Powers of Horror*, Julia Kristeva sees abjection, the aversive affect that constitutes a form of disgust reaction, as "what disturbs identity, system, order. What does not respect borders, positions, rules."[16] Sianne Ngai is interested in "the aesthetics of negative emotions" and explores the close relationship between disgust and desire, especially in their social-political contexts and uses, in proposing "A Poetics of Disgust."[17] This intersection of disgust and desire would be where one could locate questions about Spenser and the Bower, and where questions of genre and writing, in their connections to shame and desire, could also be probed.

Bataille's well-known aphorism on economies of knowledge applies to both systematizing affect theory and traditional Spenser criticism: "For academic men to be happy, the universe would have to take shape."[18] Yet the very energy expended in systematizing affect theory to distinguish and pin down, arrest shame, disgust, and embarrassment seems to suggest the deterritorializing tendency of affects, their mobility tacitly acknowledged even by those who would have them in fixed categories. This is arguably similar to systematizing allegorical criticism in Spenser studies where the blush renders Guyon shamefast and tethers him and the text to a restricted moral economy of temperance. Take, for example, Michael Schoenfeldt's binary view of Book 2, in which "Spenser frames his narrative in terms of an opposition between two kinds of pleasure: illicit, immoderate pleasure, which is to be resisted, even eradicated, and the salutary pleasure made possible by control, which is to be enjoyed, even relished," in the Castle of Alma.[19] In the scene of blushing, however, the "regulated pleasure" of the Castle encounters a crisis of less than governable affects. The blush seems to suggest a different sort of relationship to pleasures, one which seeps out of the frame and does not secure distinctions. Like the systematizing affect theorists, the boundaries delineated in the careful construction of what Schoenfeldt calls "Spenser's castle of moral health" would thus seem to open and close, unsteadily oscillating.[20]

If temperance is the policing of behavioral or affective boundaries, and if affects are distinct and separable, then the systematicity – theological, Aristotelian – seen in conventional Spenser criticism reigns in *The Faerie Queene*, and affect theory provides a key to reading it, even as Spenser's epic affirms the key claims of conventional affect theory. One norming reading affirms or mirrors the other. For cultural historians, too, the blush is one cultivated link to the self-discipline and aversive conditioning of the civilizing process and, thus, a crucial part of what belongs to temperance in *The Faerie Queene*.[21] Schoenfeldt, who reads Book 2 as affirming the moral value of temperance, stresses the "positive aspects of the self-regulation Spenser . . . endorses."[22] Temperance marks liberation from the tyranny of disordered and ungoverned passions, a personal and social victory in the struggle between the two powerful forces. He has little more to say about the blush than to mark the episode as a "strange, almost surreal, encounter [that] involves a wary affirmation of emotion in the well-regulated moral life," and he sees the blush as signifying embarrassment or shamed recognition of a self that can order emotion.[23]

Yet, as my epigraphs suggest and Book 2 shows, simply linking the blush to shame seems half the story. Spenser's Guyon and Shamefastnes, in the Legend of Temperance, present a more complicated narrative when seen in their connection to canto 12. Guyon's actions suggest strongly that affects like shame and disgust defy or even escape the boundaries that temperance or set ideas on temperance would maintain. Guyon's display of violent disgust in canto 12, in which he destroys the Bower of Bliss, legibly transforms instances of shame in Book 2, and arguably derives, consequentially, from Guyon's blush in canto 9.

Canto 9 of Book 2, among the most schematic episodes of Spenser's epic, finds Arthur and Guyon entertained in the Castle of Alma where, appropriately and schematically, they are partnered with female figures who surprise them by outwardly revealing essential inner qualities, aspects they immediately recognize in themselves. In this ethical-psychic anagnoresis Arthur meets a pensive Praysde-sire, whose serious preoccupation with fame mirrors and exposes Arthur's own desire for glory. In another instance of dramatic self-recognition Guyon finds himself with a lady whose blushing creates a dynamic, "straungely passioned" facial drama (41.9):

> The bashfull blood her snowy cheekes did dye,
> That her became as polisht yuory,
> Which cunning Craftesman hand hath ouerlayd
> With fayre vermilion or pure Castory. (2.9.41.4–7)

Passion and modesty, visually represented in the red and white of her face, do battle:

> . . . more abasht for shame,
> [she] Held downe her head, the whiles her louely face,
> The flashing blood with blushing did inflame,

> And the strong passion mard her modest grace,
> That *Guyon* meruayld at her vncouth cace. (2.9.43.1–4)

Guyon first projects a role for himself as threatening to her – "Fayre Damsell, seemeth, by your troubled cheare, / That either me too bold ye weene, this wise / You to molest, or other ill to feare" (42.1–3) – and offers his aid, "To ease you of that ill, so wisely as I may" (42.9), but Alma intervenes with a tutelary reading:

> Why wonder yee
> Faire Sir at that, which ye so much embrace?
> She is the fountaine of your modestee,
> You shamefast are, but *Shamefastnesse* it selfe is shee. (2.9.43.6–9)

In Alma's textbook allegoresis Guyon confronts the quality of temperance as the shaming discipline that, as the main figure of The Book of Temperance, he would programmatically embrace; that which is within him is externalized and visually, vividly concretized in his partner. His reaction, however, is to dissemble, and, like characters elsewhere in the text, to conceal his own blush.

In Book 3 Britomart presents herself to Merlin and "The doubtful Mayd, seeing her selfe descryde, / Was all abasht . . . / Whereof she seems ashamed inwardly" (3.3.20.1–2, 7), trying to conceal even as she exposes her love for Artegall. Later, in Book 5, Radigund, speaking with Clarinda on seducing Artegall, averts her face and "turn'd her head / To hide the blush which in her visage rose" (5.5.30.1–2). For Britomart and Radigund the blush confesses or, involuntarily, unveils an erotic truth as well as something about selfhood. When, averting his face, Guyon blushes "in privitee," he tries to conceal what is inside. He is literally "shamefast," bound by a sign of shame, and his anima shows her complicity by pretending not to see what he would conceal:

> Thereat the Elfe did blush in priuitee,
> And turnd his face away; but she the same
> Dissembled faire, and faynd to ouersee. (2.9.44.1–3)

More than shame is at work here. As Shamefastnes reveals in the changing color of her face, and as readers of the passage like David Lee Miller have noted, the repressive actions of modesty – that is, shame – overcome but also underscore or "reinscribe" the energy of passion in the blush.[24]

Both Arthur and Guyon blush to acknowledge the lessons that their soul mates teach them, lessons that reveal their identities. But it is Guyon, the central figure of Book 2, for whom the blush is most telling. His blush may reveal an impassioned battle, but it is also one part of an affective itinerary that takes him to his confrontation with Acrasia and Verdant in the Bower, a confrontation with the self as well. In this Book of Temperance, Guyon moves from erotically inflected Shamefast blushing to revulsion and disgust, to violent destruction in the Bower where disgust and its deterritorializing allure are most fully developed. Despite the Palmer's lessons on steadfastness and his teacherly interventions, Guyon remains mobile, his emotions on the move, and the blush marks an unpoliced boundary. But if it is not and cannot be confined to shame, what is a blush for Spenser? How does it find its way to the abject and disgust? And when it does in canto 12, what kind of self is revealed?

Conventional affect theory, as we have seen, regards the blush as the signifier of shame; certainly, its frequent representation in classical and early modern literature lends support to this claim. The Open Access Shakespeare Concordance lists 107 appearances of blush and blush forms (blushing, blushes, etc.), which include both blush and shame in the same line. In *Venus and Adonis*, for example, Venus is described as "Forgetting shame's pure blush and honour's wrack" (578); Hamlet's apostrophe in the closet scene: "O shame! where is thy blush? (3.4.81); and, famously, the chiasmus in *The Rape of Lucrece*, representing chastity in the description of Lucrece's facial battle: "When virtue bragg'd, beauty would blush for shame; / When beauty boasted blushes, in despite / Virtue would stain that o'er with silver white" (105–7).[25]

Spenser's *Faerie Queene* has no lack of scenes of shame: Redcrosse's literally debasing encounter with Orgoglio in Book 1, canto 9; Guyon's shame and debilitating exhaustion after resisting Mammon's temptations in canto 7; Artegall's transvestite enslavement by Radigund in Book 5; Britomart's confrontation with a cross-dressed Artegall she, for shame, can barely recognize; the men who are restored from Acrasia's bestializing spell to human appearance, their humanness (as Tomkins would agree) signified by their shamed reactions; and Gryll's shamelessness as a sign, for the Palmer and many Spenser critics, of his obdurate bestiality, his refusal of the shame that would brand him with humanness.[26] Some episodes combine shame or shaming and disgust as well: most notably, the exposure of Duessa and her fecally soiled netherparts in Book 1 canto 8, and her re-exposure in Book 2 canto 1, when the narrator recalls and revisualizes her humiliation and exposes her deception as forgery, despoiled of "proud ornaments / And borrow'd beauty" (2.1.22.6–7). Shame is everywhere in Book 2 canto 1; it is the frame that the theme of temperance promises.

Spenser's representation of these negative affects in the figure of Guyon and the treatment of temperance seems rather to view shame and disgust as more closely related, through the affect hinge of the blush, in an affect constellation in which the uncategorizable affect of desire functions to situate shame and disgust on a continuum. As Shamefastnes reveals in the changing color of her face, those who blush tacitly but visually confess to intemperate thoughts, in part reined in by self-shaming and an attempt at distancing that points toward aversion or disgust, loathing or self-loathing. A blush, then, is the collision of and the ongoing, indeterminate struggle between shame, disgust and an underwriting desire, a struggle that ultimately puts the schematic, morally affirmative reading of *The Faerie Queene* in question. If the blush is the opening signifier of affect, then temperance is its gatekeeper. But that division of labor is not how the blush operates in Spenser, since the blush is, in effect, itself an incompetent gatekeeper that exposes temperance's anaclitic relationship to shame and disgust. The blush can both mark a boundary between shame and desire and expose the permeability of that boundary. It can neither obey the law nor impose a law, and in its intensified status, poised between shame and desire, it suggests the vulnerability or openness of the blushing subject.[27]

The theme of Book 2, "The Legend of Sir Guyon, or, Of Temperaunce," suggests its moralizing frame and introduces Guyon as one "In whom great rule of Temp'raunce goodly doth appeare" (Proem.5.9). Belatedly alluded to at the beginning of canto 12 – "Now ginnes this goodly frame of Temperaunce / Fayrely to rise" (2.12.1–2) – this frame is veiled at the beginning, when the Proem presents a reflexive defense of Spenser's project against charges that the work is a "painted forgery" and the work of "an ydle braine" (Proem.1.4, 3), pointing to discoveries of the Amazon and Virginia as at least suggesting if not evidencing the materiality of Faerie Land. Spenser addresses and raises doubts not only about real and imagined realms but about his epic as art and in effect calls attention to the work itself as just such a painted forgery, anticipating the crisis of art that Spenser confronts in canto 12. Appearances, either as painted forgeries or the "certein signes" of existing or yet undiscovered worlds, come into question, not into focus, and seem inseparable.[28] What Roland Greene calls this "worldmaking" Proem suggests links between a thematic constellation of the self-governance of temperance and the discovery and domination, colonial and authorial, of worlds both real and imagined.[29] In this constellation, the blush serves as one of the "certein signes" Spenser would – programmatically – see as verifying knowledge: the sign of tempering and self-discipline.[30] It is no painted forgery but a non-cosmetic coloring, an affective inscription of self-recognition. But the recognition that Guyon experiences testifies to an inner and authentic conflict in which a very strange, open self, and not some more stable, more shaped self emerges.

Book 2 is filled with thematically anchoring utterances, even as it inventories and interrogates such received wisdom. Guyon's sententious "All wrongs have mendes but no amendes for shame" (2.1.20.6) is soon followed by Guyon and the Palmer's exchange on temperance after witnessing the suicide of Amavia, a sight which produces Guyon's strong empathic reaction:

> . . . for griefe his hart did grate,
> And from so heauie sight his head did wreath,
> Accusing fortune, and too cruell fate,
> Which plonged had faire Lady in so wretched state. (2.1.56.6–9)

Guyon turns to the Palmer, bemoaning passion that "Robs reason of her dew regalitie, / And makes it seruaunt to her basest part" (2.1.57.6–5). He does not recognize the personal resonance, but the Palmer responds pointedly to the plights of Mordant and Amavia and more than tacitly touches upon Guyon's grief:

> But temperaunce (said he) with golden squire
> Betwixt them both can measure out a meane,
> Nether to melt in pleasures whott desyre,

Nor frye in hartlesse griefe and dolefull tene.
Thrise happy man, who fares them both atweene. (2.1.58.1–5)

Is Guyon that "thrise happy man"? The introductory description of Guyon – "His carriage was full comely and vpright, / His countenance demure and temperate / But yet so sterne and terrible in sight" (2.1.6.1–3) – presents him as the model of self-discipline, yet his reaction to Amavia's suicide and other empathic reactions make him less a model, more a symptom of what the Palmer's didactic labor, described chiastically, aims to prevent or rein in:

But when strong passion or weake fleshlinesse
Would from the right way seeke to draw him wide,
He would through temperaunce and stedfastness,
Teach him the weak to strengthen and the strong suppresse. (2.4.2.6–9)

As his immoderate grief reveals, Guyon is a piece of work-in-progress for the Palmer, and as the text proceeds toward its narrative and thematic goal, the capture of Acrasia, the triumph of masculine temperance over intemperate female sexuality in canto 12, it is critically compromised in canto 9 and Guyon's blush.[31]

In Book 1, in an episode that anticipates Guyon's confused and violent action in the Bower, the Redcrosse Knight, awakened from his wet dream, is confounded by Duessa's eroticized impersonation of Una:

In this great passion of vnwonted lust,
Or wonted feare of doing ought amis,
He starteth vp, as seeming to mistrust,
Some secret ill, or hidden foe of his:
Lo ther before his face his Ladie is,
Vnder blacke stole hyding her bayted hooke,
And as *halfe blushing* offred him to kis. (1.1.49.1–7)[32]

Caught in his own conflict between both "vnwonted lust" – unusual, involuntary – and "wonted fear" – a welcomed self-censorship – Redcrosse witnesses an act that has a strongly disorienting allure and misrecognizes a very unchaste and duplicitous Duessa as Una. It is Duessa who secures the existence of Una, for without that negative and threatening part of the binary opposition, there is no Una: her figure leans, anaclitically, on Duessa. Duessa's allure underwrites Una's chastity and subjects both to the duplicity, doubling, and doubt that fill the errant epic and compromise claims of its thematic-moral unity, even its generic identity.[33] His temperately aborted action underscores the violence it suggests in its very suppression. Redcrosse's arousal and revulsion combine shaming recognition of his desire and violent, nearly murderous disavowal of it in disgust, both with himself and with his disillusionment with and desire for Una.

Redcrosse does not blush, but Duessa does, or at least she "halfe" blushes. It is only when Redcrosse hands off to Guyon at the beginning of Book 2 that this comes to fruition in 2.12. What this episode also shows is that, like the Bower itself, the blush can be a "painted forgery." Duessa's "halfe blushing" suggests the (un)reliability of the blush: indeed, this half-blush that troubles Redcrosse becomes a crisis for Guyon in Book 2 canto 12.

In Guyon's journey to take on Acrasia and obliterate the Bower, the blush functions chiastically as a mirror in which shame, disgust, and desire cross and confront each other. It is an affective chiasmus, an oscillating crossing. Instances of the blush appear in the text not as an authorizing signifier but as an interpretive knot or crux. Nowhere, however, is that knot more apparent than in Guyon's arrival at the Bower.

In canto 12 the Palmer warns his pupil against Guyon's reaction to the mysterious Crying Maiden, whose "resounding plaints" suggest "some great misfortune," echoing Amavia's distress, that beckons the knight (2.12.27.2, 8). The Palmer instructs Guyon to suspect her "womanish fine forgery" as an insidious performance: "Her guilefull bayt / She will embosome deeper in your mind, / And for your ruine at the last awayt" (2.12.29.3–5). With this policing lesson on penetrating and mentally enfeebling threats, Guyon ends his struggles with the empathic capacity that had him grieving for Amavia and that led him to dedicate his quest to destroying Acrasia.

The Palmer's advice is recalled in stanza 66 when Guyon encounters the wanton Maidens. Like Shakespeare's young man "of burning blushes" in *A Lover's Complaint*, accused in her lament by the maid for seducing and abandoning her, the wanton Maidens put on a show:

> In him a plenitude of subtle matter,
> Applied to cautels, all strange forms receives,
> Of burning blushes, or of weeping water,
> Or swooning paleness; and he takes and leaves,
> In either's, aptness, as it best deceives,
> To blush at speeches rank, to weep at woes,
> Or to turn white and swoon at tragic shows. (302–8)[34]

The sexual hypocrite of Shakespeare's poem and the enticing maidens specialize in something artful. When Guyon first approaches them, they are frolicking in the fountain and, like Shamefast's disingenuous disregard of Guyon's blush, studiously disregarding his presence. Seemingly without regard for observers, though acting *for* observers, when they register their awareness of Guyon their blushes suggest a theatrical performance, titillating and affective. These blushes are all eros, without shame:

> The wanton Maidens him espying, stood
> Gazing a while at his vnwonted guise;
> Then th'one her selfe low ducked in the flood,
> Abasht, that her a strdunger did auise:
> But thother rather higher did arise,

And her two lilly paps aloft displayd,
And all, that might his melting hart entyse
To her delights, she vnto him bewrayd:
The rest hidd vnderneath, him more desirous made. (2.12.66)

The maiden instrumentalizes the blush, and she uses it like the hair that she unbinds, Lady Godiva-style, to conceal her body in a way that intensifies Guyon's erotic interest: "Withall she laughed, and she blusht withall, / That blushing to her laughter gaue more grace, / And laughter to her blushing, as did fall" (2.12.68.1–3). Already exercised by his rough encounters with the feeble gatekeepers Agdistes and Excesse,[35] and finding himself in the endless summer and artless art of "the most daintie Paradise" (12.12.58.1), Guyon's reaction to the beckoning maidens is revealed in his "sparkling face" which discloses "The secrete signes of kindled lust" (12.2.68.5–6).

Redcrosse does not blush in response to Duessa's allure, but Guyon's facial fire recalls and refigures the embattled countenance of his allegorical mate in canto 9. From here, with his aroused and inflamed, "sparkling face," and, it is suggested, his sexually aroused body – he has been shown "many sights, that corage cold could reare" (12.2.68.9)[36] – Guyon approaches Acrasia and Verdant. In Verdant Guyon encounters a fellow knight who recalls and repeats, with a difference, first the past encounter with the slain Mordant, and then Cymocles, idling with Phaedria. In some ways the scene of emasculating seduction in canto 12, doubly anticipated, is overdetermined. Like Mordant and Cymocles, Verdant is a sort of perverse mirror of chivalry, another Guyon, whose place beside Acrasia suggests the place where Guyon's sparkling face would place him. Here Guyon's blush – for that is what it is – is one of self-recognition; the self, as Tomkins stated, resides in the face and what it expresses. But the self that Guyon confronts is something outside the stable subject of temperance, something that presents a problem for Spenser as well.

Spenser has just given a lengthy and exquisite description of the Bower, and located Acrasia in an eight-stanza description that spares no sensual detail. By now Guyon and the text have meandered through an anthology of erotic affects and affective experiences, and Spenser has thoroughly devoted himself to constructing the Bower and making a place for it in his epic project. At its most critical point, Acrasia and Verdant offer another scene of recognition for the hero when he gazes upon the post-coital Verdant, cradled in the arms of Acrasia as "His warlike Armes, the ydle instruments / Of sleeping praise, were hong vpon a tree" (2.12.80.1–2). Guyon confronts this crisis of enervating pleasure, "wastefull luxuree" (7), dishonored knighthood and manhood, and reacts to it with abjecting disgust, but Spenser's exquisitely wrought Bower places *him*, Spenser, in his own dilemma, aesthetic and generic. Not just Guyon but his author as well confronts this crux, which now takes on a dimension in which the stakes are very high. Generically, the epic text approaches another text that would undermine it: Guyon and Spenser risk finding themselves as the hero and the author of an early modern epyllion.

The violence that erupts as Guyon captures Acrasia and destroys the Bower reflects what may be considered Spenser's strong response to his investment in allure and pleasure: converting the epyllion to an anti-epyllion more than restoring an epic. What ensues is generic, thematic confusion reordered in the obliteration of an exquisitely constructed painted forgery: it is Spenser taking action against his own art in what Georgia Brown calls a "belated act of shamefast iconoclasm,"[37] and what we could also call aesthetic disavowal in which shame, desire, and disgust are joined by the blush of self-recognition, the hinge that opens to affect.

It is unlikely that Spenser would be against the notion of an affect system or against systematicity in general, since the very organization of *The Faerie Queene* holds out the promise of a Christian-Aristotelian ethical-moral structure filled with edifying truths, but the text itself doesn't manage to close the deal on the systems it advances in the six books and their thematic statements. This is especially the case with Book 2 and its troubling conclusion. In relation to affect theory, Spenser's positioning of the blush and its role in *Faerie Queene* 2 resists systematizing and pluralizes emotion. Does Spenser have Guyon destroy the Bower to cover up his own desire to indulge in sensual, even pornographic poetry? The Bower, its exquisite beauty and pleasures, may be destroyed, but Spenser has managed to undermine and unsettle the categories, of both selfhood and literature, he would officially hold up and affirm.

Perhaps it would be digressive to include in this reading what may arguably be the canto's coda, the concluding encounter with Gryll, but I will take that risk. As the last word, and with the Bower obliterated, Guyon proving his moral mettle, Acrasia's victims returned to manhood, it would seem that Gryll should provide a final affirmation of temperance. But rather than acting as the misguided figure who secures Spenser's project, Gryll may function as an unsettling force in Book 2. In Spenser's source, Plutarch's *Moralia*, the clever and articulate Grillus retains his swinish form and ably debates Odysseus on the moral superiority of animals in a demonstration of equivocating irony. Spenser's unblushing Gryll is human, restored by the Palmer but entirely ungrateful – he laments and rails against his liberator – and shamelessly longing for his bestial form. Guyon's scorn – "See the mind of beastly man, / That . . . / . . . chooseth with vile difference / To be a beast, and lacke intelligence" (2.12.87.1–2, 4–5) – and the Palmer's hasty dismissal – "Let *Gryll* be *Gryll*, and haue his hoggish minde" (2.12.87.8) – underscore Gryll's refusal of shame, the distinguishing affect of humans, as a man's active refusal of his species status. If Spenser's purpose is to establish a moral boundary that would expel Gryll, he opens an area of permeability, uneasy and supplementary, in which moral categories are also suspended. Gryll's cohorts, too, are left less than restored: "Yet being men, they did vnmanly looke, / And stared ghastly" (86.3–4). Despite the narrator's assigning them "inward shame" and "wrath" (4, 5), their ghastly stares hold them in some eerily melancholy state. They, like Gryll and Plutarch's Grillus, are suspended in an interspecies moment, both beast and human but neither one nor the other. The destruction of the Bower and the putative but never completed or successful restoration of Acrasia's victims end Book 2 on this uncertain note.

What Guyon encounters in his meeting with Shamefastnes and her embattled visage in which shame/modesty and passion/desire confront each other in the blush is what temperance, despite the promises from Guyon and the Palmer's sententiae, can only be pinned down to be: policing bodily and affective boundaries that leans on the transgression of boundaries, a structural conflict that is ultimately unsettled and in which temperate ordering or reordering is belied by an affect constellation in which the blush opens to shame and desire, crossed by disgust. The blush obstructs the attempt to enforce a boundary or a distinction between disgust and shame or a cultural law. Canto 9 and the imbricated affects signified by the blush anticipate Guyon's pulling toward the desire and abjecting horror that destroys the Bower of Blisse and say much about Spenser's own relationship to passion and temperance in his art. What happens in canto 12 begins with Guyon's blush in canto 9; in the end, Guyon's blush may also be Spenser's.[38]

Notes

1 Greenblatt, *Renaissance Self-Fashioning*, 178. Quotations from the 2nd edition of the Longman *The Faerie Queene*.
2 Further discussion follows below. See also the Introduction to this volume.
3 Shouse, "Feeling," attempts to distinguish among the three: "Feelings are *personal* and *autobiographical* . . . emotions are *social*, and affects are *prepersonal*." Ngai discusses and summarizes work on affect-emotion distinctions in *Ugly Feelings*, 25–7. Ngai, like myself, uses the two terms interchangeably.
4 Berger, Jr., *Allegorical Temper* and *Revisionary Play*. Among many other examples, we could mention work such as Goldberg's early *Endlesse Worke* and the more recent *Seeds of Things*.
5 An admirable and pedagogically useful reading of Book 2 as a "conversation" can be found in Webster, "Challenging the Commonplace."
6 Miller, *Anatomy*, 34. In his introduction, Miller sees consensus rhetoric as "invitational," apparently to skirt the problems posed by (gender, sexuality, class, ethnicity) difference which appeals to consensus only to highlight difference.
7 Miller, *Anatomy*, 35.
8 Miller, *Anatomy*, 35.
9 Sedgwick and Frank note Tomkins's non-heterosexist psychology, something which also separates his work from Miller's remarks on (hetero) masculine anxieties about the anus, for him self-evidently disgusting (as opposed to what some might consider a site for sexual pleasure): "I need not spell out just how contaminating, how disgusting, the anus is. It is the essence of lowness . . . Even those penetrations consented to . . . lower the status of the person so penetrated." Miller, *Anatomy*, 100.
10 Sedgwick and Frank, "Shame," 73, 74. Sedgwick's famous "Paranoid Reading and Reparative Reading, or, You're So Paranoid, You Probably Think This Essay Is About You," in *Touching Feeling,* 123–52, argues for a "reparative" or ameliorative reading that values the body and emotion over "paranoid" (post-structuralist) critique.
11 It is hardly necessary to mention Tomkins's opposition to psychoanalysis' theories of development and socialization, such as Freud's notion of the superego, addressed in the section, "Some errors of Freud resulting from the confusion of drive and affect," *Shame*, 49–50.
12 Tomkins, *Shame*, 74, 134. Tomkins could look for support from Cicero as quoted in my epigraph. Translation of the Latin is mine.
13 Tomkins, *Shame*, 136–7. Probyn's *Blush*, while offering perceptive, often unblushingly personal remarks about the political uses of shame, really encapsulates this conventional, ultimately reductive view.

14 Sedgwick and Frank, "Shame," 24.

15 Menninghaus, *Disgust*.

16 Kristeva, *Powers*, 4.

17 Ngai, *Ugly Feelings*, 1; Ngai, "Raw Matter."

18 Bataille, "Formless," 31.

19 Schoenfeldt, *Bodies and Selves*, 68.

20 Schoenfeldt, *Bodies and Selves*, 40.

21 See Georgia Brown's summary of Norbert Elias on shame and the civilizing process and Gail Kern Paster on embarrassment, as well as criticisms of their shortcomings, in *Redefining*, 13–14. Brown's position on the late sixteenth-century epyllion as work that capitalizes on shame, authorship, and the role of vision has been fruitful for my reading of canto 12 as anti-epyllion.

22 Schoenfeldt, *Bodies and Selves*, 70. Schoenfeldt takes issue with two major critical positions: Greenblatt's reading of canto 12, which links civilizing discipline to the violence of colonization, and David Lee Miller's interest in the erotic and Book 2's failed attempts to hide (abounding) genital signifiers. As Goldberg has pointed out, Schoenfeldt's position, summed up in his claim that in Book 2 "Spenser's portrait of the temperate subject has more traffic with the conduct of the colon than with the suppressions of Colonialism," 73, misreads Foucault on care of the self in subject formation and, worse, assigns to the colon "only a purgative function; facing excrement, he [Schoenfeldt] evacuates sexuality." Goldberg, *Seeds*, 89–90. Although less squeamish or at least less interested in writing about the anus and the colon than William Ian Miller, Schoenfeldt's position, firmly separating the pleasures of the digestive from the necessary excremental, is tacitly aligned with Miller's homophobic statements.

23 Schoenfeldt, *Bodies and Selves*, 64.

24 In *Poem's Two Bodies*, 174, Miller interprets the repression as the attempt, unsuccessful and auto-deconstructive, to censor the genital: "The displacement through which genital eros finds its way into representation within the temperate body is enacted silently by this allegorical "framing" of sexuality in the heart. There it emerges in an unstable ratio of shamefastness, which denies access to the genitals . . . Feigning to oversee is thus an integral part of the representational strategy by which the reinscription of sexuality proceeds. Spenser . . . brings his knights into the human heart to confront the displacement and reinscription of their desires." Krier, *Gazing,* 159, reads the embarrassment and abashedness of this encounter as awkward and comedic: "the language of both Guyon and the narrator . . . is all of the embarrassment-arousing phenomena of mistaken erotic intentions, flashes, and inflamings."

25 Open Source Shakespeare: Concordance of Shakespeare's Complete Works. Accessed April 10, 2014. http://www.opensourceshakespeare.org/concordance.

26 Plutarch, *Moralia XII*, 389–91.

27 On vulnerability and the subject, see Kuzner, *Open Subjects*, especially his reading of Book 4, 39–83.

28 On the colonial resonances and a reading of Book 2 that stresses its references to Ireland, see McCabe, *Spenser's Monstrous Regiment*.

29 Greene, "Primer."

30 And, one must add, as the racial signifier of whiteness. See Iyengar's fascinating chapter on "Heroic Blushing" in *Shades of Difference*, 103–22.

31 Clearly, Guyon's affective responses have attracted attention from Spenser scholars. Berger's chapter on Guyon's faint in canto 7 in *Allegorical Temper* is just the beginning. Among the others to address the faint, see Tonkin, "Discussing Spenser's Cave of Mammon"; Swearingen, "Guyon's Faint"; Yoon, "Significance of Guyon's Faint" ; Kessler, "Guyon's Faint"; Hubbard, "Send Your Angel."

32 One *OED* definition of "half" seems appropriate here: "4. As a measure of degree: Attaining only half-way to completeness or to the actual action, quality, or character in question; falling short of the full or perfect thing; partial, imperfect, incomplete."

33 Goldberg, *Seeds*, 82, 97, describes Duessa's key role eloquently: "The doubleness that she announces as her identity . . . is a shared condition in the poem and constitutes the site of its unending scene of work . . . The 'doubtfull Damzell' [Una] (vi.12.1) confronts the dubious truth that shapes the plot of the poem from its initial path of 'diverse doubt' (i.10.9) through its doubtful forms." He later writes of "the poem's attachment to what it ostensibly refuses."

34 *A Lover's Complaint*, in *Complete Sonnets and Poems*, ed. Colin Burrows (New York: Oxford University Press, 2008).

35 As Schoenfeldt, "Construction," 235, notes, those gates "seem to be erected simply for the erotic pleasure of transgressing them," in contrast to the fortified entrances to the Castle of Alma.

36 Glossed by A.C. Hamilton in his edition of Spenser's *Faerie Queene*, 282, as "arouse; or in the explicitly erotic sense, 'cause to stand up.'"

37 Brown, *Redefining*, 9. Guyon's iconoclasm may have contemporary parallels, as Nussbaum's discussion of the "Homosexual-Provocation" defense in *Hiding*, 137, strongly suggests.

38 Special thanks to Daniel Juan Gil and Ineke Murakami for helpful comments, questions, and nudgings.

References

Bataille, Georges. "Formless." In *Visions of Excess: Selected Writings, 1927–1939*, 31. Edited by Allan Stoekl and translated by Stoekl et al. Minneapolis: University of Minnesota Press, 1985.

Berger, Harry, Jr. *The Allegorical Temper: Vision and Reality in Book II of Spenser's "Faerie Queene."* New Haven: Yale University Press, 1957.

———. *Revisionary Play: Studies in the Spenserian Dynamics*. Berkeley: University of California Press, 1988.

Brown, Georgia. *Redefining Elizabethan Literature*. Cambridge: Cambridge University Press, 2004.

Cicero, Marcus Tullius. *De Oratore Book III*. In *Cicero IV*, 2–185. Translated by H. Rackham. Loeb Classical Library 349. Cambridge, MA: Harvard University Press, 1942.

Goldberg, Jonathan. *Endlesse Worke: Spenser and the Structures of Discourse*. Baltimore and London: Johns Hopkins University Press, 1981.

———. *The Seeds of Things: Theorizing Sexuality and Materiality in Renaissance Representations*. New York: Fordham University Press, 2009.

Greenblatt, Stephen. *Renaissance Self-Fashioning: From More to Shakespeare*. Chicago: University of Chicago Press, 1980.

Greene, Roland. "A Primer of Spenser's Worldmaking: Alterity in the Bower of Bliss." In *Worldmaking Spenser: Explorations in the Early Modern Age*, edited by Patrick Cheney and Lauren Silberman, 9–31. Lexington: University of Kentucky Press, 2000.

Hubbard, Gillian. "'Send Your Angel': Augustinian Nests and Guyon's Faint." *Spenser Studies: A Renaissance Poetry Annual* 27 (2012): 107–32.

Iyengar, Sujata. *Shades of Difference: Mythologies of Skin Color in Early Modern England*. Philadelphia: University of Pennsylvania Press, 2005.

Kessler, Samuel R. "Guyon's Faint and the Elizabethan Soteriological Debate: Double Predestination in The Faerie Queene, Book 2, Canto 8." *Sixteenth Century Journal: Journal of Early Modern Studies* 43, no. 1 (Spring 2012): 19–45.

Krier, Theresa M. *Gazing on Secret Sights: Spenser, Classical Imitation and the Decorums of Vision*. Ithaca: Cornell University Press, 1990.

Kristeva, Julia. *Powers of Horror: An Essay on Abjection.* Translated by Leon S. Roudiez. New York: Columbia University Press, 1982.

Kuzner, James. *Open Subjects: English Renaissance Republicans, Modern Selfhoods and the Virtue of Vulnerability.* Edinburgh: Edinburgh University Press, 2011.

McCabe, Richard. *Spenser's Monstrous Regiment: Elizabethan Ireland and the Poetics of Difference.* Oxford: Oxford University Press, 2002.

Menninghaus, Winfried. *Disgust: Theory and History of a Strong Sensation.* Translated by Howard Eiland and Joel Golb. Albany: SUNY Press, 2003.

Miller, David Lee. *The Poem's Two Bodies: The Poetics of the 1590* Faerie Queene. Princeton: Princeton University Press, 1988.

Miller, William Ian. *The Anatomy of Disgust.* Cambridge, MA: Harvard University Press, 1997.

Ngai, Sianne. "Raw Matter: A Poetics of Disgust." In *Telling It Slant,* edited by Mark Wallace and Steven Marks, 161–90. Tuscaloosa: University of Alabama Press, 2002.

———. *Ugly Feelings.* Cambridge, MA: Harvard University Press, 2005.

Nussbaum, Martha C. *Hiding from Humanity: Disgust, Shame, and the Law.* Princeton: Princeton University Press, 2004.

Plutarch. *Moralia XII.* Translated by Harold Cherniss and William C. Helmbold. Loeb Classical Library 406. Cambridge, MA: Harvard University Press, 1957.

Probyn, Elspeth. *Blush: Faces of Shame.* Minneapolis: University of Minnesota Press, 2005.

Schoenfeldt, Michael. *Bodies and Selves in Early Modern England: Physiology and Inwardness in Spenser, Shakespeare, Herbert, and Milton.* Cambridge: Cambridge University Press, 1999.

———. "The Construction of Inwardness in *The Faerie Queene,* Book 2." In *Worldmaking Spenser: Explorations in the Early Modern Age,* edited by Patrick Cheney and Lauren Silberman, 234–43. Lexington: University of Kentucky Press, 2000.

Sedgwick, Eve Kosofsky. *Touching Feeling: Affect, Pedagogy, Performativity.* Durham, NC: Duke University Press, 2003.

———, and Adam Frank. "Shame in the Cybernetic Fold: Reading Silvan Tomkins." In *Shame and Its Sisters: A Silvan Tomkins Reader.* Edited by Eve Kosofsky Sedgwick and Adam Frank, 1–28. Durham, NC: Duke University Press, 1995.

Shouse, Eric. "Feeling, Emotion, Affect." M/C Journal 8, no. 6 (December 2005). Accessed November 15, 2014. http://journal.media-culture.org.au/0512/03-shouse.php.

Spenser, Edmund. *The Faerie Queene.* 2nd ed. Edited by A.C. Hamilton. London: Longman, 2001.

Swearingen, Roger G. "Guyon's Faint." *Studies in Philology* 74 (1977): 165–85.

Tomkins, Silvan. *Shame and Its Sisters: A Silvan Tomkins Reader.* Edited by Eve Kosofsky Sedgwick and Adam Frank. Durham, NC: Duke University Press, 1995.

Tonkin, Humphrey. "Discussing Spenser's Cave of Mammon." *SEL: Studies in English Literature, 1500–1900* 13, no. 1 (Winter 1973): 1–13.

Webster, John. "Challenging the Commonplace: Teaching as Conversation in Spenser's Legend of Temperance." In *Approaches to Teaching Spenser's* Faerie Queene, edited by David Lee Miller and Alexander Dunlop, 82–92. New York: Modern Language Association, 1994.

Yoon, Jung-Mook. "The Significance of Guyon's Faint in Book 2 of The Faerie Queene." *Journal of English Language and Literature* 35, no. 1 (Spring 1989): 13–27.

3   Desiring disgust in Robert Herrick's epigrams

Natalie K. Eschenbaum

According to one of Robert Herrick's nineteenth-century editors, *Hesperides* (1648) is a collection "abounding in passages of outrageous grossness."[1] Take, for instance, the epigram, "Upon Pimpe":

> When *Pimpes* feet sweat (as they doe often use)
> There springs a sope-like-lather in his shoos. (H-1113)[2]

Poems about sudsy foot sweat, syrupy diarrhea, maggot-producing bad breath, and other disgusting bodily effusions appear throughout Herrick's collection of over 1,400 poems. When *Hesperides* was rediscovered at the turn of the nineteenth century, Herrick's editors were appalled by this aversive verse. Francis Turner Palgrave, compiler of the well-known *Golden Treasury of English Songs and Lyrics*, proclaims, "We have, probably, no poet . . . to justify the invidious task of selection . . . more fully and forcibly than . . . Herrick."[3] Herrick found great success as a selected and anthologized poet. He became known for his church hymns, *carpe diem* lyrics, and poems about country ceremonies, Julia's clothing, and the pleasures and perils of alcohol consumption. By the mid-twentieth century, almost one hundred editions of Herrick's verse had been published, but only a few scholarly editions included the disgusting poems.[4] Today, they are rarely anthologized – and thus rarely read or taught.

   In a study of disgust, it is helpful to consider Herrick's critical reception because in a way that reception demonstrates the aversive affect in action. The disgust Herrick's early editors and critics felt in response to *Hesperides* is palpable. Robert Southey calls Herrick "a coarse-minded and beastly writer, whose dunghill, when the few flowers that grew therein had been transplanted, ought never to have been disturbed."[5] Thomas Ashe "wonders that a man who could exhibit such delicacy at times, could at others be so disgusting – coarse is too weak a word."[6] Content-wise, the epigrams were the problem: "The sole blot of his verse, the dull and dirty epigram section, is rather an excrescence than a fault in grain."[7] But Herrick's editors and readers were not simply disgusted by the epigrams. They were disgusted by Herrick's apparent lack of taste. Palgrave implies that Herrick's inability to edit himself was his primary fault: "Whatever may have been the influences . . . which determined the contents of his volume, severe taste was not one of them."[8] To write and publish poems about disgusting things makes Herrick himself coarse, disgusting, and tasteless.

George Saintsbury even goes so far as to critique the tastes and talents of critics who read Herrick's epigrams, about which, he says, "no human being who has any faculty of criticism can say any good."[9] I am not the first to risk revealing I have no "faculty of criticism" by addressing poems like "Upon Pimpe." In the second half of the twentieth century, a few scholars rightly note that Herrick's poems fulfill the generic conventions of the classical epigram.[10] Robert W. Halli, Jr. explains that epigrams were popular in seventeenth-century England because they appealed "to their readers' sense of humor, since the Renaissance followed the ancient principle that physical and moral ugliness was the basic cause of laughter."[11] Halli insists that Herrick's epigrams be read in their historical as well as their textual context: "The scurrilous epigrams contrast drastically with the pretty poems, and contribute substantially to the artistic effect of the book."[12] Ten years later, Anne Baynes Coiro expands on this idea in *Robert Herrick's* Hesperides *and the Epigram Book Tradition* and argues that *Hesperides* "should be read in its entirety" because the epigrams "work in direct tension with his lyric poems of delicate beauty."[13] Michael Schoenfeldt similarly argues that Herrick uses disgust for the "grotesque body" to generate "throughout *Hesperides* a narrative which delineates the characteristics of the exalted and the base."[14] He cites Mary Douglas and Norbert Elias to argue that Herrick shows how bodily control, especially of fluids, had become a sign of civilization and class in the Renaissance.[15]

Halli, Coiro, and Schoenfeldt all imply that Herrick uses disgust to mark his presumed superiority over lower-class citizens. Schoenfeldt states that disgust "allows Herrick to pretend that he is temporarily superior to the flesh he inhabits and shares with the lower-class figures he mocks."[16] Inclusion of the epigrams does not mark Herrick's lack of taste, as his nineteenth-century editors presumed; rather, the epigrams demonstrate that Herrick recognizes what is disgusting and makes fun of those who do not. "Upon *Sudds* a Laundress," for instance, describes a woman who washes and then stiffens collars with urine and phlegm:

> *Sudds* Launders Bands in pisse; and starches them
> Both with her Husband's, and her own tough fleame. (H-237)

The implied punch line of the joke is the contradiction that produces disgust: Sudds *cleans* her clothes with *unclean* bodily wastes. She is a tasteless individual because she neither recognizes nor cares that she is polluting rather than cleansing and thus negating her identity as a "laundresse." If we, as readers, laugh with Herrick, we too place ourselves above poor Sudds in regard to civility.

Mary Thomas Crane challenges some of these conclusions. She considers Herrick's experience as a goldsmith and his interest in the "transitions among three states of matter – solid, liquid, and gas" to argue that Herrick's disgusting poems instead show the connections between the upper and lower classes: "It might seem that the effusion of liquid from an open and grotesque body is linked, in *Hesperides*, with lower class subjects, but this is not entirely the case."[17] Crane demonstrates that "other poems hint, if nervously, that the bodies of Herrick's friends and patrons . . . are also subject to such indignities."[18] She agrees that Herrick attempts to mark his superiority, but she sees that he also embraces a "universalized grotesque with as much excited fascination as the beautiful."[19] Herrick is interested in exploring attraction and repulsion; it is misleading to focus solely on the former.

Halli, Coiro, Schoenfeldt, and Crane, in work published twenty-five years ago, demonstrated that the aversive verse in *Hesperides* is critically compelling. Since then, scholars have had little or nothing to say about it. A case in point is Ruth Connolly and Tom Cain's recent collection, *Lords of Wine and Oile: Community and Conviviality in the Poetry of Robert Herrick*. Two contributors – Leah S. Marcus and Katharine Eisaman Maus – mention the epigrams only to note that Herrick's "rougher poems interrupt the mesmerizing perfection" of the lyrics, and that he "loves to juxtapose poems that jar incongruously in tone."[20] The fact that none of the essays in Connolly and Cain's collection focuses on disgust is an observation rather than a critique because the collection instead centers on the theme of community-building, but study of Herrick's disgusting epigrams is elusive in *all* recent publications.

Perhaps this is simply because the epigrams are not readily available. Before Oxford published Cain and Connolly's new edition in hardcover in 2013, the complete *Hesperides* had been out of print since 1968. But, what if the nineteenth-century, anthologized version of Herrick perpetuates because readers are, in a sense, critically disgusted by the epigrams? Schoenfeldt notes, "it is tempting to censor or ignore those poems that resist traditional critical vocabularies."[21] Also, disgust, by its very nature, repels us from reading and analyzing the epigrams: who would want to do a close reading of sudsy foot slime or piss-encrusted laundry? Thomas Aquinas identified aversion as a concupiscible passion that is the contrary of desire.[22] For him, desire draws us toward things that are pleasurable, and aversion repels us: repulsive things, quite literally, repulse us.[23]

Recent work on the affect of disgust, however, problematizes this Thomistic view of aversion and reveals that Herrick may have been challenging medieval views, too. In *Savoring Disgust*, Carolyn Korsmeyer explains that "although this emotion seems to represent pure aversion, disgusting objects can also fascinate – and even attract."[24] William Ian Miller agrees: "The disgusting itself has the power to allure" and "the fair does not lurk behind a wall of disgust; the disgusting is precisely what is fair."[25] There is something attractive about aversion, desirable about disgust. I will argue that it is this paradox that Herrick explores in *Hesperides*.

As we have seen, a number of recent Herrick scholars argue that the epigrams need to be read alongside the lyric verses because, as Coiro puts it, disgust works to "puncture and destroy lyric elegance."[26] But this conclusion presumes that disgust is always a repulsive and destructive force, that disgust is always disgusting. Schoenfeldt claims that, in *Hesperides*, "desire and disgust are segregated in unequivocal poems of elegant praise and visceral disgust."[27] While I agree that Herrick frequently juxtaposes desirable and disgusting images, poem by poem, I will argue that his epigrams demonstrate how desire and disgust are *not* segregated;

they are intimately connected. Herrick's commoners might have failed the "civilizing process" encouraged by Renaissance conduct books, but Herrick works through a more complex understanding of disgust. In his imaginary, things, people, and actions are not inherently disgusting; he employs disgust in order to upset the very affect it is supposed to elicit. Coiro says that the contrast of the lyric and the epigram "bring[s] into question the ontological status of beauty itself."[28] But even without this contrast, Herrick's epigrams cross disgust and desire.

Herrick is the first to admit that his poems might disgust, but he makes disgust relative. *Hesperides* opens with a number of poems addressed to the book and its readers, including "To the soure Reader":

> If thou dislik'st the Piece thou light'st on first;
> Think that of All, that I have writ, the worst:
> But if thou read'st my Booke unto the end,
> And still do'st this, and that verse, reprehend:
> O Perverse man! If All disgustfull be,
> The Extreame Scabbe take thee, and thine, for me. (H-6)

Herrick implies that none of his poems is inherently disgusting, and it is the reader who makes them so. If "this, and that verse" remains disgusting in context, Herrick says, then you deserve to be cursed with a vile, scabby illness. He implies that if you are disgusted by his poem, you are the one who is disgusting. This accusation would be difficult to stomach if you first opened *Hesperides* and lighted upon a poem like "Upon Reape":

> *Reapes* eyes so rawe are, that (it seemes) the flyes
> Mistake the flesh, and flye-blow both his eyes;
> So that an Angler, for a daies expence,
> May baite his hooke, with maggots taken thence. (H-879)

What, besides disgust, can a reader feel in response to this poem? The image of a man with diseased, maggot-ridden eyes turns the stomach. As Schoenfeldt says in his discussion of a poem about diarrhea, it "seems to revel inexplicably in filthiness," but "is mildly funny, if one can stomach the wit."[29]

Humor might be one response to these poems, but something else might explain the filthiness. Korsmeyer suggests that poetry, perhaps uniquely, has the power to transform something disgusting into something desirable "because of its exacting attention to the form and shape of expression – the eloquence that converts onerous subject matter to beauty."[30] Does routing the image of maggoty eyeballs through constructed language – through rhyme and meter – make "Upon Reape" beautiful? I am not convinced, but it helps to draw us toward the disgusting rather than to repel us. Coiro argues that Herrick sees poetry "as a veneer and an artifice that he has created to cover a grim reality."[31] But these unapologetically disgusting epigrams do not cover over disgust. Instead, they bring it to the surface and invite us to experience it fully.

In addition to humor or curiosity, one could argue that "Upon Reape" should inspire pity. It would be horrifically painful to have eyes so diseased that flies mistake them for rotting flesh. Reape appears to be an innocent victim of poor health and bad luck, which is the case for many of the epigrams' characters. Megg, for instance, has a cold "which, this night hardned, sodders up her nose" (H-945.2). Spalt has so many pus-filled pimples and boils on his face that "he needs a Tucker for to burle his face" (H-594.2). Shopter, an old widow, "when so ere she cryes, / Lets drip a certain Gravie from her eyes" (H-1107.1–2). And, Linnit "playes rarely on the Lute" and "sweetly sings," but his rancid breath "sayes no," or defiles the beautiful playing and singing (H-381.1, 2, 2). Some characters deserve pity for their disgusting plights, but Herrick suggests that others deserve their vile punishments. He describes a man with sweaty palms whose physical flaw mirrors his moral flaw: "*Pauls* hands do give, what give they bread or meat, / Or money? no, but onely deaw and sweat" (H-731.1–2). And, in "Upon Brock. Epigram," Herrick argues that disgusting behavior is more disgusting than a physical ailment:

> To clense his eyes, *Tom Brock* makes much adoe,
> But not his mouth (the fouler of the two.)
> A clammie Reume makes loathsome both his eyes:
> His mouth worse furr'd with oathes and blasphemies. (H-273)

Still other characters perform disgusting actions, even though they themselves might be physically desirable. "Upon Sibilla" describes a woman who uses almond paste to scour her hands, but "then gives it to the children to devoure" (H-561.2). In addition, "in Cream she bathes her thighs (more soft then silk) / Then to the poore she freely gives the milke" (3–4). Sibilla might appear desirable on the surface and look much like the praised Julias, Antheas, and Silvias who also populate *Hesperides*, but *she* is disgusting. Although most would find it disgusting to ingest almonds and cream from somebody else's beauty rituals, the actions of the children and the poor are not what disgust here. *Sibilla* disgusts.

This survey of Herrick's vile verses in *Hesperides* demonstrates that disgust never *simply* disgusts. It is part of a complex web that might inspire curiosity, humor, or pity, and only sometimes actually repels. Disgusting states and actions might reflect the vileness of specific individuals, but, more significantly, they might not. What disgusts in one situation does not disgust in another. In sum, Herrick explores the relative nature of disgust. Considering the word "disgust" was new to the English lexicon when Herrick wrote *Hesperides*, such a claim might be remarkable. Perhaps Herrick is wrestling with an emotion his contemporaries deemed important enough to assign a new word.[32]

Schoenfeldt claims that Herrick's exploration of disgust is informed and purposeful: "Herrick laughs not because the practices he cites are unhealthy but rather because they are socially constructed as repulsive."[33] In a sense, Herrick flaunts his knowledge of what his culture deems disgusting at the expense of the "lower-class characters" who "confuse the very categories that define their social abjection."[34] But if Herrick deconstructs disgust, he does not do it simply to mark his own superiority or to question its social construction. For Crane, when we look closely at the epigrams about bodily effusions, we see Herrick's "universe . . . consists of surfaces which conceal, but may at any moment be ruptured by a constant cycle of material change from solid to liquid to gaseous states."[35] These natural cycles and processes do not discriminate based on class, but "some of these processes produce results such as gems, sweet odors, a blush, which are beautiful, while in other cases the same processes are disgusting and threatening."[36] Crane is right to see that Herrick explores the ways in which the "beautiful and grotesque are as interchangeable as the states of matter themselves."[37] But he also explores the very nature of this newly named aversive affect. He does not always categorize things as either beautiful or disgusting, but sometimes shows that they are the same.

If we read the complete *Hesperides*, as Coiro and others advise, it seems important to note that Herrick's first uses of disgust are focused on his book and its readers. As we already saw, "To the soure Reader" curses those who read *Hesperides* and find everything about it "disgustfull" (H-6.5). The verse that precedes it similarly curses those who might use the pages of *Hesperides* to wipe "the place, where swelling *Piles* do breed" (H-5.2). The verse that follows begs the book to not be like "those men, who are like *Bread* / O're-leven'd; or like *Cheese* o're-renetted" (H-7.1–2). Leavening and rennet are necessary components of bread and cheese, but too much of either spoils the food. Like many of his contemporaries, including his "father" Ben Jonson, Herrick attempts to craft his readership. He hopes his book will be read – rather than used as toilet paper – and read fully – from beginning to end – and that its ingredients – the poems – are well balanced and pleasing. In the opening poems Herrick admits that his book might contain the disgusting, be read by disgusting individuals, and be used for disgusting purposes. By attaching disgust first to himself, his project, and his – presumably – upper-class readers, he diffuses the aversive nature of disgust. Thus, in a series of introductory poems that mean to attract readership, he employs an affect that is supposed to repel.

Herrick next uses disgust in *Hesperides*'s first epigram about a lower-class Dean Prior resident, "Upon Blanch":

> *Blanch* swears her Husband's lovely; when a scald
> Has blear'd his eyes: Besides, his head is bald.
> Next, his wilde eares, like Lethern wings full spread,
> Flutter to flie, and beare away his head. (H-99)

J. Max Patrick glosses "scald" as "an inflammatory disease."[38] According to the *Oxford English Dictionary*, "scald head, n." is "a person's head diseased with ringworm or some similar affliction."[39] Blanch's husband has a fungus growing on his head that blurs his vision, but this illness only accentuates his ugliness, as he already has a bald head with flapping, leathery ears. Halli argues that Blanch makes "a claim which observation reveals to be absurd."[40] She "swears" her diseased husband is "lovely," even though he is decidedly *not* lovely. Blanch, not her husband, is the one with distorted vision. There might "be a moral here about self-delusion," Halli says, but "the poem seems more to be a humorously distorted application of the proverb that beauty lies in the eye of the beholder."[41] Herrick certainly employs humor in this verse, but the moral about self-delusion is stronger than Halli claims. Blanch *should* be disgusted by her husband; however, not only is she not disgusted, but she finds her husband "lovely." Love can change something foul into something fair.

"Upon Blanch" contributes to a tradition of early modern poems that praise people – usually women – for their defects. Shakespeare's Sonnet 130 ("My mistress' eyes are nothing like the sun") is the most famous example.[42] The speaker says that his mistress's breasts are greyish brown, rather than pure white; that her hair is coarse and black, rather than golden wire; and that her breath stinks, rather than exudes perfume. Shakespeare concludes, "And yet, by heaven, I think my love as rare / As any she belied with false compare" (13–14). In a simple reading, Shakespeare critiques the tradition of the Petrarchan blazon: he claims that his beloved is as beautiful as the goddess-like beauties described in most Renaissance poetry. If you say your mistress's teeth look like pearls, for instance, then you are lying. Herrick's "No Loathsomnesse in love" similarly lists a number of ugly physical traits of women but, he claims, "*No Dislike there is in love*" (H-21.2). His mistress might have a huge nose ("an *Acre* hath of Nose") or black teeth ("her grinders black as jet") or little or no hair ("Ha's she thinne haire, hath she none"), but he still finds her lovely ("She's to me a *Paragon*") (H-21.6, 12, 13, 14).

"Upon Blanch" differs from Shakespeare's sonnet and "No Loathsomnesse in love" in a couple of important ways. First, it more obviously employs the affect of disgust. Shakespeare's and Herrick's mistresses might have ugly features, but they are not cursed with diseased eyes or pus-filled sores. A fungus-ridden face is more likely to disgust than a large nose, primarily because disease reminds of death. Or, as Julia Kristeva explains, diseased rashes and effusions disgust because "these body fluids, this defilement, this shit are what life withstands, hardly and with difficulty, on the part of death."[43] Second, "Upon Blanch" is about someone else's love, rather than the speaker's. This difference in perspective is something John Donne explores in "Elegy 8: The Comparison," a poem that might also be placed in this vile-mistress poetic tradition. Donne's mistress's droplets of perspiration "seem no sweat drops, but pearl carcanets" (6), whereas "rank sweaty froth thy mistress' brow defiles, / Like spermatic issue of ripe menstruous boils" (7–8).[44] Donne points out that the same aspects of a woman can be desirable or disgusting, depending on one's perspective. Blanch loves her husband, and she is not disgusted by his appearance as we might be. Blanch's lack of disgust might be a sign of the depth of her love.

Miller believes "that disgust has a firmer hold on us, that it is more basic to our definition of self, than most other passions."[45] This is partly because disgust is linked to rank, putrid, fermenting death, as Kristeva implies. But this is also because "our very core, our soul, is hemmed in by barriers of disgust, and one does not give them up unless one is in love or is held at the point of a gun."[46] Miller claims that disgust uses our orifices and senses to police the surfaces of our bodies and to protect our cores: the rules of disgust "mark the boundaries of self; the relaxing of them marks privilege, intimacy, duty, and caring."[47] In other words, the same fluids that ooze from a stranger lose their power to disgust when they ooze from a loved one. Perhaps love is the overcoming or acceptance of disgust; it enables parents to change soiled diapers and lovers to exchange bodily fluids. The problem with Miller's definition is that it assumes disgust is the starting point of all human relationships. That is, we are essentially disgusted by others' bodily fluids unless we have reason – love or fear of death – to feel something other than disgust. If we add erotic desire or religious devotion to the list of reasons we relax our boundaries, we discover that some fluids are not inherently disgusting. Some fluids, or actions of fluid exchange, are desirable before they even hold the potential to disgust. Or, perhaps, because they hold this potential.

In *Hesperides*, Herrick explores the fluid connections among these essential definers of self: love, disgust, desire, and devotion. In some ways, his interest in disgust is congruent with our own. In Bernardo Bertolucci's contemporary erotic thriller *The Dreamers* (2003), based on Gilbert Adair's novel *The Holy Innocents* (1988), Matthew, a young American film student, is studying abroad in Paris. He meets and becomes fast friends with two French students, Théo and Isabelle, a brother and sister who are Siamese twins that were separated at birth. Matthew moves into their home, falls in love with Isabelle, and discovers that Théo and Isabelle's relationship borders on incest. They sleep naked together, they bathe together, and they watch each other masturbate. The morning after Matthew's first night in their home, Isabelle wakes him by licking away his sleepies, or the drainage from the corners of his eyes.[48] He seems surprised, but not disgusted, by her action. When he asks her why she does this, she tells him that this is how she wakes her brother. Matthew tells her it is strange, but she tells him that he enjoyed it.[49]

Adair's novel and Bertolucci's film are rich for analysis, but here I am most interested in Herrick's similar intersection of desire and disgust. His epigram "Upon Loach" describes the same early morning ritual, this time between a husband and wife:

> Seeal'd up with Night-gum, *Loach* each morning lyes,
> Till his Wife licking, so unglews his eyes.
> No question then, but such a lick is sweet,
> When a warm tongue do's with such Ambers meet. (H-816)

This short epigram might disgust, but it also is intimate, lovely, and perhaps erotically charged.[50] Herrick does not simply critique a lower-class citizen; instead, he challenges the very idea of disgust by making a vile action desirable. We might cringe at the thought of tasting another's coagulated eye drainage, but Herrick says there is "no question" that his wife's action is "sweet" because it reveals loving devotion. Loach's name refers to "'A kind of Confection or Electuary that is to be licked, or suffered to melt in the mouth without chewing' (Phillips, *New World*, s.v. 'Loach, *or* Lohoch')"; to his wife, Loach's eye gunk is candy.[51] We also are reminded that desire drives people to lick all sorts of bodily effusions that would disgust in other contexts. In *The Dreamers*, Matthew is aroused by Isabelle's "warm tongue," as are many of the film's viewers. Film critic David Edelstein finds this scene and others where the main characters get "smeary with various secretions . . . a huge turn-on and kinda gross."[52] If Herrick meant "Upon Loach" solely to disgust, he could have ended the epigram at the first period. The final two lines, if taken out of context, contain little that disgust. By the end of the poem, the "glew"-like eye effusions are simply and beautifully described as "Ambers."[53]

Reading Herrick's desirable disgust alongside *The Dreamers* – and together with recent sociological and philosophical studies (e.g., Miller, Korsmeyer) – reveals that early modern disgust is similar to contemporary disgust in compelling ways. Such a conclusion, of course, risks anachronism. But we see similar instances of desirable disgust if we look back to medieval Christian devotional traditions. On its surface, "Upon Loach" does not appear to be a religious poem.[54] However, if, as Achsah Guibbory suggests, we "reconsider the genre of 'religious' poetry and . . . look again at *Hesperides*," we discover fascinating parallels.[55] Guibbory argues that the "nastiest epigrams" are probably directed toward the Puritans and present "the body devoid of spirit and grace," and that this "graceless materiality is for Herrick both the consequence and appropriate punishment for those (Puritans) who would presume to draw neat lines between the holy and the profane, the spirit and the flesh."[56] The first line of "Upon Loach," which simply describes a diseased bleary-eyed man, might serve as a representative example of the spiritless and graceless body Guibbory believes Herrick deplores. However, in the second line, Loach's wife brings a version of grace to the epigram that blurs "the categories of the sacred and the profane."[57]

In religious writing, disgust frequently is the response to the profane, fleshy, earthly body. As Alexander Cuffel explains, "in Jewish, Pagan, and Christian writings about the nature of God, a primary concern was to separate divinity from the biological functioning of the human body."[58] Specifically, "the intake of food and the excretion of feces and urine as well as all bodily fluids and their accompanying odors served as tangible, despised reminders of this process that was so incompatible with a pure, unmoved, and uncorrupted deity or deities."[59] Things like skin disease and leprosy were frequently considered to be punishments from God for transgressions or impiety.[60] Yet the body and its effusions could also be desirable and compatible with religious expression. As Leo Steinberg powerfully demonstrates in his study of Renaissance art, the *body* of Christ – from naked infant to bleeding corpse – was celebrated during this period because it represented that he was "very man, very God."[61] The fact that Christ was fully human meant that he was subject to the same fleshy processes as the rest of humanity. In addition, the tradition of the Eucharist is a Christian celebration of the body and its effusions. Whether or not the bread and wine *become* the flesh and blood of Christ when they are consecrated, the sacrament celebrates the body and the very human – as opposed to divine – need for food and drink.

The Eucharist also reminds us again, but in a different way, that disgust is relative. Cuffel explains, "Christians compared the Eucharist to honey; Jews called it stinking and nauseating."[62] In the Christian context, consuming human – albeit also Godly – flesh and blood is desirable, but in other contexts it is disgusting. In Herrick's own poem about Eucharistic devotion, "To Christ" (N-129), drinking Christ's blood does not disgust for an instant: "My mouth I'le lay unto Thy wound / Bleeding, that no Blood touch the ground" (N-129.4–5). Herrick reminds of Richard Crashaw here, and his impassioned lyrics on Christ's wounds: "O these wakeful wounds of thine! / Are they mouths? or are they eyes? / Be they mouths, or be they eyen, / Each bleeding part some one supplies" (1–4).[63] Is it possible that "Upon Loach" is part of this tradition of Eucharistic devotion? Might Loach's wife be taking in her husband's bodily effusions as an act of sacramental love?

Herrick's use of the word "sweet" to describe Loach's wife's lick offers a compelling connection to Eucharistic devotion. Caroline Walker Bynum explains, "the food-body God gives in the eucharist is received by Christians as both erotic and nourishing sweetness."[64] In *Holy Feast and Holy Fast*, Bynum chronicles the lives of medieval female beguines and saints who used food and drink to manipulate their bodies and to demonstrate their faith. The Eucharist was central to these manipulations and many of these women were unable to eat anything but consecrated bread and wine. A few women even sought out diseased bodily effusions as Eucharistic stand-ins: "Like Catherine of Siena, who drank pus, and Catherine of Genoa, who ate lice, Angela [of Foligno] drank water that came from washing the sores of lepers. One of the scabs stuck in her throat, she said, and tasted 'as sweet as communion.'"[65] Although the diseased effusions tasted sweet to these women, the disgust they initially felt was, in part, what transformed the vile into the desirable. In the case of Catherine of Siena, "She twice forced herself to overcome nausea by thrusting her mouth into the putrefying breast of a dying woman or by drinking pus." Her reward for the second instance was a vision of Christ in which he tells her, "Yesterday the intensity of your ardent love for me overcame even the instinctive reflexes of your body itself: you forced yourself to swallow without a qualm a drink from which nature recoiled in disgust." In the vision, Christ pulls Catherine to his side and "she fastened her lips upon that sacred wound . . . and there she slaked her thirst." Diseased pus tasted as sweet to Catherine as the Eucharist, and she lived on them for the rest of her life.[66] Sweetness is thus both gustatory pleasure and a metaphor for love.

Catherine of Siena's story unites Herrick's "Upon Loach" and "To Christ" in a surprising way. Licking a person's coagulated eye drainage and sucking blood from Christ's side are both examples of sweet, devotional love. In fact, the first might represent stronger, sacrificial love because it requires that disgust be overcome, or that disgust be transformed into desire. Drinking directly from Christ's body is a potential reward for taking care of diseased human bodies. Other stories of medieval saints similarly complicate our readings of Herrick's epigrams. For instance, Bynum describes a royal saint, Margaret of Hungary, who never washed her own body, but whose "wash water from her hair, when held in the mouth or swallowed, cured ill sisters and even a brother in another monastery."[67] Herrick's Sibilla, who gave the milk and almonds she used on her hands and thighs to the poor, might disgust less in this context. Perhaps she gave the cream and nut paste freely because she believed it had healing powers? Perhaps she simply never considered they might disgust?

To argue that some of Herrick's disgusting epigrams are devotional is not to negate the argument that they hold erotic potential; the devotional aspects actually encourage erotic readings. Bynum notes that Eucharistic devotion frequently "had erotic or sensual overtones." The desire to eat and drink from Christ was a desire for "fusion" as well as union that was both ecstatic and erotic.[68] In *Closet Devotions*, Richard Rambuss reads seventeenth-century religious verse to discover "devotion that is – and not just is like – an erotic experience, an affective shock that seldom registers as 'just' spiritual."[69] Even poems that describe Christ's crucified body, "begored and putrescent," present a penetrable – wounded with spears – and ejaculatory – blood spewing forth – man in erotic terms.[70] In *Hesperides*, acts of devotion – religious and secular – might also be acts of erotic desire: for instance, when Herrick's speaker drinks Christ's blood saying, "My mouth I'le lay unto Thy wound" (N-129.4); when Loach's wife licks her husband's eyes with a "warm tongue" (H-816.4); and when the poor drink the cream that bathed Sibilla's "thighs (more soft then silk)" (H-561.3). These actions connect the bodies of people in sensual ways that might disgust or titillate or both. As Isabelle demonstrates with her eye lick in *The Dreamers*, a disgusting action can be erotically exciting when it *should* disgust, but doesn't. Isabelle asks Matthew if he enjoyed her licking away his morning eye gunk; he responds, "was I supposed to?" and she answers with a simple, "naturally."[71] Sometimes desire is the *natural* response to disgust.

Some of Herrick's most erotic verses also play with the boundaries of disgust, desire, and devotion. For instance, "Fresh Cheese and Cream" celebrates one of Herrick's most beloved mistress's breasts:

> Wo'd yee have fresh Cheese and Cream?
> *Julia's* Breast can give you them:
> And if more; Each *Nipple* cries,
> To your *Cream*, her[e]'s *Strawberries*. (H-491)[72]

In part, the poem describes the utilitarian function of Julia's breasts. They produce milk, and milk can be made into cheese. But the verse also is sexually charged. The breasts do not just produce cream; they *are* cream that surrounds Julia's strawberry-like nipples.

A contemporary reading might lead us to lactophilia, a fetish that disgusts many in contemporary Western culture.[73] A devotional reading might instead link the image, again, to the Eucharist. As Bynum reminds us, breast milk was thought to be "transmuted blood" at this time, and some "spoke of drinking blood from the breast of mother Jesus."[74] But whether erotic, devotional, or both, there is still something disturbing about the image of a woman's breasts as edible cheese. Milk is a pure bodily effusion, but cheese is processed and coagulated, and often moldy and rank – albeit tasty. When Herrick connects Julia's breasts first to cheese, one might imagine pale, milk-white cheese, riddled with fine blue veins. But to imagine blue-veined cheese is to imagine something like a ripe Roquefort, together with the pungent smell that reminds of foot sweat. Indeed, the same bacteria are responsible for the scents of both blue cheese and feet.

Disgust thus links an erotic poem about a woman's breasts back to the poem about Pimpe's frothy foot sweat that opened this chapter. The link might also explain why both "Upon Pimpe" and "Fresh Cheese and Cream" were excluded from nineteenth-century editions of Herrick, and why they still are so rarely anthologized. Alternative eroticisms can disgust just as much as diseased bodies. Aversion is a dangerous affect to employ, especially when it dances with attraction. Breast milk, holy blood, eye drainage, and foot sweat are all bodily effusions that can be desirable, disgusting, or both. Perhaps it is the "both" that makes people most uncomfortable.

In *Hesperides*, Herrick employs disgust while questioning the status of the affect itself. Disgust might repulse, but it also might express erotic desire and reveal intense devotion. Herrick reminds us that feelings of disgust are relative – to time, to culture, to scenario, to subject. By ignoring the disgusting epigrams, and by manufacturing a seemingly "tasteful" Herrick, the nineteenth-century editors and critics erased an essential component of *Hesperides*. The development of discriminating taste, and the upholding and relaxing of the rules of disgust, is intimately connected to the rise of the early modern subject. In *A History of Private Life*, Philippe Ariès explains, "Between 1500 and 1800 people developed new attitudes toward their own bodies and toward the bodies of others."[75] People created the "protected zone around the body" that we now describe as our personal space.[76] Herrick's poetry challenges these boundaries of selfhood. His poems ask us to be disgusted, to test our judgments of taste, and to recognize that our relationship to disgust is fluid.[77]

Notes

1 Hazlitt, "Preface," viii.
2 Text references are to numbered poems (poems from *Hesperides* are prefaced with an "H-" and poems from *His Noble Numbers* are prefaced with an "N-") and lines of this edition. If no line numbers are indicated, the poem is quoted in full.
3 Palgrave, "Introduction," xi.
4 Gertzman, *Fantasy*. Gertzman's book includes an appendix that details ninety-eight unique editions of Herrick's verse published between 1810 and 1968.
5 Southey, *Lives*, 85.
6 Ashe, "Robert Herrick," 129. Even Herrick's greatest supporters were compelled to qualify any praise they gave. Simpson, "Preface," vi, muses, "it is one of the paradoxes of literature that this exquisite artist, experimenting in minute satire, should have composed a monotonous and, on the whole, pointless series of poems on merely nauseous themes." Saintsbury, "Introduction," xxvi, finds that "part of his work disgusts those who are most prepared to be delighted with other parts of it." Grosart, "Introduction," cxxi, notes that the epigrams are "'spots' of putridity placed among the good things of the banquet."
7 Saintsbury, "Introduction," lii–liii.
8 Palgrave, "Introduction," xi.
9 Saintsbury, "Caroline Poetry," 355.

10 See, for instance, Kimbrough, "Critical Study," 211–12; Rollin, *Robert Herrick*, 79–80. Even Saintsbury, "Introduction," xxxvi, comments on Herrick's place in the epigram tradition, but he argues that "Herrick's epigrammatic work is comparably the worst, in a literary point of view, that he has left; and it is, even among all of the dull, coarse epigrams which the late sixteenth and early seventeenth century has left us, exceptionally coarse and dull."

11 Halli, "Epigrams," 31.

12 Halli, "Epigrams," 37.

13 Coiro, *Robert Herrick's* Hesperides, 3, 160. Coiro devotes a chapter to the "mocking" epigrams that target the "poor (or nouveau riche), uneducated members of the lower class," 156.

14 Schoenfeldt, "Art of Disgust," 128.

15 Douglas, *Purity and Danger*; Elias, *Prozeß*.

16 Schoenfeldt, "Art of Disgust," 150.

17 Crane, "Cultural Materialism," 22, 33.

18 Crane, "Cultural Materialism," 33.

19 Crane, "Cultural Materialism," 43.

20 Marcus, "Conviviality," 70; Maus, "Why Read Herrick?," 29.

21 Schoenfeldt, "Art of Disgust," 150.

22 Miner, *Thomas Aquinas*, 53–5.

23 These generalizations are treated with more complexity in King's and Correll's chapters.

24 Korsmeyer, *Savoring*, 3.

25 Miller, *Anatomy*, 111.

26 Coiro, *Robert Herrick's* Hesperides, 162.

27 Schoenfeldt, "Art of Disgust," 142.

28 Coiro, *Robert Herrick's* Hesperides, 160.

29 Schoenfeldt, "Art of Disgust," 133.

30 Korsmeyer, *Savoring*, 175.

31 Coiro, *Robert Herrick's* Hesperides, 161.

32 See the Introduction for further discussion of the word "disgust" and its relationship to the word "taste."

33 Schoenfeldt, "Art of Disgust," 134.

34 Schoenfeldt, "Art of Disgust," 134.

35 Crane, "Cultural Materialism," 39.

36 Crane, "Cultural Materialism," 39.

37 Crane, "Cultural Materialism," 39.

38 Patrick, *Complete Poetry*, 48, n. 1.

39 *Oxford English Dictionary Online*, June 2014, s.v. "scald head." Accessed July 3, 2014. http://www.oed.com/view/Entry/171720.

40 Halli, "Epigrams," 34.

41 Halli, "Epigrams," 34.

42 Shakespeare, "Sonnet 130," 375.

43 Kristeva, *Powers*, 3.

44 Donne, "Elegy 8: *The Comparison*," 103.

45 Miller, *Anatomy*, 250.

46 Miller, *Anatomy*, 250.

47 Miller, *Anatomy*, xi.

48 The lick is Bertolucci's addition. In Adair's novel, Danielle (Isabelle's equivalent) just picks away and examines Matthew's eye gunk: "Her tongue protruding over her lower lip, her hand unshaking, half schoolboy and half surgeon, Danielle inserted her finger slowly into the soft crevice at the corner of his left eye and slowly, avidly, meticulously, excavated the tiny, brittle stalactite of sleep that was lodged there. After subjecting it to a thorough examination on the tip of her finger, she flicked it off, then proceeded to

draw a similarly scabby, yellowish fragment from the right one. These two nocturnal incrustations looked absolutely minute on her finger but felt, from Matthew's own point of view, like a pair of dice that had been extracted from his eyes." Adair, *Holy Innocents*, 49.

49 "Visions of Garbo."
50 I read "Upon Loach" as a poem that explores the sense of taste in Eschenbaum, "Robert Herrick."
51 Cain and Connolly, *Complete Poetry*, 2:723, n. 816.
52 Edelstein, "Godard and Man in Paris."
53 The eye effusions are like flies encased in amber, or instances of vile beauty that attract rather than disgust. To reinforce this idea, the poem that follows "Upon Loach" describes the rich beauty of "a Flie within a Beade / Of Amber cleanly buried" (H-817.1–2).
54 See Ainsworth, "Rise to life with These." Ainsworth argues that Herrick's mocking epigrams demonstrate how "even these disgusting and lowly people will receive God's grace and be made immortal in Heaven," 147.
55 Guibbory, "Enlarging," 28.
56 Guibbory, "Enlarging," 33, 36, 37.
57 Guibbory, "Enlarging," 30.
58 Cuffel, *Gendering*, 22.
59 Cuffel, *Gendering*, 26.
60 Cuffel, *Gendering*, 40.
61 Steinberg, *Sexuality*, 10.
62 Cuffel, *Gendering*, 154.
63 Crashaw, "Wounds," 453. On the abundance and erotic charge of images of Christ's penetrable, bleeding body in Crashaw, see Rambuss, "Christ's Ganymede." On disgust in and of Crashaw, see also Rambuss, "Crashaw and the Metaphysical Shudder."
64 Bynum, *Holy Feast*, 155.
65 Bynum, *Holy Feast*, 144–5.
66 Bynum, *Holy Feast*, 171–2.
67 Bynum, *Holy Feast*, 136.
68 Bynum, *Holy Feast*, 246.
69 Rambuss, *Closet Devotions*, 84.
70 Rambuss, *Closet Devotions*, 20.
71 "Visions of Garbo."
72 Brackets in Patrick's edited poem.
73 See, for instance, the outcry in response to a breast milk ice-cream shop that opened in London in 2011. Zoe Williams, a restaurant critic, said she was repulsed by the idea of the shop but tried the product: "In summary: at first I liked it; then I didn't mind it; then I hated it; then I wanted to be sick." Williams, "Breast Milk Ice-Cream." But despite (or perhaps because of) people's disgust, the shop sold out of the ice cream within days of its initial production. Chappell, "Breast Milk Ice Cream a Hit."
74 Bynum, *Holy Feast*, 270, 271.
75 Ariès, "Introduction," 4.
76 Ariès, "Introduction," 4.
77 Thanks to Richard Rambuss for inspiring this essay years ago, and to Barbara Correll for helping me to complete it.

References

Adair, Gilbert. *The Holy Innocents: A Romance*. London: Heinemann, 1988.
Ainsworth, David. " 'Rise to life with These': Salvation and Herrick's Mocking Epigrams." *ANQ: A Quarterly Journal of Short Articles, Notes, and Reviews* 25, no. 3 (2012): 147–53.

Ariès, Phillipe. "Introduction." In *Passions of the Renaissance: A History of Private Life*, vol. 3, edited by Roger Chartier, translated by Arthur Goldhammer, 1–11. Cambridge, MA: Belknap Press, 1989.

Ashe, Thomas. "Robert Herrick." *Temple Bar* 68 (May 1883): 120–32.

Bynum, Caroline Walker. *Holy Feast and Holy Fast: The Religious Significance of Food to Medieval Women*. Berkeley: University of California Press, 1987.

Cain, Tom, and Ruth Connolly, eds. *The Complete Poetry of Robert Herrick*. 2 vols. Oxford: Oxford University Press, 2013.

Chappell, Bill. "Breast Milk Ice Cream a Hit at London Store." *National Public Radio*, February 25, 2011. Accessed July 16, 2014. http://www.npr.org/blogs/thetwo-way/2011/02/25/134056923/breast-milk-ice-cream-a-hit-at-london-store.

Coiro, Ann Baynes. *Robert Herrick's* Hesperides *and the Epigram Book Tradition*. Baltimore: Johns Hopkins University Press, 1988.

Connolly, Ruth, and Tom Cain, eds. *Lords of Wine and Oile: Community and Conviviality in the Poetry of Robert Herrick*. Oxford: Oxford University Press, 2011.

Crane, Mary Thomas. "Herrick's Cultural Materialism." *George Herbert Journal* 14, nos. 1 & 2 (Fall 1990/Spring 1991): 21–50.

Crashaw, Richard. "On the Wounds of Our Crucified Lord." In *Seventeenth-Century British Poetry: 1603–1660*, edited by John P. Rumrich and Gregory Chaplin, 453–54. New York: Norton, 2006.

Cuffel, Alexandra. *Gendering Disgust in Medieval Religious Polemic*. South Bend, IN: Notre Dame University Press, 2007.

Donne, John. *John Donne: The Complete English Poems*. Edited by A.J. Smith. 1971. Reprint, London: Penguin, 1986.

Douglas, Mary. *Purity and Danger: An Analysis of the Concepts of Pollution and Taboo*. London: Routledge, 1966.

Edelstein, David. "Godard and Man in Paris: The Movie World Meets Reality in Bernardo Bertolucci's *The Dreamers*." *Slate*, February 6, 2004. Accessed November 28, 2014. http://www.slate.com/articles/arts/movies/2004/02/godard_and_man_in_paris.html.

Elias, Norbert. *Über den Prozeß der Zivilisation*. Basel: Verlag Haus zum Falken, 1939. Translated by Edmund Jephcott as *The Civilizing Process*. Edited by Eric Dunning, Johan Goudsblom, and Stephen Mennell. Rev. ed. Malden, MA: Blackwell, 2000.

Eschenbaum, Natalie K. "Robert Herrick and the Five (or Six) Senses." In *The Senses in Early Modern England, 1558–1660*, edited by Simon Smith, Jackie Watson, and Amy Kenny, 113–29. Manchester: Manchester University Press, 2015.

Gertzman, Jay A. *Fantasy, Fashion and Affection: Editions of Robert Herrick's Poetry for the Common Reader, 1810–1968*. Bowling Green, OH: Bowling Green State University Popular Press, 1986.

Grosart, Alexander B. Introduction to *The Complete Poems of Robert Herrick*. Edited by Alexander B. Grosart, v–cclxxvi. 3 vols. London: Chatto & Windus, 1876.

Guibbory, Achsah. "Enlarging the Limits of the 'Religious Lyric': The Case of Herrick's *Hesperides*." In *New Perspectives on the Seventeenth-Century English Religious Lyric*, edited by John R. Roberts, 28–45. Columbia: Missouri University Press, 1994.

Halli, Robert W. Jr. "Robert Herrick's Epigrams on Commoners." *South Atlantic Bulletin* 43, no. 1 (January 1978): 30–41.

Hazlitt, W. Carew. Preface to *Hesperides: The Poems and Other Remains of Robert Herrick Now First Collected*, by Robert Herrick. Edited by W. Carew Hazlitt, v–ix. 2 vols. London: John Russell Smith, 1869.

Herrick, Robert. *The Complete Poetry of Robert Herrick*. Edited by J. Max Patrick. New York: Norton, 1968.

Kimbrough, Joe Arthur. "A Critical Study of Robert Herrick." PhD diss., University of Illinois, 1965.

Korsmeyer, Carolyn. *Savoring Disgust: The Foul and the Fair in Aesthetics*. New York: Oxford University Press, 2011.

Kristeva, Julia. *Powers of Horror: An Essay on Abjection*. Translated by Leon S. Roudiez. New York: Columbia University Press, 1982.

Marcus, Leah S. "Conviviality Interrupted, or Herrick and Postmodernism." In *Lords of Wine and Oile: Community and Conviviality in the Poetry of Robert Herrick*, edited by Ruth Connolly and Tom Cain, 65–82. Oxford: Oxford University Press, 2011.

Maus, Katharine Eisaman. "Why Read Herrick?" In *Lords of Wine and Oile: Community and Conviviality in the Poetry of Robert Herrick*, edited by Ruth Connolly and Tom Cain, 25–38. Oxford: Oxford University Press, 2011.

Miller, William Ian. *The Anatomy of Disgust*. Cambridge, MA: Harvard University Press, 1997.

Miner, Robert. *Thomas Aquinas on the Passions*. New York: Cambridge University Press, 2009.

Palgrave, Francis Turner. Introduction to *Chrysomela: A Selection from the Lyrical Poems of Robert Herrick*. Edited by Francis Turner Palgrave, ix–xxvi. London: Macmillan, 1877.

Patrick, J. Max, ed. *The Complete Poetry of Robert Herrick*. New York: Norton, 1968.

Rambuss, Richard. "Christ's Ganymede." In *Closet Devotions*, 11–71. Durham, NC: Duke University Press, 1998.

———. *Closet Devotions*. Durham, NC: Duke University Press, 1998.

———. "Crashaw and the Metaphysical Shudder; Or, How to Do Things with Tears." In *Structures of Feeling in Seventeenth-Century Cultural Expression*, edited by Susan McClary, 253–71. Toronto: University of Toronto Press, 2013.

Rollin, Roger B. *Robert Herrick*. New York: Twayne, 1966.

Saintsbury, George. "Caroline Poetry." In *A History of Elizabethan Literature*, 354–93. London: Macmillan, 1887.

———. Introduction to *The Poetical Works of Robert Herrick*. Edited by George Saintsbury, xxv–liii. 2 vols. London: George Bell & Sons, 1893.

Schoenfeldt, Michael C. "The Art of Disgust: Civility and the Social Body in *Hesperides*." *George Herbert Journal* 14, nos. 1 & 2 (Fall 1990/Spring 1991): 127–54.

Shakespeare, William. *The Arden Shakespeare: Shakespeare's Sonnets*. Third Series. Edited by Katherine Duncan-Jones. Walton-on-Thames: Thomas Nelson, 1997.

Simpson, Percy. Preface to *The Poetical Works of Robert Herrick*. Edited by F.W. Moorman, iii–vii. London: Oxford University Press, 1921.

Southey, Robert. *The Lives and Works of the Uneducated Poets*. Edited by J.S. Childers. London: Humphrey Milford, 1925.

Steinberg, Leo. *The Sexuality of Christ in Renaissance Art and in Modern Oblivion*. 2nd ed. Chicago: University of Chicago Press, 1996.

"Visions of Garbo." *The Dreamers*. DVD. Directed by Bernardo Bertolucci. Century City, CA: Twentieth Century Fox, 2003.

Williams, Zoe. "Breast Milk Ice-Cream: The Taste Test." *The Guardian*, February 27, 2011. Accessed July 16, 2014. http://www.theguardian.com/lifeandstyle/2011/feb/27/breast-milk-ice-cream-taste.

4 Discerning (dis)taste

Delineating sexual mores in Shakespeare's *Venus and Adonis*

Marcela Kostihová

She seizeth on his sweating palm . . .
And, trembling in her passion, calls it balm –
Earth's sovereign salve to do a goddess good.

—*Shakespeare*, Venus and Adonis (25–7)

One of the most startling traits of Shakespeare's retelling of the romance of Venus and Adonis, compared to the source material in Ovid's *Metamorphoses*, is the absence of the very romance that originally defines it. The mutually satisfying tryst between the goddess of love and the fair youth – one of the many interspecies relationships Ovid describes – is transformed into a distasteful, wrong-headed pursuit of Adonis by Venus. In this farce, which preserves little but the bare-bones plot – they meet, he hunts, he dies, she cries – the two central characters are translated so drastically that the only characteristics that link them to their Ovidian predecessors are their names and their general identificatory categories: fair human youth and goddess of love.

Adonis' admiring ardor for Venus is nixed, and the Adonis we encounter in Shakespeare's poem meets Venus' advances with shame and anger. His passing fancy for general hunting is replaced by an all-consuming desire to hunt "the boar," which he claims is his only love. While Ovid's Adonis is trampled accidentally by a random boar who unexpectedly charges as the hunter is looking around the woods for unspecified prey, Shakespeare's Adonis meets his end in a clandestine, complex, and highly sexualized encounter wherein the very boar he has been after "sheathed" a "sharp tusk" in the eager Adonis' "soft groin."[1] The independent, powerful goddess of Ovid's tale, who dispenses hunting advice but otherwise tends to her own business, becomes a groveling, distastefully overconfident wretch. Dripping with sarcasm and ridicule, Shakespeare's narrator revels in detailing the range of wooing attempts, subterfuges, and loquacious arguments Venus employs to explore the depth of the cringing shame and visceral disgust her behavior elicits in the fair Adonis and, it might be expected, the reader.[2]

This disgust creates the lynchpin around which the signifying order of the poem turns: in providing a revolting spectacle for the reader, Venus' distasteful behavior cements her degradation from awe-inspiring goddess to a common, animalistic wench. Inversely, in documenting Adonis' distaste and enumerating his every blush of shame, Shakespeare proposes an alternative, cultured and elite structure of behavior that distinguishes Adonis and his homoerotic world of the hunt from the vulgar, bestial world of heterosexual pleasure and procreativity. It is my contention here that the poem moves beyond the usual level of misogyny that often provided entertainment in popular Renaissance texts to bank on the profound appeal of that which is culturally pegged as disgusting to force an evaluative distinction between two gendered modes of sexual behavior.

Drawing on contemporary moral treatises that use disgust with lower class behaviors to promote cultured courtly humanism, Shakespeare's poem seeks to uncouple homosexual acts from bestiality, coupling base animalism, instead, with heterosexuality. Thus, disgust is harnessed as a tool in an attempt to (re)establish homosexual desire as the logical provenance of polite society. This reversal is underscored by the pigheaded determination of both protagonists of the narrative to effect vertical movement counter-intuitive to their symbolic position; whereas Venus is pulled to earth by the gravity of her passion and focuses exclusively on literally tumbling to the ground pinning Adonis beneath her, Adonis battles gravity to move upward toward heavenly love that would provide ways to transcend the earthly constraints that bind him. The ultimate metamorphosis enables Adonis to achieve just that, elevating him from the world of vulgar love to the elite realms of cultured society inaccessible to the uninitiated, presumably common reader.

The binary between the elite and the commons is carried out throughout the poem, beginning with its very premise. Prior even to Shakespeare's dedication of the poem to the "honourable" Henry Wriothlesley, the Earl of Southampton, in which Shakespeare mentions "honour" no less than seven times, Shakespeare calls on Ovid's *Amores* to provide the poem's epigraph. This epigraph – "Vilia miretur vulgus; mihi flavus Apollo / Pocula Castalia plena minister aqua," translated by Christopher Marlowe as "Let base conceited wits admire vile things, / Fair Phoebus lead me to the Muses' springs" – prophesizes that the text will lend itself to two separate interpretations by two discrete groups of readers.[3] On the one hand, the epigraph suggests, the commons will be entertained by the vulgar subject matter the poem promises to deliver. On the other, the epigraph proposes, a few discerning readers of taste, presumably familiar with both Latin and Ovid's erotic tome, could use the poem as a springboard to further cultivate taste. Such an inscription inescapably creates a symbolic gap between undesirable (though entertaining) common vulgarity and a highly desirable and presumably attainable membership in an implied exclusive community, providing an entry point for any willing reader to think critically about the implications of Venus-ridicule. Sure, Venus is ridiculously funny – if you like that sort of humor – but what are we to do with it?

The world of Shakespeare's Venus is gleefully vulgar. It undermines her nominally elevated status position as a powerful goddess and, by representative association, the status of all women as objects worthy of male desire. After all, as she loquaciously contends – and the poem does nothing to dispute such claims – she is female perfection embodied. If one is to go by Shakespeare's contemporaries' standards of female beauty and flair, she has "no defects" (133–8). The poem revels not merely in the unsuccessful wooing effort of an over-confident individual – though elements of that sort of righteous ridicule are undeniably present – but, more importantly, in the inability of any imaginable woman to succeed where Venus herself fails. Venus' presumed superiority, deriving from her heralded female perfection and divine status, unravels in the face of a steadfast youth bent on stalwart pursuit of truly perfect love. While Venus does possess expected supernatural elements – at one point, she reposes on a bed of tender violets and primroses without bending a single stem (125, 151–2) – they do nothing to provide the distinguishing features one would expect from a member of a preeminent global elite. If anything, Venus is literally accessible and down to earth: the sole aim of her arguments and actions in the poem is to impede any movement other than downward, to bring both herself and Adonis to the ground, tangled in an amorous embrace.

While her speech aspires to the usual elevated courtly love discourse, the content of Venus' message further documents her descent to gross vulgarity and demonstrates the denigrating dangers of heterosexual passion. Venus' attempts to persuade Adonis to amorous play betray comical misapplication of her affection. One of the most appalling fixations of the supposedly heavenly creature is on earthly bodily fluids, which she inexplicably celebrates. Early on, she smears herself with Adonis' sweat, which she deems "Earth's sovereign salve to do a goddess good" (26–7). She revels in the "steam" of his frustrated breath, calling it "heavenly moisture, air of grace," deliberately ignoring Adonis' struggles to escape her ironclad embrace (62–5). One of the most infamous metaphors she employs is of inviting Adonis to imagine himself a "deer" to "graze" in her "park" (231, 233) wherein she underscores the places below the neck where Adonis might consider refreshing himself at the "pleasant fountains" (234) of her own bodily fluids. She does not shy away from referring suggestively to body parts, whether they be "round rising hillocks" or "high delightful plain," and refers to abundant pubic hair that provides ample hiding places, whether in "sweet bottom-grass" or the more explicitly coarse "brakes obscure and rough" (237). Lest the reader let imagination run away with pleasant erotic thought, the narrator hastens to point out the coarseness of the goddess's fluid production, noting her dripping "sweat" (175), which later turns into frustrated "reek and smoke" in her repeated and fruitless seduction attempts (555).

Contrary to her intent, Venus' invitation to animal role-playing further alienates Adonis' discerning affection by underscoring the base urges she represents and celebrates throughout the poem. In addition to the deer/park metaphor, one of the central exemplars of her seductive discourse is Adonis' own amorous horse, which breaks its reins to pursue a passing mare. But where Venus sees the horse gloriously achieving freedom from the humiliating servility of "petty bondage," from being "mastered with a leathern rein . . . like a jade" (394, 391–2), Adonis sees a gross dereliction of duty and descent into chaos. In its diction and point of view, the poem supports Adonis' assessment, documenting the disintegration of the once-glorious courser into a collection of uncooperative body parts:

> Round-hoofed, short-jointed, fetlocks shag and long,
> Broad breast, full eye, small head, and nostril wide,
> High crest, short ears, straight legs, and passing strong;
> Thin mane, thick tail, broad buttock, tender hide –
> Look what a horse should have he did not lack,
> Save a proud rider on so proud a back. (295–300)

Venus' exhortation to Adonis to follow the horse's example and to "learn from him" (404) only accentuates the warning the poem poses against the detrimental effects of heterosexual passion.

Venus' final argumentative card, perhaps the most overplayed in the deck of courtly love discourse and one that has become suspect in its ineffectiveness, is to present heterosexual amorous play as a way to pay the debt to nature which, the argument goes, requires procreation. She plays this card forcefully, exhorting Adonis repeatedly to fulfill this prerogative, such as when she impresses upon him that "to get is [his] duty" (163–8). Here the poem parallels the argument of Shakespeare's early sonnets, written – as far as scholars have been able to determine – at the time of *Venus and Adonis*. Like Shakespeare's procreation sonnets, Venus exhorts her fair youth to reproduce. And, like the subsequent sonnets, the poem rejects the boundaries of so-called natural behavior for someone of Adonis' superior perfection.[4] But where the sonnets propose poetry as the antidote to procreation and as the means to achieve immortality, *Venus and Adonis* poses the possibility of transcending common life via metamorphosis. This metamorphosis is the reward for proper moral behavior, exemplified in modest comportment, distaste for that which is to be recognized as disgusting, maintaining of privacy and decorum and, most importantly, stalwart refusal of everything that Venus represents.

Animalistic characteristics, particularly when it comes to things procreative, have been culturally classified as repugnant, as researchers of things disgusting in Western culture have pointed out. Presumably, as Carolyn Korsmeyer has proposed, this disassociation from such behavior is rooted in the realization that disgust is one of the distinguishing characteristics that separate humans from animals. Animals, she points out, might recoil from objects or situations that created distress in the past, but they do not feel disgust. Disgust, then, serves as a warning system that helps humans to recoil "from indicators of our animal nature, thereby protecting the human 'soul' from descent to a bestial condition and guarding our moral and spiritual being against degradation and pollution."[5] Similarly, Susan B. Miller suggests that human repudiation of natural procreation, broadly defined, bolsters a human need for ontological and epistemological structures of meaning. The frequent deployment of disgust with overabundant fecundity and sexuality seen in the animal and plant kingdoms aims to bolster humans' sense of existential importance: "Nature is the mother that so abounds in fertility that she cares little about the individual scion . . . Progeny will come and go, in great numbers and in endless forms. As individuals, we are eclipsed; we utilize disgust to argue for our own significance."[6]

While, ontologically speaking, disgust seems to be a broadly universal emotion, seen in most of the world's cultures, I am far more interested in the epistemological questions of its delineation. Research on disgust suggests that the overwhelming majority of humans experience disgust. However, the triggers of the emotion are not identical across geography and time, suggesting how much what is considered disgusting varies. While some forms of visceral disgust – such as that with human waste and unsuitable food – seem generally similar, others have clearly been culturally developed and engrained to police the boundaries of humanity that, in turn, help to stratify the human population along socially constructed hierarchies. It is undeniable, for instance, that the Renaissance and humanism, in their intensified scrutiny of the natural world, used disgust to establish a value-laden dichotomy that helped distinguish true "humanity" – aspirationally defined – from its presumably "beastly" origins.

As a greater proportion of literate and leisured readers turn to printed text, deliberate representation of didactically distasteful behavior proliferates. By the late sixteenth century when *Venus and Adonis* was published, disgust had become a central policing emotion that – while predominantly culturally constructed as to what triggered it – served as an instructive tool in establishing the normative boundaries of human subjectivity. The core of Renaissance humanism, as Alan Stewart has demonstrated, assumed a certain performance of "humanity" that was to differentiate humans from animals. This performance depended on cultivated taste and sensibility that were the result of careful study of classical sources.[7] Since "not all mankind could achieve humanity," Stewart argues, those who failed to perform successfully according to these carefully defined tastes and sensibilities could therefore be classified as "beasts."[8]

The passions, in particular, were blamed for countering this careful construction of the human self, being blamed for reducing "the mind to the level of the beasts."[9] Margaret Healy further elucidates the specific concerns – first articulated in popular medical books contemporaneous with the writing of Shakespeare's poem – with heterosexual amorous play, usually euphemized as "Venus," as the prime agent in this dehumanizing process: "Anxious discussion and warnings about losing reason, succumbing to dangerous ungovernable passions and becoming beast-like . . . emerged in the vernacular medical books from the second half of the sixteenth century."[10] Potential patients were counseled in when to best "engage in Venus" or how to properly restrain "matters of Venus" to achieve optimal balance of the body.[11]

Disgust as a tool of delineating acceptable behavior came to police not only everyday interactions between individuals, but also the unfolding and changing social hierarchy. As Norbert Elias' early historical research of manners demonstrated, the Renaissance saw a newly defined distinction for the cultured but non-aristocratic Western European ranks.[12] Differentiating themselves equally from the vulgar and beastly commoners as well as from the artificially over-refined courtly aristocrats, cultured "middling sorts" sought to see themselves as the cradle of essential civilized behavior.[13] In this differentiation, the distinction between low class and bestiality collapses. Elias' close scrutiny of Renaissance conduct books reveals that aspiring members of polite culture were to engender disgust at improper behaviors associated with lower classes because of the assumed impropriety of the involved actors: the articulated deterrent to bad behavior here is not just that it is disgusting, but, more likely, it is disgusting because it is "rustic" or "bestial."[14] Finally, Elias contributes a very useful observation on the development of normative "good manners," suggesting that admirable behavior increasingly necessitated restraint in expression, whether in terms of polite speech, table manners, or bodily functions. Polite refinement calls for a certain delicacy that moves unrestrained expression of one's self and its urges into the private sphere, calling on shame and embarrassment as potent policing tools in maintaining general decorum and differentiating between increasingly visible social class.[15]

My argument is most indebted, however, to William Ian Miller's work in *The Anatomy of Disgust*. Miller argues that disgust is one of the central cultural building blocks in delineating differences between social strata. His research echoes Elias' in demonstrating the use of disgust in distancing upper classes from the commons through their disgust with them and their ways, suggesting that such disgust provides an important political tool that facilitates the hierarchization of the political order, whether it is the work of "maintaining hierarchy," providing "claims for superiority," or underscoring the "indication of one's placement in the social order."[16] In the early elicitations of explicit disgust – Miller finds the first use of the word itself toward the end of the seventeenth century, though not of the emotion or its stratifying use – polite disgust had precisely to do with the degree of self-restraint an individual could demonstrate:

> The vulgar are those given to the excessive, the cloying, the fulsome and facile; the refined are those who can discern vulgarity and reject it in advance by the mechanism of good taste, which is disgust. Taste thus manifests itself by refusing, by turning away in disgust, by recoiling at that which bears the marks of the vulgar, easy, cloying, and cheap. The disgusting is that which poses no resistance; it is the easy, that which just happens unless we cultivate and train to avoid and to reject it; it is the path of least resistance, the allure of sinking back into the belly.[17]

Such calculated recoil thus poses that while disgusting bodily urges are universal, their indulgence is not. It is precisely the manner of this indulgence – whether one gives in to a temptation and, if so, how, when, and where – that determines one's position in the social order.

Shakespeare's *Venus and Adonis* betrays all the marks of enforcing the boundaries of polite society – through restraint, reticence, privacy, and shame – to create a loaded dichotomy between two gendered forms of sexual desire. Venus, and the heterosexuality she represents, is denigrated as an instantiation of those unbridled – and uncontrollable – passions that rule the vulgar commons, who hardly recognize the extent of their own depravity. After all, one of Venus' most reprehensible qualities is that she fails to recognize her behavior as shameful or inappropriate. The homoerotic desire Adonis represents, in stark contrast, is discreet, restrained, and appropriately private. This distinction between elevated homoerotic and base heteroerotic love is explicitly articulated by Adonis who, once he has given over any hope of maintaining the polite discourse that should have ruled the encounter of two courtly individuals, explodes in Venus' face:

> Call it not love, for love to heaven is fled
> Since sweating lust on earth usurped his name,
> Under whose simple semblance he hath fed
> Upon fresh beauty, blotting it with blame . . .
> Love comforteth, like sunshine after rain,
> But lust's effect is tempest after sun;
> Love's gentle spring doth always fresh remain;
> Lust's winter comes ere summer half be done;
> Love surfeits not; lust like a glutton dies:
> Love is all truth, lust full of forgéd lies.
> More I could tell, but more I dare not say;
> The text is old, the orator too green. (793–806)

Adonis' apt reference to venerable classical texts here exemplifies his very aspiration toward the cultivated ideals of contemporary conduct literature, as well as his desire to pursue divine ideals even if their fulfillment is not readily available on earth. After all, as Adonis says, true love has "fled" from common desires to heaven and is no longer accessible to mere mortals. Its characteristics, as well as those of base, earthly love, are voluminously described in the "texts" Adonis modestly but expertly references. Among them, Plato's *Symposium* and Plutarch's *Eroticus* stand as the most cited sources.[18]

Both Plato and Plutarch explicitly separate two forms of love – Heavenly and Earthly Aphrodite – as mutually exclusive relations that apply to different segments of the population. Earthly or common love, Plato instructs, is absolutely necessary to the continuation of the human species, despite its many flaws. Usually linked to the common masses and afflicting only the unlearned or inexperienced among the cultured classes, it is beastly in nature. Earthly love, according to Plato, is "the love felt by the vulgar [men], who are attached to women no less than to boys, to the body more than to the soul, and to the least intelligent partners, since all they care about is completing the sexual act." Heavenly love, in comparison, caters to those who wish to transcend the common urges of the body toward a superior understanding of the universe. The Heavenly Aphrodite's "descent is purely male (hence love [of men] for boys), is considerably older and therefore free from the lewdness of youth. That's why those who are inspired by her Love are attracted to the male: they find pleasure in what is by nature stronger and more intelligent."[19]

Like the didactic distinctions in Plato's *Symposium*, Plutarch's *Eroticus* takes the form of a debate between stakeholders. The scenario is so similar to that of

Venus and Adonis that it likely served as the classical template that supplemented the plot-poor episode in Ovid's *Metamorphoses*: "An older, in all other respects honorable woman of no mean beauty and wealth desires to marry a fair youth, Bacchus. Because he is not likely to agree to the marriage – in fact, he is at the time openly attached to an older man, and his hunting friends vocally protest the match – she kidnaps him to persuade him in private."[20] In the ensuing argument, Protogenes, one of the defenders of Heavenly Aphrodite, here also called "true love," and the "love of boys," states that "true love . . . has nothing whatever to do with the women's quarters . . . there is only one genuine love, that of boys, and it is not 'dripping with desire.'"[21] Pisias, Bacchus' older male lover, who not surprisingly adds his two cents to the heavenly Aphrodite camp as well, provides a graphic description of the heterosexual act that clearly means to disgust the audience and, inversely, point out the comparable virtues of homoerotic relations. Earthly Aphrodite has men "hitched on to the female of the species by their sexual organ, just like dogs." This, he claims, has little to do with true love.[22]

Adonis' distinction between heavenly and earthly loves clearly echoes this classical preference, defining Venus' "device in love" (789) as disgusting and unworthy. The love Adonis claims to prefer – and which Venus lacks – clearly tends toward the genteel and courtly. His discourse seeks to be polite and with-drawn, providing Venus with the courtesy of doubt, staying silent when no words would do in upbraiding her, and deferring to classical sources. The actual erotic encounter between Adonis and the boar provides an instructive juxtaposition to Venus' lewd advances. While Venus' wooing and forceful fondling of Adonis is grossly open, visible for scrutiny of any reader, Adonis' encounter with the boar is scrupulously private. In fact, we are never told what exactly happens. We hear a few confused noises, see the self-satisfied boar carry off "froth like milk" on the penetrating tusk (901–2), and rely on Venus to explain the event, as she pieces together the clues of the encounter.

Considering how unreliable Venus' critical insight has been, she is hardly a dependable detective. Nevertheless, perhaps as a reminder of the presumed vulgar perspective of most of the poem's readers, she is the only one we have. According to this record, what has transpired in the woods is radically uncertain. While we are told of death and gore, Venus' exclamation, "behold two Adons dead!" (1070), suggests that she also catches titillating glimpses of two underdressed youths intertwined in the grass, both of whom have presumably simultaneously expired. The sequence of events as she imagines it is inevitably charged and per-ceived as mutually pleasurable: Adonis' spear clashes with the boar's tusk, and the "loving swine" "sheathed" his tusk in Adonis' "soft groin" (1111–16).

The focus on death here is similarly ambiguous. While death for Adonis is certainly prescribed by Ovid's *Metamorphoses*, Shakespeare's poem refuses to take the demise literally. Throughout the poem, we stumble on repeated and, in the world of Renaissance euphemisms, common wordplay that equates death with sexual climax. Venus makes this wordplay an annoying leitmotif of her rhetoric, begging Adonis to "kill" her (499), frustrated that this "death" which she calls "lively joy" (498) is not forthcoming. At one point Venus even feigns death to solicit physical contact (467–80). The narrator revels in telling us that Adonis' beauty produces a quick death in the observer (250) and quips that in Venus' arms Adonis "could not die" (1246). Venus subsequently worries that the boar will outdo her in providing Adonis with the very "death" she so desires to share with him (660). The most telling of these examples is perhaps Venus' desperate wail once she has found Adonis dead. In that moment, Venus wishes for a "tusk" of her own, for, as she says, "had I been toothed like him, / With kissing, I would have killed him first" (1117–18). While Venus seems to be grieving that Adonis has departed this world, she is equally devastated by imagining that he has found sexual fulfillment in the arms of another "Adon," and by realizing that she had had no chance all along. After all, no matter how perfect the goddess of love might be, she does not, and cannot, wield a "tusk." The failure here is portrayed as a sexual one, privileging the private performance of the male homoerotic sexual act over heterosexuality.

It is decidedly ironic that Adonis' supposedly superior sexual encounter is with a symbolic animal, given that Adonis' disgust has taught us that beastly behavior is to be avoided.[23] Beyond observing that the boar's act adds insult to Venus' injury – suggesting that the boar provides a far more elevated and fulfilling encounter than anything the perfect Venus might offer – it is worth noting that contemporary notions of disgust tend not to sanitize sex. Sex is sex, and while one form might be superior to another – as this poem suggests – what makes Adonis' encounter with the boar fall into the category of the cultured is that the expression of desire is shrouded in polite privacy.

While other scholars have recognized the characterization of desire in *Venus and Adonis* along much the same lines I have, documenting Shakespeare's playful setup of tensions between the homoerotic world of the hunt for the boar and Venus' heteroerotic universe, Adonis' death has inevitably been interpreted as the ultimate warning against consummation of homoerotic desire. This approach has best been articulated by Goran Stanivukovic, who interprets Adonis as a "queer figure" who resists a heterosexual relationship with Venus in favor of a homoerotic, "sodomitical" connection with the boar.[24] The boar, in Stanivukovic's view, symbolizes virility, a male love object that the "effeminate" Adonis prefers over the lusty Venus. Adonis' gory death under the loving boar's tusk serves as a didactic heteronormative ending that counteracts reading the poem as an endorsement of sodomy, which, to the Renaissance audience, would have been a "gross sin."[25] Hence, Adonis' castrating death marks a "final victory of normative moralism over illicit desire."[26]

The ending of the poem, I contend, ultimately resists such moralistic reading. Adonis' death is too titillatingly ambiguous to be taken at face value. In fact, it is likely that, in Shakespeare's hands, the ultimate death as found in Ovid undergoes revisions, similar to those to the rest of the plot. Where Ovid presents us with a tragic accident that ultimately frees Venus to do other things, Shakespeare suggests that Venus loses access to the fair youth. Adonis' death literally removes him from Venus' clutches. The fact that she is alone with his body further underscores this likelihood, for a successful consummation of Adonis' homoerotic desire would not take him out of this world, but, as he "melts" from "her" sight (1166), he drifts outside the boundaries of heteroerotic love. In other words, he is no longer subject to the "matters of Venus": as far as Venus is concerned, Adonis is as good as invisible.

Adonis' metamorphosis thus provides transubstantiation between two social strata that may as well be different worlds. In proving his good taste, Adonis proves his superiority. By demonstrating his disgust at Venus' common advances, which he easily resists, and about which he merely "smiles in disdain" (241), Adonis earns the privilege not only of reaching the fulfillment of his own desires, but also of transcending the limiting boundaries of the common class. Nested with the cultured elite of restrained, polite society – here represented as tending solely toward the homoerotic – he is no longer tainted with the vulgar world of the common reader where Venus holds sway. Shakespeare's *Venus and Adonis* thus goes beyond mere misogyny in celebrating one man who conquered that which others have found irresistible. It seeks to institutionalize heterophobia in order to delineate the normative boundaries of a cultured homoerotic subjectivity that transcends the pedestrian temptations of distasteful, beastly humanity.

Notes

1 Ovid, *Metamorphoses*, 247–8; Shakespeare, *Venus and Adonis*, 601–35. My in-text references refer to line numbers.
2 For a more detailed account of Shakespeare's transformation of Venus see, for instance, Mortimer, *Variable Passions*, 15–17.
3 Ovid, *Amores*, I.15; Marlowe, *Ovid's Elegies*, 65.
4 As has been copiously documented, sonnets 1–17 urge the fair youth to procreate for much the same reasons that Venus lays out, not least of which is the necessity to make his beauty immortal through succeeding generations. Sonnet 18, however, puts a stop to this argumentative train, proposing instead that a workable solution to the immortality of beauty is the sonnet itself, promising the fair youth,

But thy eternal summer shall not fade
Nor loose possession of that fair thou ow'st,
Nor will death brag thou wander'st in his shade,
When in eternal line to time thou grow'st.
So long as men can breathe or eyes can see,
So long lives this, and this gives life to thee. (7–12)

This nimble solution, as Valerie Traub has articulately argued, ensures that "the power to create life is transformed into the exclusively male power of the poet's invocation to an exclusively male audience." Traub, *Desire and Anxiety*, 140.

5 Korsmeyer, *Savoring*, 34.
6 Miller, *Disgust*, 56.
7 Stewart, "Humanity," 9.
8 Stewart, "Humanity," 10.
9 Cummings, "Animal Passions," 26.
10 Healy, "Bodily Regimen," 54.
11 Healy, "Bodily Regimen," 55, 57.
12 Elias' research, published in 1939, has repeatedly been attacked for inconsistencies, inaccuracies of detail, and glossing over some aspects of that which usually falls

under the disgusting, such as women's sexuality or menstrual blood. For more detailed account of responses to Elias work, see a sub-chapter in Miller, *Anatomy*, 170–78. I generally agree with Miller that, while the detail might sometimes be incomplete, the overall arc of development of the "civilizing process" Elias proposes is seminal and worth consideration.

13 Elias, *Civilizing Process*, 62.

14 Elias, *Civilizing Process*, 73, 74, 77, 107.

15 Elias, *Civilizing Process*, 93, 94, 110.

16 Miller, *Anatomy*, 18, 8–9.

17 Miller, *Anatomy*, 169.

18 Similar considerations of same-sex relationships can be found, for instance, in Montaigne's *Essais* or Bacon's *Essays*, both aptly entitled "On Friendship." English Renaissance scholars have provided exhaustive accounts of the structures of same-sex desire and its representation in the literature and culture of the period. For representative examples, see Goldberg's *Queering the Renaissance* and *Sodometries*, Bray's *Friend*, or Traub's *Desire and Anxiety*.

19 Plato, *Symposium*, 14.

20 Plutarch, *Essays*, 248.

21 Plutarch, *Essays*, 249–50.

22 Plutarch, *Essays*, 253. Robert P. Merrix comes close to making a similar distinction between two spheres divided along gender lines. Though he does not see Adonis' encounter with the boar as explicitly sexual, settling instead for a homosocial world of a masculine hunt, he does equate Venus explicitly with the stereotypical domain of institutional heterosexuality, namely domesticity: "The conflict between Venus and Adonis is not moral or ritual; it is social and sexual and concerns conflicting lifestyles, one domestic, fruitful, and secure, and the other exotic, sterile, and dangerous . . . In the first section of the poem, various formal elements – narration, rhetorical description, dialogue – combine to reveal a world filled with fecundity, security, and domesticity in which Venus, as the major procreative and domestic force in the world, attempts to fulfill her nature." Merrix, "Lo," 343, 346.

23 As the most dangerous animal for Renaissance hunters which simultaneously functioned as a symbol of "dangerous virility," Edward Berry reminds us, the boar embodies the ultimate "venereal rage," being of "boiling complexion," and so "he desireth nothing but copulation." Berry, *Shakespeare and the Hunt*, 47. Berry looks to Edward Topsell's *The Historie of the Foure-Footed Beasts* to argue that the boar's forceful sexuality is often equated with death. As an undeniable instrument in Adonis' "death," the boar has been posited on a spectrum of agencies from embodying Venus' violent lust, to the cruel random forces of nature, to representing the self-destructive force of sodomy that will inevitably result in literal death.

24 Stanivukovic, "Kissing the Boar," 91.

25 Stanivukovic, "Kissing the Boar," 89.

26 Stanivukovic, "Kissing the Boar," 103. Shying away from earlier readings that gleefully endorsed misogynist ridicule of Venus as the "muscular rapist," recent scholarship has puzzled over the various forms of desire presented in the poem, exploring the conflict of sexual preferences that make the crux of Venus' disappointment, and the "queerness" of the discourse between the two characters, neither of whom falls into Renaissance normative categories. Adonis has been traditionally placed in the anxiety-producing category of the effeminate male, whereas Venus has been read as a female character transgressing normative gender roles. Anthony Mortimer has attempted to shift the "queerness" of desire to Venus: "If nature dictates mutual attraction between sexes, what are we to make of the fact that Venus is attracted to Adonis by his feminine qualities. . .? If sexual intercourse is, as she argues, the fruit of maturity, how do we take her own admission that she wishes to taste Adonis while he is still 'unripe.' And, if it is an initiation into manhood, how does this fit with her repeated attempts to reduce

him to the level of a child to be tempted with "honey secrets" and protected from the dangerous world by the playpen of a maternal body? Ambivalence reigns." Mortimer, *Variable Passions*, 127–8. Madhavi Menon, in contrast, reads *Venus and Adonis* as a "failure" of desire, as a text that ultimately does not satisfactorily lend itself to any established modern or Renaissance readings since it fails to deliver sexual climax of any kind. Menon, "Spurning," 509.

References

Berry, Edward. *Shakespeare and the Hunt: A Cultural and Social Study*. Cambridge: Cambridge University Press, 2001.

Bray, Alan. *The Friend*. Chicago: University of Chicago Press, 2003.

Cummings, Brian. "Animal Passions and Human Sciences: Shame, Blushing, and Nakedness in Early Modern Europe and the New World." In *At the Border of the Human: Beasts, Bodies, and Natural Philosophy in the Early Modern Period*, edited by Erica Fudge, Ruth Gilbert, and Susan Wiseman, 26–50. London: Macmillan, 1999.

Elias, Norbert. *The Civilizing Process: The History of Manners and State Formation and Civilization*. Translated by Edmund Jephcott. Oxford: Blackwell, 1994.

Goldberg, Jonathan. *Queering the Renaissance*. Durham, NC: Duke University Press, 1994.

———. *Sodometries: Renaissance Texts, Modern Sexualities*. Stanford: Stanford University Press, 1992.

Healy, Margaret. "Bodily Regimen and Fear of the Beast." In *At the Border of the Human: Beasts, Bodies, and Natural Philosophy in the Early Modern Period*, edited by Erica Fudge, Ruth Gilbert, and Susan Wiseman, 51–73. London: Macmillan, 1999.

Korsmeyer, Carolyn. *Savoring Disgust: The Foul and the Fair in Aesthetics*. Oxford: Oxford University Press, 2011.

Marlowe, Christopher. *Ovid's Elegies*. In *The Collected Poems of Christopher Marlowe*. Edited by Patrick Cheney and Brian J. Striar. New York: Oxford University Press, 2006.

Menon, Madhavi. "Spurning Teleology in *Venus and Adonis*." *GLQ: A Journal of Lesbian and Gay Studies* 11, no. 4 (2005): 491–519.

Merrix, Robert P. " 'Lo, in This Hollow Cradle Take Thy Rest:' Sexual Conflict and Resolution in *Venus and Adonis*." In *Venus and Adonis: Critical Essays*, edited by Philip C. Colin, 341–58. New York and London: Routledge, 1997.

Miller, Susan B. *Disgust, the Gatekeeper Emotion*. Hillsdale: The Analytic Press, 2004.

Miller, William Ian. *The Anatomy of Disgust*. Cambridge, MA: Harvard University Press, 1997.

Mortimer, Anthony. *Variable Passions: A Reading of Shakespeare's Venus and Adonis*. New York: AMS Press, 2000.

Ovid. *Metamorphoses*. Translated by A.D. Melville. Oxford: Oxford University Press, 1986.

Plato. *Symposium*. Translated by Alexander Nehamas and Paul Woodruff. Cambridge: Hackett, 1989.

Plutarch. *Selected Essays and Dialogues*. Translated by Donald Russell. Oxford: Oxford University Press, 1993.

Shakespeare, William. *The Sonnets*. In *The Norton Shakespeare*. Edited by Stephen Greenblatt, 1915–91. New York and London: W.W. Norton, 1997.

———. "Venus and Adonis." In *The Norton Shakespeare*. Edited by Stephen Greenblatt, 601–35. New York and London: W.W. Norton, 1997.

Stanivukovic, Goran V. "Kissing the Boar: Queer Adonis and Critical Practice." In *Straight with a Twist: Queer Theory and the Subject of Heterosexuality*, edited by Calvin Thomas, 87–108. Urbana: University of Illinois Press, 2000.

Stewart, Alan. "Humanity at a Price: Erasmus, Bude and the Poverty of Philosophy." In *At the Borders of the Human: Beasts, Bodies, and Natural Philosophy in the Early Modern Period*, edited by Erica Fudge, Ruth Gilbert, and Susan Wiseman, 9–25. London: Macmillan, 1999.

Traub, Valerie. *Desire and Anxiety: Circulations of Sexuality in Shakespearean Drama*. London and New York: Routledge, 1992.

Part II
Cultural encounters

5 Indecorous customs, rhetorical decorum, and the reception of Herodotean ethnography from Henri Estienne to Edmund Spenser

Galena Hashhozheva

Ethnographic writing rarely stood by itself as a genre in the Renaissance. But – along with geography, history, political and legal analysis, and the survey of trade and travel opportunities – it did form one component in the multi-layered exposition of knowledge about foreign lands. Examples of more purely ethnographic texts are not entirely lacking, such as the *Fardle of Facions* (1541) by the German humanist Johannes Boemus. Yet the integration of ethnography into works with a more comprehensive scope – works as disparate as Jean Bodin's *Method for the Easy Comprehension of History* (1566), Peter Martyr's *Decades* (1511), and the popular sixteenth-century cosmographies – lent it greater seriousness and complexity.

These were desirable features in ethnographic writing, which always lay open to accusations of fabricating sensational falsehoods about faraway realms in the notorious manner of John Mandeville's mid-fourteenth-century account *Travels*. Judged by the standards of one culture, the differing customs of another appeared arbitrary and inconvenient at best, and absurd and disgusting at worst, in which case their description could strain the limits of believability. It was a problem that ethnography had faced since its beginnings in the fifth century BCE: to be both praised for its delightful revelations of foreign exotica, which expanded the worldview of the author's countrymen, and reviled for its indulgence in improbable marvels, monstrosities, and abominations.[1] The first European text to make a substantial contribution to ethnography, Herodotus' *Histories*, was criticized from antiquity through the Renaissance for spinning tales about foreign cultures as much as it was disparaged for giving misleading accounts of wars, reigns, and nations standing at historic crossroads. Occasionally, Herodotus' Renaissance critics went as far as to revise the more generous classical assessments of his work: if Cicero had called Herodotus *pater historiae* (the father of history), Juan Luis Vives insisted that he was *mendaciorum pater* (the father of lies).[2]

Beyond having doubts about his veracity, Herodotus' enemies objected to his apparent sympathy with the barbarians and his appreciation for their religious traditions and habits of everyday life.[3] While the *Histories* may well bear the mark of Greek national pride as a chronicle of the Greco-Persian wars, its ethnographic sections betray an extraordinary fascination with foreign cultures. This fascination mutes Herodotus' bias toward his native country to the point that his critics suspect he has forgotten where his loyalties lie. Such accusations are an unwitting testimony to the rhetoric of restraint that typifies Herodotus' accounts of foreign customs: he could be taken for a "lover of the barbarians" because, contrary to what would be expected from a civilized Greek, he did not subject them to a sweeping negative judgment.

His tone is especially tactful in the rare cases when he cannot withhold his disapproval. But more often than not, he reports with deadpan detachment in the face of even the most sordid customs. One nation likes to eat lice; another drinks human blood and makes napkins out of human skin; yet another forces its women to a rite of sacred prostitution whose abuses pollute them and leave them averse to sexual intercourse.[4] Nauseating details are hard to avoid in ethnographic reports about foreign diet, religion, funeral rituals, and gender relations. Yet, Herodotus maintains the decorum of his monumental work, in which valorous deeds and grand historic events are related alongside apparently foul customs. His discreetness is a matter of both his style and ethical outlook. He is no less loath to offend the barbarians' unconditional love for their customs than to make his civilized Greek audience shudder with disgust. Notwithstanding his Greek origin, Herodotus is an ethnographer of the whole inhabited world, and a humane thinker with a profound interest in cultural diversity.

While Herodotus was not the only classical model of ethnographic writing available to Renaissance readers, his *Histories* possess a rhetorical sophistication that ranks them a cut above Pliny's *Natural History* or the Hippocratic treatise *Airs, Waters, Places*. In recognition of the *Histories*' literary and scholarly prestige, Renaissance translations observed its traditional editorial division into nine books, honorifically named after the nine Muses. With its marvels and exotic locations, Homer's *Odyssey* in particular provided a precedent for Herodotus' ethnography. Ever since the Hellenistic period, Herodotus' style had been deemed sufficiently Homeric for his prose masterpiece to earn the same regard as the epic poems.[5]

The fifteenth-century rediscovery of the *Histories* coincided with the era of exploration, and Europeans who created accounts of the New World benefited from the Herodotean paradigm of conceptualizing customs and classifying peoples.[6] A writer of the untamed geographical peripheries and their uncouth populations, Herodotus was a welcome inspiration in an age when maps were constantly redrawn on a global scale and yesterday's peripheries could become tomorrow's centers. Like Renaissance travelers, Herodotus knew the value of first-hand experience: he pioneered foreign travel as a method of collecting systematic information of the sort that would merit inclusion in a sustained written account like the *Histories* rather than remaining, as other travelers' tales did, in the realm of folklore. Having journeyed through Egypt, a familiar destination for Greek merchants and curious tourists, and Scythia, a dreaded brink of the known world, Herodotus describes these two countries in his ethnographic centerpieces – the second and fourth books, which had a rich post-classical afterlife as a source of cultural and natural-historical comparanda.

In contrast to most Renaissance travelers, however, Herodotus did not explore foreign lands with the motives of an imperialist. He did not study the natives to make them easier to conquer or to condemn their barbarism to make their conquest appear more just. Though witness to the birth of Athenian imperialism, the *Histories* are permeated by a pathos of hope that the Hellenic peoples might yet avoid the pitfalls of empire manifested in the course of Persia, which had after all invaded Greek lands in a not-too-distant past. Herodotus holds empire responsible for both "corrupting the original condition [and culture] of its own nation and compromising those of other peoples."[7] Empire is the enemy of Herodotean ethnography, insofar as it poses a threat to cultural difference, the proper material of the ethnographer.[8]

Yet, in this respect Renaissance readers of the *Histories* were unwilling to learn from Herodotus. Europe pursued its colonial ventures in the New World, and it engaged in internecine conflicts, often in the name of religion, that pitted one European nation and its imperialist advances against another. The reception of the *Histories* can tell us a lot about the later authors' ethical orientation toward the extended landscape of humankind with all its permutations of objectionable customary practices. Continental authors like Henri Estienne and Michel de Montaigne, and English authors like Barnabe Rich and Edmund Spenser offer a representative range of sixteenth-century responses to Herodotean ethnography in three distinct cultural contexts – French Catholic, Caribbean, and Irish – which for many epitomized a morally and physically disgusting barbarism.

In the face of unseemly customs, only Montaigne proves himself adept at Herodotean delicacy and negative capability. The militantly anti-Catholic Estienne and the anti-Irish Rich, although translators of the *Histories*, are tendentiously blind to its philobarbarian aspect and are eager to malign contemporary ethnicities whom they perceive as kindred to the *Histories*' Egyptians, Scythians, and other non-Greeks. Finally, in Spenser's dialogue *A View of the Present State of Ireland* we encounter a complicated use of Herodotean ethnography. Spenser, who served in the late Elizabethan colonial government, was as anti-Catholic as Estienne and as anti-Irish as Rich, with whom he belonged to the same circle of English literati gathering in Dublin and outside the Pale. Yet, although Spenser can hardly be considered a philobarbarian – indeed, most modern scholars tend to brand him an apologist for genocide – his reception of Herodotus led to a paradoxical claim to decorum and an appeal to imaginative delight amid *View*'s descriptions of indecorous Irish customs.

Henri Estienne: Herodotus the iconoclast

Herodotus' tactfulness and command of style deservedly attracted the attention of ancient rhetoricians. Ethnographic passages from the *Histories* are quoted in Longinus' *On the Sublime* to illustrate various stylistic felicities and, in a single exceptional case, a lapse of propriety.[9] As an example of the figure of a "pleasantly turned periphrasis," for instance, Longinus offers an "inimitable" statement from the *Histories*: "Upon those Scythians who sacked her temple the goddess

[Aphrodite] sent a female malady."[10] The "female malady," a tasteful and yet mercilessly apposite phrase, refers to the loss of virility endemic to a distinct Scythian tribe.

In the Hellenistic period and the Byzantine Middle Ages, Herodotus' prose was widely admired, even by those who considered him a liar.[11] Because the text remained unavailable to most Western readers, it was not until the Renaissance that they could appreciate Herodotus' rhetorical strategies. With Lorenzo Valla's magisterial Latin translation, published in 1474, the *Histories* came to be recognized as a major work with literary merit. Erasmus ranked Herodotus among the "best authors" offering "sound models of style" in Greek prose.[12] Joachim Camerarius, in his 1542 edition of the *Histories*, lavishly praised its sweetness, eloquence, and variety, achieved in large part by including fables, folklore, and bizarre occurrences and customs.[13]

The philologically accomplished Henri Estienne was the next to take up the mantle of humanist enthusiasm for Herodotus.[14] Estienne published a revised version of Valla's Latin text in 1566, with a dedication to Camerarius and a preface titled *Apologia pro Herodoto*, in which he aimed to clear Herodotus' reputation of age-old slurs. This was followed in the same year by the separate publication of a much longer French *Apologie pour Hérodote* – or *A World of Wonders* in its English version from 1607 – whose two prefaces continue the defense of Herodotus, while the rest develops into a sustained anti-Catholic polemic.

In both apologies, but especially in the French, Estienne proposes that those who disbelieve Herodotus' accounts of outlandish customs among the barbarians of antiquity might change their minds if they consider the far more outlandish and objectionable practices among the unreformed nations of sixteenth-century Europe. This line of reasoning achieves a twofold goal. First, by revealing the similarities between an allegedly dubious past and a widely attested present, Estienne mounts a defense of Herodotus' veracity. Second, Estienne casts his descriptions of Catholic popular religion in the guise of Herodotean ethnography, thereby lending Catholicism the taint of the grotesque and the exotic. This emphasizes his alienation from the unreformed half of his own nation. The sordid rituals of the Catholics are so abundant that they cause Estienne's style to grow profuse in enumerating and condemning them, to the particular annoyance of his English translator. In a prefatory note, he complains of Estienne's "manifold (though not impertinent) excursions and . . . his infinite parentheses, which were enough to exercise the patience of a Saint," punning on Estienne's diatribe against the demoniacal variety of local saint cults among the Catholic.[15] Estienne has this stylistic profuseness in common with Herodotus. Bizarre foreign customs bear much of the blame for the *Histories*' famously digressive narrative structure. Herodotus himself admits that he can get carried away with the thrills of ethnography: "For from the very beginning it was always the way of my history to investigate excursuses" (4.30). The description of Scythia, for example, interrupts the historical narrative for the better part of the fourth book.

In a more constructive moment of his diatribe, Estienne argues that even the vilest ancient mores reported by Herodotus ought to be accepted as plausible and employed as a pedagogical tool, as a mirror of our own times and the "perversnesse of our nature."[16] Because the pedagogic potential that Estienne finds in the *Histories* concerns first and foremost devotional behavior, he is at pains to demonstrate that Herodotus, despite his paganism, was a deeply pious man. After providing four folio pages' worth of Herodotus' Christian-like parables and maxims, Estienne concludes: "My soul is seized with a fear that it will be Herodotus – along with the Queen of Sheba, a pagan woman, and all other pagan authors from whom such holy sayings have issued – who at the Last Judgment will charge us, the Christians . . . because we think, speak, and write so profanely."[17]

Estienne imagines Herodotus in the role of an accuser and harsh critic, and then flatters himself for following Herodotus' example while dissecting the culture of contemporary Catholic nations in a most scathing manner:

> I am not ignorant how the poore Aegyptians in Herodotus are derided and laughed to scorne for their religion (if it may be so called) and deservedly I confesse, as may appear by their exceeding trifling ceremonies. But if we come to the superstitious Masse-priests, which have bene within these three-score yeares, and narrowly search all their trash and trinkets, we shal be (in a maner) enforced to confesse, that the Aegyptians might (in comparison) even glorie and boast of their religion.[18]

Yet, Estienne is merely projecting his own revulsion at idolatry onto Herodotus' account of Egyptian religion. Herodotus, for his part, never assumes a derisive attitude toward any culture, though he could find a pretext in the Egyptians' tendency to "make all their customs and laws for the most part contrary to those of the rest of mankind" (2.35). For all its strangeness, neuroticism, and occasional unsavoriness, Egyptian culture receives a respectful treatment in the *Histories*, and even some praise (2.64). Despite his philological expertise, Estienne misreads both the tone and the content of these passages. Strikingly, Estienne warns others of Herodotus' linguistic peculiarity, rhetorical subtlety, and of the dangers of misconstruction. Estienne even detected these errors in Valla's translation while emending it for his 1566 edition. But he is himself guilty of that very same mistake.

Estienne's enlisting of Herodotus as a Protestant avant la lettre in his satiric attack against Catholic devotion would not have met with the ancient author's approval. For Herodotus, mocking the customs of other nations or communities could never be constructive because, being traditional, customs remain in large measure immune to rational consideration. He states: "For if it were proposed to all nations to choose which seemed best of all customs, each, after examination made, would place its own first; so well is each persuaded that its own are by far the best" (3.38). Herodotus adds a vivid parable:

> When Darius was king, he summoned the Greeks who were with him and asked them what price would persuade them to eat their fathers' dead bodies. They answered that there was no price for which they would do it. Then he

summoned those Indians who are called Callatiae, who eat their parents, and asked them (the Greeks being present and understanding by interpretation what was said) what would make them willing to burn their fathers at death [as in ancient Greek heroic funerals]. The Indians cried aloud that he should not speak of so horrid an act. (3.38)

What turns Darius' cultural experiment into such an intense drama of affect is its encroachment on customs involving the body and the physicality of death. By ingesting their deceased parents' bodies, the Kallatians salvage them from annihilation and create a circular continuity of substance among the members of a family. Yet to the Greeks, this custom amounts to immoral necrophagy. For their part, the Greeks incinerate bodily remains to purify them, but from the Kallatians' perspective fire denatures and all but obliterates the dead.[19] When judged by an outsider, either funeral practice can seem sacrilegious and disgusting. Disgust at ethnic practices or beliefs is in some ways the most overpowering, insofar as it feeds off the perception that an entire ethnicity, not just an isolated individual, commits the offense as a matter of time-honored habit.

For Herodotus, by contrast, such a reaction of disgust is regrettable, and often even culpable, on account of a latent aggression that underlies it. In the case of the Greeks and the Kallatians, disgust could possibly be excused since it is part of a defensive response to the emperor, who insults their ethnic dignity with his cavalier bargaining in customs. Burning one's parents sickens the Kallatians not as a Greek custom, but as a potential alien intrusion on their own cultural system. The same can be claimed, respectively, for the Greeks. Rather that blaming them for their revulsion, one ought to pity both nations as victims of a sort of cultural torture performed by Darius. What is in bad taste is neither their reciprocal disgust, nor the burning or eating of the dead in itself, but rather Darius' perverse proposal. Equally unacceptable to Herodotus would be Estienne's disgust with Roman Catholicism, which he views as a massive unseemliness that suffuses vast regions of Europe. In a parallel to Herodotus' parable about funerary rites, for example, Estienne professes revulsion at the doctrine of transubstantiation, the Roman Catholic interpretation of the Eucharist. He calls the Eucharist as celebrated in the Roman Catholic mass "theophagy": the "base" superstitious custom of eating the supposed body of one's dead and resurrected god.[20]

Herodotus incorporates Darius' disregard for Greek and Kallatian funerary rites into one of the *Histories'* great moral lessons: one ought not mock the customs of other nations because they cling to their ways as we do to ours. To show a basic respect for the customs of others is not to betray one's own, but rather to acknowledge the higher power of custom apart from its particular incarnations. Herodotus presses this obligation even upon imperial nations and emperors and presents those who refuse to honor it as exempla of degradation and atrocious irrationality. The gratuitous disrespect toward the religion of Egypt, one of his conquests, earns the Persian emperor Cambyses the epithet "madman" (3.38). Cambyses commits sacrileges in mockery of Egyptian customs, viewing them as abominations that the conquered – at least in his paranoid imperial fantasies – exploit to insult his authority. He breaks open ancient coffins to gaze profanely at the mummies and burns the images of local deities whose dwarfish appearance offends him (3.37). He sadistically kills the sacred bull Apis because the Egyptian elite runs off to honor it on its annual festival, rather than attending to him. Cambyses jeers: "Wretched wights, are these your gods, creatures of flesh and blood that can feel weapons of iron? That [pointing at the bleeding bull] is a god worthy of the Egyptians" (3.29). We may note, at Estienne's expense, that it is Cambyses, one of the *Histories'* most lurid monsters, who epitomizes the mockery of supposedly idolatrous foreign customs that Estienne mistakenly ascribes to Herodotus.

How Estienne could have overlooked the lesson of this well-known tyrant's life is a mystery. Cambyses' hubris and mindless iconoclasm were of great interest to the Renaissance against a backdrop of rising absolutism. In England alone they inspired Thomas Preston's fittingly indecorous *Cambises King of Percia*, published in 1569, and Christopher Marlowe's rhetorically avant-garde *Tamburlaine the Great*. Renaissance readers well versed in the mirror-for-princes tradition would also have been interested in the latter part of Cambyses' reign, when he turns into a Nero-like tormentor of his own nation and court. Thus, Herodotus tells us that the emperor who started out by reviling and eradicating the customs of the conquered ends up violating his native customs (3.31).

Cambyses' earlier victims, the Egyptians, make this connection explicit with their claim that the stabbing of Apis brought a curse upon Cambyses. It is this curse, they assert, that triggers Cambyses' madness and his subsequent iniquities against Persians (3.33). Moreover, Cambyses dies of a self-inflicted wound in the thigh, exactly where he had stabbed the bull. In the eyes of the Egyptians, this is a punishment for Cambyses' overall immorality and tyranny and, more specifically, a symbolic retribution that custom exacts for having been compromised by the emperor. Custom is king, Herodotus affirms following Pindar, a king who will not yield without struggle to the brute force of foreign conquerors (3.38). Nor, one might add, will it yield to the harsh criticism of intellectuals like Estienne.

Michel de Montaigne: Herodotus the relativist

Estienne's misconstruction of Herodotean ethnography is all the more surprising since in the 1560s he published two further ancient texts that could have instructed him in an attitude of neutrality when faced with unpalatable foreign customs: the Hellenistic philosopher Sextus Empiricus' *Outlines of Pyrrhonism* and the anonymous *Dissoi Logoi* (*Contrasting Arguments*), a Sophistic manual originally composed in the same era as the *Histories*, but often appended to manuscripts of Sextus' works. In the *Outlines* Sextus expounds Pyrrho's skeptic teachings about the impossibility of finding truth and certainty, which he supports with arguments from both phenomenological subjectivism and cultural relativism. The Pyrrhonians refused to call cannibalism, incest, or pederasty bad customs and urged a suspension of judgment about them, as about any other human belief, perception, or action.[21] For its part, the *Dissoi Logoi* is interested in rhetorical disputes about what is seemly and what unseemly, and it contains a section on mutually repugnant ethnic customs that can be used in such disputes.[22] The parallels between this part of the *Dissoi Logoi* and various ethnographic details from the *Histories* have long been noticed.[23] Both the Sophists and the Pyrrhonians collected shocking foreign customs and used them to demonstrate either that judging customs is pointless because, sealed by the authority of convention, they all have equal validity within their respective society, or that for each custom – and that included any purportedly superior Greek customs – one could argue *in utramque partem* (on both sides of an issue).

Like antiquity, the European Renaissance produced some consummate questioners of its customs and mores. The most erudite among them was Michel de Montaigne, whose views were largely shaped by reading the Pyrrhonians and the Sophists, very likely including the same editions that Estienne labored to bestow on the international humanist community. Apart from the *Essays*, Montaigne left us his *Travel Journal*, a private record of his travels through France, Switzerland, Germany, and Italy, marked by a Herodotean attentiveness to local customs in their endless permutations from one village to the next. The lands through which Montaigne travels offer nothing as exotic as the nations visited by Herodotus the tourist. Nevertheless, even the European countries boast distinctive local manners whose unfamiliarity Montaigne finds eye-opening, enriching, and worth recording. Many an ethnographic passage in the *Histories* sounds not unlike Montaigne's ostensibly trivial remark on the Bavarian diet: in Bavaria, they have "a great abundance of cabbage, which they chop up small . . . put a great quantity of it thus chopped up into vats with salt and make soups out of it all winter."[24] Montaigne has such a Herodotean curiosity about foreign ways that to observe them first-hand is not enough. He must also subject himself to them: in order "to essay completely the diversity of manners and customs, [he] let himself be served everywhere in the mode of each country, no matter how much difficulty it caused him."[25]

Montaigne's most Herodotean reflection on foreign customs is his essay "Of the Caniballes," which gleans insights from the *Histories* regarding the Scythians, cannibals of the Old World, whom the Caribbean cannibals resemble in more than their diet. Montaigne finds, for example, that both the Scythians and the Caribs punish lying prophets especially strictly. An enemy of imposture, Montaigne praises this custom, which he explains with the Scythians' and the Caribs' barbarian innocence.[26] In a Herodotean spirit, Montaigne views the customs of the Caribs as a fairly elaborate and coherent system with commendable features not reducible to the consumption of human flesh.

Most of Montaigne's contemporaries, however, especially the supporters of colonial conquest, fixated on the exceptional loathsomeness of cannibalism and viewed it in isolation from other aspects of New World culture. Montaigne faults the Europeans for their simplistic construal of anthropophagy. He also compares cannibalism to violent customs prevalent across Europe that desecrate the human body in ways more appalling than the cannibals could ever invent. Indeed, as

Montaigne underlines, when the Caribs witnessed the grisly torture methods that the Portuguese used on captives, they reasoned that cannibalism would be an inadequate requital and began imitating the Portuguese.[27] Montaigne echoes the Herodotean thesis that barbarism is a relative category: "Men call that barbarisme which is not common to them."[28]

To wit, Herodotus had no reservations about showing that for the Egyptians, it was the Greeks, along with all other nations, who were barbarians, and very disgusting barbarians at that.[29] To the Egyptian mind, the Greeks defiled themselves by consuming the flesh of cows, which were sacred to Isis: "For this reason no Egyptian man or woman will kiss a Greek man, or use a knife, or a spit, or a cauldron belonging to a Greek, or taste meat . . . that has been cut up with a Greek knife" (2.41). Firmly convinced that a nation that eats cows was no good, the Egyptians devised a way to turn the Greeks' dietary customs against them. In Egyptian sacrificial rituals animal heads were associated with evil, so the Egyptians handed them off to the Greeks:

> The [Egyptians] flay the carcass of the victim, then invoke many curses upon its head and carry the same away . . . No Egyptian will taste of the head of anything that had life . . . Where there is a market, and Greek traders in the place, the head is taken to the market and sold to them; where there are no Greeks, it is thrown into the river. (2.39)

The Greeks become a figurative cesspool for animal parts that have undergone a scapegoating ritual. Already disgusting enough, the European barbarians are now also cursed.

Herodotus calmly describes this arrangement, in which his fellow countrymen are abused by the Egyptians. Elsewhere, with similar poise, he explains that Greek gods and customs that resemble Egyptian gods and customs must be derivative (2.50–51). Greek traditionalists would have found this opinion just as offensive as the French and other Europeans probably found Montaigne's accusations of being more barbarous and violent than the natives of the New World.

Barnabe Rich: Herodotus the reticent prattler

The *Histories* were first partially translated into English in 1584, under the title *The famous hystory of Herodotus*. Identified only by the initials B.R. in the dedication and address to the reader, the translator has traditionally been thought to be Barnabe Rich. Rich was a professional soldier with literary ambitions, who devoted a considerable part of his life and military service to the English colonial endeavor in Ireland.[30] The unruly native population and its resilient culture had given occasion for hostile ethnographic accounts of Ireland since at least the Norman Conquest. Rich contributed several texts to this tradition of English writing on Ireland, the most important of which is *A New Description of Ireland*, published in 1610.

Rich's reading and translation of the *Histories* seems influenced by his negative leanings as an ethnographic observer. Compare the following sentence from the *Histories* with Rich's English version:

> Other people live apart from their beasts, the Egyptians live with them (τοῖσι μὲν ἄλλοισι ἀνθρώποισι χωρὶς θηρίων ἡ δίαιτα ἀποκέκριται, Αἰγυπτίοισι δὲ ὁμοῦ θηρίοισι ἡ δίαιτα ἐστί). (2.36)

Whereas Rich translates:

> Moreover, the people of all lands use to make difference betweene their owne diet and the foode of beastes, saving in Aegypt, where in barbarous and swinish maner men and beasts feede joyntly together.[31]

Apart from mistranslating δίαιτα (manner of living) as "diet," Rich adds the evaluative phrase "barbarous and swinish."[32]

Similarly, Rich embellishes Herodotus' comment concerning Egyptian portrayals of Pan with two sarcastic litotes. Herodotus states:

> Now in [the Egyptians'] painting and sculpture the image of Pan is made as among the Greeks with the head and the legs of a goat . . . but why they so present him I have no wish to say. (2.46)

Whereas Rich translates:

> the cause whereby they are mooved to portray and shadow [Pan] in such sort, *is no greate and handsome tale* to tell, and therfore we are willing to omit it by silence, sufficeth it that we knowe how as well bucke as dooe goates *are no pety saincts* in this country.[33]

Herodotus' "I have no wish to say (οὔ μοι ἥδιόν ἐστι λέγειν)" is expanded into "is no greate and handsome tale to tell, and therfore we are willing to omit it by silence."

Rich's version of a comment concerning the Egyptian sacrifice of pigs is likewise coarser and longer than the original. Herodotus writes:

> The Egyptians have an account of the reason why they sacrifice swine at this festival yet abominate them at others; I know it but it is not fitting for me to mention it. (2.47)

Whereas Rich translates:

> The reason why the people of Aegypt kill swyne at this time, and at all other times boyle in so great despight and hatred against them, bycause mine eares glowed to heare it, I thought it maners to conceale it.[34]

Rich's "bycause mine eares glowed to heare it" is a gratuitous addition to Herodotus' "it is not fitting for me to mention it (οὐκ εὐπρεπέστερος ἐστι λέγεσθαι)" (2.47).

Rich mars Herodotus' famous moments of decorous silence that often serve him to pass over a morally or physically indecorous fact. Herodotus keeps his reticence only as a last resort, as though following the Aristotelian recommendation that when faced with "impiety or foulness," one can always choose between "the language of disgust" and a "discreet reluctance to utter a word."[35] Herodotus certainly knows how to give "the language of disgust" a controlled outlet in quoted speeches, thereby delegating it from his narrative persona to characters who represent their cultures and those cultures' prejudices. This leaves him with endless possibilities for portraying reciprocal disdain between nations with contrary lifestyles. Yet even within quoted speeches, Herodotus tries to season the disgusting with a clever turn of phrase or an apt laconism. For instance, the Ethiopians were famous for their longevity, which they associated with their diet of milk and boiled meat. Other diets struck them as deficient:

> [The Ethiopian king] asked further what food the [Persian] king ate, and what was the greatest age to which the Persians lived. The [ambassadors] told him their king ate bread, showing him how wheat grew; and said that the full age to which a man might hope to live was eighty years. Then said the Ethiopian, it was no wonder that their lives were so short, if they ate dung. (3.22)

These facets of Herodotus' rhetorical delicacy are lost on Rich.

Although Rich seems to favor reticence, he does not use it decorously. Rich's *occultatio* is a mannerism that intensifies his scathing rhetoric of disgust in *New Description of Ireland*. When Rich protests that he "will not speake of" something, he usually babbles it all out within a paragraph or two, often with torrents of negative adjectives. His graphic revelations about Irish dairy making, for instance, belie his initial promise: "Neither will I speake of their unmannerly manners in making of their Butter."[36] Visceral reactions in the vein of "mine ears glowed," which he adds to Herodotus' prose, become a staple of his style in *A New Description*. Early in his ethnographic account Rich avers: "If I should set downe the sluttish and uncleanly observations of the Irish . . . especially of those manners and conditions whereunto they inure themselves in the remote places of the Countrey, I might set downe such unreverent and loathsome matter, as were unfit for every queasie stomacke to understand of."[37]

Irish dairy making generally presents Rich with deliberate dirtiness where he expects cleanliness:

> It is holden among the Irish, to bee a presagement of some misfortune, to keepe their milking vessels cleanly, and that if they should either scald or wash them, some unlucky misadventure would surely betide them . . . I my selfe have seene, that vessell which they hold under the Cow whilst they are in milking, to be furred halfe an inch thicke with filth, so that *Dublyne* it self

is served every Market day with such Butter, as I am sure is much more loath-some then toothsome.[38]

Fynes Moryson, another witness of Irish mores, also bemoans how the Irish "straine their milke taken from the Cow through a . . . handfull of straw, none of the cleanest, and so clense, or rather more defile the pot and milk."[39] Their hygiene itself is, paradoxically, unhygienic. It is no surprise that many an Englishman in Ireland "would not touch [cheese and butter] with his lippes, though hee were halfe starved."[40]

Rich frames all housekeeping procedures in Ireland as exactly contrary to the commonsensical ones in use elsewhere: "Throughout the whole Realme of *Ireland,* in those thinges wherein they should be most neate and cleanly they doe shew themselues to be most sluttish and filthy."[41] Rich's Irish share this perversity with Herodotus' Egyptians, who are said to "knead dough with their feet, and gather mud and dung with their hands" (2.36) and generally to practice customs contrary to common sense and to the customs of other nations (2.35). The Irish even surpass the Egyptians in that they use body parts filthier than feet to prepare the meal for their cakes. Rich reports having seen "a woman sitting with a Mustarde Quearne betweene her bare thighes, grinding of Oatmeale."[42] This meal out of which the Irish make their unappetizing cakes is "as ill in complexion (to looke uppon) as a little durt under a mans feet."[43] Rich's rhetoric is not far removed from the Ethiopian king's equation of bread with dung in the Persian diet.

The same alleged perversity also causes the Irish to consider carrion a greater delicacy than fresh meat. Yet, in a mutual comparison between the English and Irish diets, the English are not the only party that looks down on the other. Moryson recounts how, while he served as a secretary in the army, on one occasion the fleshier parts from certain horse cadavers went missing. The horse eater was found to be Irish-born and, "being brought to the Lord Deputy, and asked why he had eaten the flesh of dead Horses, thus freely answered, Your Lordship may please to eate Pheasant and Partridge, and much good doe it you that best likes your Taste; and I hope it is lawfull for me without offence, to eate this flesh that likes me better than Beefe."[44] The soldier answers as though he had been instructed in Herodotean relativism: to the common Irishman, horse carrion is as pheasant to the English nobleman, so why can't each have his respective preference? Barnabe Rich notes that the Irish make a point of not allowing the clash between their customs and those of the English to proceed exclusively at their expense; they too regard the purportedly more decorous English customs as incomprehensible and repugnant: "the unnurtered sort among them are no lesse admiring our decencie, then wee their rudenesse and unciuility."[45] But unlike Herodotus, Moryson and Rich are not ready to tolerate such reciprocation in the realm of cultural difference, for they write against what they perceive to be the inferior culture of a colonized people.

Edmund Spenser: Herodotus the delightful antiquarian

Spenser's dialogue *A View of the Present State of Ireland* is ultimately a hostile work similar to Rich's *New Description*. Nevertheless, its road to that position of hostility is neither consistent nor unambiguous. Proof of this is the relatively small amount of text that James Ware had to cut when he decided to expurgate the harsher passages concerning Irish culture from *View* before publishing it in the political climate of reconciliation of the early 1630s. Had Ware tried to do the same with Rich's *Description*, he would have found it difficult to keep much text together after disentangling its profuse rhetoric of disgust. Spenser's *View* observes a higher standard of decorum both because of its classically inspired dialogic frame and because of the influence of Herodotus, whom he mentions several times and often borrows from without acknowledgment.

Granted, for a number of these instances it is difficult to prove that Spenser was borrowing directly from Herodotus rather than via Diodorus, Strabo, Boemus, or Olaus Magnus.[46] But as Rich's translation of the *Histories* signals, Herodotus was a prestigious author for the circle of literati in which Rich and Spenser must have crossed paths. Moreover, Gabriel Harvey compliments Spenser in a letter on his – now lost – *Nine Comoedies* "wherevnto in imitation of Herodotus [Spenser] gave the names of the Nine Muses."[47] If Spenser chose to imitate Herodotus, he must have read the Greek's work with interest. The significance of the *Histories* to *View* goes beyond sundry ethnographic details that Spenser could borrow. Although its anti-imperialist stance would not have appealed to Spenser, the *Histories* offered an attractive model of ethnographic writing that seeks to engage its readers' aesthetic sense, bold imagination, and intellectual powers.

Most bewilderingly, with its tales of the Irish "salvage brutishnes and loathly filthines"[48] (this being one of Ware's expurgated phrases) *View* proposes to delight rather than to disgust. One may think this impossible, considering that Spenser is working with the same nightmarish material that Rich and Moryson included in their reports of Ireland: feeding on filthy dairy and horse carcasses, drinking human and animal blood, howling like beasts, and turning into wolves. Yet throughout the first half of *View*, in which Irenius, an English-born resident of Ireland, describes such customs and theorizes that they reveal the Scythian origin of the Irish, his English interlocutor Eudoxus cannot stop averring that this doubly barbaric ethnographic-cum-genealogical discourse "is verye pleasinge unto [him] and indede savorethe of good conceite and some readinge withal."[49]

"Some reading withall" signals a key aspect of the dialogue's claim to being one of the more decorous texts on Ireland. Its insistent reliance on authoritative sources and scholarly methods transmutes sordid customs into something orderly and intellectually appealing.[50] According to his letter to Raleigh, when Spenser set out to write *The Faerie Queene*, he read "Aristotle and the rest." Similarly, when he undertook his project on Ireland, he read "sundrie Aucthours,"[51] such as Herodotus, Lucian, Diodorus, Camden, and many others. For each repugnant Irish custom, Irenius can argue that it "is reade in all histories to have bene used of the Scithians,"[52] with an emphatic *all* signaling the comprehensiveness of his research.[53] Eudoxus responds appreciatively to the learned mode of Irenius's ethnography, and includes not only the use of authorities but also the correction of predecessors' errors: "Beleve me this Observacion of yours Irenius ys verye good and delightefull far beyonde the blinde Conceipte of some . . . as namelye, mr Stannihurst."[54] James Ware pays the same compliment to Spenser himself, whose ethnographic and genealogical "proofes" he finds to be "full of good reading" and to "shew a sound judgment."[55]

The aura of scholarly expertise that elevates the disgusting materials of *View* is all the more pleasing for being concerned with the deep past – here, the Scythian past – in its relevance to the titular "Present State" of Ireland. Spenser had proven his talent for resurrecting times beyond living memory in *The Faerie Queene*, "The Ruines of Time," and other works. In *View*, he remains no less an antiquarian than a poet.[56] Antiquity lends the customs described in *View* not only a time-honored raison d'être but also a patina of quaintness and, indeed, of enchantment:

> Surelye, Iren[ius,] I have in these fewe wordes hearde that from youe which I woulde have thoughte had bene ympossible to have bene spoken of times so remote and Customes soe ancieente: with delighte wheare of I was all that while as it weare entraunced and Carried so far from my selfe, as that I ame now righte sorie that yee ended so sone.[57]

Seemly or unseemly, the customs described by Irenius have "carryed" Eudoxus mystically back into the past, which for him seems to be an isle of intellectual beatitude. Eudoxus is as enchanted by the Scythian origins of the Irish as *The Faerie Queen*'s Arthur is "quite rauisht with delight" to read the Briton Moniments of his own nation (2.10.69). Eudoxus's enchantment seems to reverberate also in the Proem to the Legend of Courtesy:

> The waies, through which my weary steps I guyde,
> In this delightfull land of Faery,
> Are so exceeding spacious and wyde,
> And sprinckled with such sweet variety,
> Of all that pleasant is to eare or eye,
> That I nigh rauisht with rare thoughts delight,
> My tedious trauell doe forget thereby;
> And when I gin to feele decay of might,
> It strength to me supplies, and chears my dulled spright. (6.Proem.1)

It is no accident that, at the end of his edition of *View*, Ware added two excerpts of the most ecstatic poetry Spenser ever wrote: the river marriage from the Legend of Friendship and the Cantos of Mutabilitie. Apparently, for Ware *View* was as literary as it was scholarly.[58]

The above stanza celebrates *The Faerie Queene* as a literary narrative: its redirections, exuberant swerves, and endless continuances. Similar excursuses, albeit on a non-epic scale, also occur in *View*. Like Fairy Land, the ethnographic section of *View* has the appearance of a vast landscape: "a faire Champian laide open unto youe, in which yee maye at lardge stretche out your discourse into manye swete remebraunces of Antiquityes from whence it semeth that the Customes of that nacion [the Irish] proceeded."[59] The ethnographic wanderings of *View* cunningly disguise themselves as a distraction, long and somewhat hard to justify, from the more straightforwardly political, legal, and military problems at hand.[60] Acknowledging this, both interlocutors continually negotiate how much attention they should devote to ethnography. Eudoxus at first tries to keep Irenius on the political line of the dialogue. Gradually, however, the more entranced Eudoxus becomes by the tales of Scythian-Irish customs, the more lax he grows about insisting on discursive discipline. He even encourages Irenius to spend more time on customs and antiquities: "Then I praye youe whensoever in your discourse youe mete with them [customs] by the waye doe not shunn but bouldlye tuche them."[61] Once again, we are reminded of Herodotus, a virtuoso of digression, and of the way in which the *Histories* abandons its more linear politico-historical narrative for the sake of ethnographic description.

The detours that typify Spenser's epic, Spenser's dialogue, and Herodotus' *Histories* are a preeminently literary technique. Herodotus is said to have entertained crowds at the Olympic Games with recitations of the *Histories*. He would have used this technique to embed tales of the curious and the fantastical into his main historical plot and to create suspense, thus positioning himself against the athletes, his competition in the business of entertaining. In the fifteenth century, the *Histories* captivated Boiardo, who produced a "romancified" translation for his Ferrarese courtly audience.[62] For Boiardo, the *Histories* were a universe of exotic lands and marvels traversed via a rambling narrative path, not unlike that of an epic romance. Herodotus thus emerges as a model of literariness and aesthetic delight that would have been useful to Spenser in writing both romance and ethnography. In Eudoxus's desire for pleasure and entrancement Spenser signals how his readers, too, should respond to the dialogue's ethnographic sections.

Notwithstanding its monstrous political proposals, *View* aspires to literary merit and contains "some of the most gripping prose passages in English Renaissance literature."[63] Apart from Herodotean ethnography, the Renaissance dialogue – a literary form much given to demonstrations and discussions of refinement and civility – also put aesthetic pressure on *View*.[64] Clearly, Spenser took up a peculiar challenge when he decided to write about a people who eat filthy dairy in a genre that, from Plato to Castiglione, included elegant table talk among its rhetorical paradigms. Although Spenser occasionally employs the rhetoric of disgust for Irenius's speeches, he is also interested in transforming the disgusting into witty stylistic coups, along the lines of Herodotus' "female malady." For example, rather than calling the dairy processing of the Irish filthy, Spenser incorporates it into a comment on their perjury: in court, they "make no more scruple to passe againste an Inglishman or the Quene, thoughe it be to straine theire oathes, then to drinke milke unstrained."[65]

Like a proper dialogue, *View* speaks in two voices that allow for two distinct perspectives.[66] Initially, only Irenius identifies with an aggressive stance against Irish culture. By contrast, for much of the debate Eudoxus is of the opinion – which he shares with Herodotus – that the conquered should be able to continue in loyalty to their native ways in their everyday lives. Eudoxus scolds Irenius for demonizing customs, such as the wearing of mantles and long hair, which while indecorous, do not appear all that bad or important.

Concerning the mantle, Irenius explains that for men on the road it serves as a house, protecting them from gnats and rain, and that when wrapped around the left arm, it gives the same benefit as a small shield. Further, "for a bad huswif" the mantle is:

> Haulfe a wardrope for in sommer ye shall finde her arayed Comonlye but in her smocke and mantle to be more readye for her lighte services. In winter and in her travell [labor] it is her Cloake and safegarde and allsoe a Coverlett for her Lewed exercises. And when she hathe filled her vessell under it she maye hide bothe her burden and her blame. yea and when her bastarde is borne it serves in steade of all her swadlinge cloutes.[67]

Soiled with the bodily fluids of dissolute women and their bastards and tossed about by men in their lives of Irish lawlessness, the mantle is objectionable to Irenius, and he calls for its prohibition.

In response to this diatribe, Eudoxus exclaims, "O evill minded man that havinge reckoned up so manye uses of a mantell will yeat wishe it to be Abandoned; Sure I thinke Diogenies dishe did never serve his master more turnes notwithstandinge that he made his dishe his Cupp his cap his measure his waterpott, then a mantle dothe an Irishe man."[68] Armed with his dish, club, and tub, the Cynic Diogenes led a quasi-primitive lifestyle, not only pragmatic but also ethically superior to the urban decadence of Athens. In this respect Diogenes seems even more philobarbarian than Herdotous, and Eudoxus's Diogenean comment suggests approval of the barbarians' practical ingenuity in their uncivilized state. Eudoxus is impressed by the many ways in which the Irish can use the mantle for the same reasons that Herodotus is amused by the clever cooking methods of the Scythians, although they are among the more backward barbarians Herodotus describes.[69]

At times, Eudoxus suggests that Irenius may be hypocritical for criticizing Irish customs as loathsome that have close parallels in English customs. For instance, Eudoxus tentatively defends the Irish long front hair or "glib." Irenius may find it disagreeable, but in Eudoxus's eyes it resembles a well-accepted English fashion: "But what blame laye youe to the glibbe; Take hede I praye youe that youe be not to busye thearewith for feare of your owne blame seinge our Inglishemen take it up in suche a generall fassion to weare theire haire so unmesurable longe that some of them excede the Irishe glibbes."[70] The mischievousness in Eudoxus's tone may hint that he himself belongs to the club of Englishmen with long – though probably not "unmeasurable long" – hair.

Eudoxus shows sufficient independence from Irenius's opinion of the Irish for *View* to be a genuine dialogue. It takes considerable persuasion to convert him to Irenius's views, which however seem irresistible in the end. Irenius asserts that ethnic customs cannot be evaluated merely in themselves, but must also answer to colonial politics. Absorbed as he is in pleasant antiquarian thinking, Eudoxus is not ready to argue with this position. In any case, he has already bestowed his sympathy on Irenius the ethnographer and proceeds to do the same for Irenius the

colonial tactician and his proposal to eradicate Irish culture as a political expedi-
ent, in the vein of the Tacitean reason of state.[71] Irenius does not shy from meas-
ures as extreme as famine and violent resettlement. Catholicism in particular is
something that the debaters in *View*, no less than Estienne's *Apologie*, would see
disappear, although they acknowledge that this would be a slow and difficult process even in a reconquered Ireland.

One of Irenius's solutions for eradicating disgusting Irish customs is so sly that
it can itself qualify as an abomination:

> In everye Cantred or baroney they shoulde kepe [a] Scholmaster which sould
> enstructe them in grammar and in the principles of sciences to whom they
> shoulde be Compelled to sende theire youthe to be dissiplined, whearby they
> will in shorte space growe up to that Civill Conversacion that bothe the Chil-
> dren will loathe the former rudenes in which they weare bredd and allsoe theire
> parentes will even by thensample [the example] of theire younge Children per-
> ceave the fowlenes of theire owne brutishe behaviour Compared to theires.[72]

Nothing could be less Herodotean than this exercise in social engineering. Irenius
plans to force the most helpless part of Ireland's population – children who have
not yet settled completely into the practice of their native customs – to internalize
the colonists' disgust with Irish culture. The germ of disgust will then be trans-
ferred from the children to the parents who, in order not to be alienated from their
offspring and the future of the family, will submit to the new customs and spurn
their Irish heritage. Irenius's trick thus makes the disgusting nation itself a means
for defeating ethnographic disgust. Judged in light of the Herodotean sovereignty
of custom, this scheme seems more nefarious than the famine proposal that modern readers of *View* usually single out as Irenius's worst crime – in word if not in
deed – against Ireland. Perhaps even death amid swarms of creeping emaciated
ghosts of human beings, who have begun to cannibalize one another,[73] is not as
punitive and detrimental to the future of a nation as the insidious murdering of its
customs in the minds of its children.

Of the texts in which we discern echoes and citations of the *Histories*, Spenser's *A View of the Present State of Ireland* has emerged as the most unsettling
Renaissance appropriation of Herodotean ethnography. Spenser opposes the per-
petuation of repugnant barbarian practices into the new era as strongly as does
Estienne or Rich. But at the same time, *View* exhibits features more proper to the
Herodotean ethos or to Montaigne's musings and interrogations, features such
as a nuanced rhetoric, scholarly aura, literary aspirations, the occasional defense
of Irish customs, and the refusal to write a monovocal text, choosing instead the
dynamic of debate and its conventions of decorum. *View* is in effect a divided text.
Even if Spenser did not adhere to cultural relativism, he understood the challenge
that the charms of Herodotean ethnography posed to the colonial domination of
England over Ireland and turned them to his own political purposes, demonstrating in the process that he was capable of writing ethnography *as though* he were
a cultural relativist.

View ends with Eudoxus reminding Irenius that he has promised to give a longer exposition of Irish culture and genealogy on another occasion.[74] Earlier, Irenius specified that for the purposes of *View* "it shall suffice to tuche suche Customes of the Irishe as seme offensive and repugnante to the good government of that realme."[75] If Irenius's focus in *View* is on the "offensive" customs, should we infer that the customs left for a future "moste ample discourse"[76] could be inoffensive or even praiseworthy? Spenser's ethnography would be still more bewildering if it showed the colonist Irenius treating any Irish practices as acceptable.

Then again, even in *View* being politically inconvenient does not preclude an aspect of Irish culture from being the object of Spenser's envious fascination. Spenser condemns the quasi-aristocratic love of freedom permeating Irish society down to its lower strata in part because such freedom could never be his, although he is aware of its desirability as he embodies it in the romantic figure of the knight-errant in *The Faerie Queene*.[77] Except for its resentfulness, Spenser's recognition of the Irish cult of personal and national freedom is not that different from Herodotus' admiration of how the Scythians, a barbarous warrior society, strive to preserve their autonomy as much as his own valiant countrymen do (4.46–7). In Irenius's promise of an ampler discourse Spenser may be revealing his intention to write a longer, more scholarly text on Ireland that would come still closer to the Herodotean spirit and gaze more calmly into the eyes of the barbarians. But like the unwritten or lost books of *The Faerie Queene*, this project is fated to remain a Spenserian enigma.[78]

Notes

1   On the "explosion of ethnography" in fifth-century BCE Greece, see Skinner, *Invention*, ch. 1.
2   For a survey of the reception of Herodotus, see Momigliano, "Place of Herodotus."
3   Plutarch, "Malice," 857.12.
4   Herodotus, *Histories*, 1.199. Subsequent references are in the text.
5   See for example Longinus, *On the Sublime*, 13.3.
6   On reading the classics in the age of colonial expansion, see Grafton et al., *New Worlds, Ancient Texts*.
7   Darbo-Peschanski, "Herodotus and *historia*," 103.
8   On Herodotean ethnography against imperialism, see Ward, *Philosophy of Empire*, 1–10, 159–61.
9   On the lapse, see Longinus, *On the Sublime*, 43.2–5.
10 Longinus, *On the Sublime*, 28.4; cf. Herodotus, *Histories*, 1.105.
11 For a grudging admission of Herodotus' mastery as a prose author, see Plutarch, "Malice," 874.43.
12 Erasmus, *Aim and Method*, 164.
13 Camerarius, "Praefatio," sig.α4r.
14 On the Renaissance reception of Herodotus, see Longo, *Hérodote*, especially 23–43 on Estienne.
15 R.C., "The Translator to the Reader," sig.A4v.
16 I quote from the English translation of Estienne's *Apologie*, titled *A World of Wonders*, sig.C1v.
17 Estienne, "Apologia," sig.3*2r.
18 Estienne, *World of Wonders*, sig.B2v.

19 For a Lévi-Straussean reading of the funeral customs, see Redfield, "Herodotus the Tourist," 32–5.
20 Estienne, *World of Wonders*, sig.B3r.
21 Sextus Empiricus, *Pyrrhoniarum*, sig.C5r.–C6v.; sig.M2r.–M6v.
22 "Dissoi Logoi," sig.G4v.–G6r.
23 Thomas, for example, notes that Herodotus' description of Egypt reads like "a long sophistic joke" and Darius' experiment like an epitome of "Sophistic relativism." *Herodotus in Context*, 130, 126.
24 Montaigne, *Travel Journal*, 891.
25 Montaigne, *Travel Journal*, 884.
26 Montaigne, "Of the Caniballes," 165–6. For the Scythian divinators and their punishment, see Herodotus, *Histories*, 4.68–9.
27 Montaigne, "Of the Caniballes," 166.
28 Montaigne, "Of the Caniballes," 163.
29 On barbarism as a perspectival category, see 2.158.
30 In *Persian Empire*, 79, Grogan offers both textual and biographical evidence in favor of attributing the translation to Rich. Grogan also points out the translator's pro-imperialist agenda (80), which makes him, like Estienne, yet another misinterpreter of Herodotus' view of empire.
31 Herodotus, *Famous Hystory*, sig.L6v.
32 Incidentally, Estienne's edition, *Herodoti Halicarnassei Historiae*, sig.D5r, contains the same error: "Apud caeteros mortales victus a ferarum secretus est consortio, aegiptii cum feris vescuntur." Grogan, *Persian Empire*, 79, likewise speculates that B.R. may have consulted translations by Estienne and others.
33 Herodotus, *Famous Hystory*, sig.M2v; my italics for the two litotes.
34 Herodotus, *Famous Hystory*, sig.M2v.
35 Aristotle, *Rhetoric*, 1408a3.
36 Rich, *New Description*, sig.G4v.
37 Rich, *New Description*, sig.E4v.
38 Rich, *New Description*, sig.F1r.–F1v.
39 Moryson, *Itinerary*, 198.
40 Moryson, *Itinerary*, 197.
41 Rich, *New Description*, sig.F1r.
42 Rich, *New Description*, sig.G4v.
43 Rich, *New Description*, sig.G4v.
44 Moryson, *Itinerary*, 199.
45 Rich, *New Description*, sig.F1v.
46 As one can infer from the *Variorum* notes, passim, in Spenser, *View*.
47 Harvey, "Letters," 471.
48 Spenser, *View*, 102.
49 Spenser, *View*, 95.
50 Spenser, *View*, 84–6.
51 Spenser, *View*, 107.
52 Spenser, *View*, 106–7.
53 On the contested scholarly status of *View*, see Van Es, *Spenser's Forms*, 78–84.
54 Spenser, *View*, 104.
55 Ware, "Preface," 532.
56 On antiquarianism and *View*, see Van Es, *Spenser's Forms*, 84–102.
57 Spenser, *View*, 109.
58 Van Es, *Spenser's Forms*, 80.
59 Spenser, *View*, 81.
60 There is increasing acknowledgement in Spenser studies that the non-pragmatic and not obviously political aspects of *View*, such as its dialogic frame and ethnographic sections, are neither subsidiary nor merely decorative.

61 Spenser, *View*, 105.
62 Looney, *Compromising*, 65–76.
63 Canny, *Making Ireland British*, 44.
64 On the dialogic form of *View*, see Coughlan, "Some Secret Scourge," 59–71.
65 Spenser, *View*, 66.
66 In this I follow Coughlan, "Some Secret Scourge," 59–71, and Van Es, *Spenser's Forms*, 87–91; but for arguments for *View*'s "monologism," see the extended exchange between John Breen, Andrew Hadfield, and Willy Maley in the journal *Connotations* (1994–1996). Accessed December 1, 2014. http://www.connotations.uni-tuebingen.de/.
67 Spenser, *View*, 101.
68 Spenser, *View*, 102.
69 Herodotus, *Histories*, 4.61.
70 Spenser, *View*, 102.
71 Hadfield, *Shakespeare, Spenser*, 90–104.
72 Spenser, *View*, 218.
73 Spenser, *View*, 158.
74 Concerning this tantalizing detail, see Hadfield, *Irish Experience*, 85–6.
75 Spenser, *View*, 82.
76 Spenser, *View*, 81.
77 I both draw on and diverge from Shuger, who does not see much room for envy in Spenser's perception of Irish freedom in "Irishmen, Aristocrats."
78 I am grateful to Jane Grogan, Theodora Hadjimichael, and J. Eric Marler for inspiring conversations about all things Herodotean, and to Barbara Correll for her comments on an early version of this essay.

References

Aristotle. *Rhetoric*. Translated by Rhys Roberts. New York: The Modern Library, 1954.
Camerarius, Joachim. "Praefatio." Herodotus. *Herodotou logoi ennea*. Edited by Joachim Camerarius, sig.α2r.–β4v. Basel: Herwagen, 1541.
Canny, Nicholas. *Making Ireland British*. Oxford: Oxford University Press, 2001.
Coughlan, Patricia. "Some Secret Scourge which shall by her come unto England: Ireland and Incivility in Spenser." In *Spenser and Ireland: An Interdisciplinary Perspective*, edited by Patricia Coughlan, 46–74. Cork: Cork University Press, 1989.
Darbo-Peschanski, Catherine. "Herodotus and *historia*." In *Herodotus and the World*, edited by Rosaria Munson, 78–105. Oxford: Oxford University Press, 2013.
"Dissoi Logoi (Dialexeis)." *Diogenous Laertiou Peri biōn . . . .* Edited by Henri Estienne, sig.G3v.–H1v. Geneva, 1570.
Erasmus. *Desiderius Erasmus. Concerning the Aim and Method of Education*. Edited by William Woodward. Cambridge: Cambridge University Press, 1904.
Estienne, Henri. "Apologia pro Herodoto." *Herodoti Halicarnassei Historiae*. Translated by Lorenzo Valla. Edited by Henri Estienne, Sig.2*5r.–sig.4*6v. Geneva, 1566.
———. *A World of Wonders*. Translated by R.C. London: John Norton, 1607.
Grafton, Anthony, April Shelfoord, and Nancy Siraisi. *New Worlds, Ancient Texts*. Cambridge, MA: Harvard University Press, 1992.
Grogan, Jane. *The Persian Empire in English Renaissance Writing, 1549–1622*. Basingstoke: Palgrave, 2014.
Hadfield, Andrew. *Edmund Spenser's Irish Experience*. Oxford: Oxford University Press, 1997.
———. *Shakespeare, Spenser, and the Matter of Britain*. Basingstoke: Palgrave, 2004.

Harvey, Gabriel. "Harvey's Letters." In *Edmund Spenser. Works*, vol. 10, edited by Rudolf Gottfried, 441–77. Baltimore: Johns Hopkins University Press, 1949.

Herodotus. *The famous hystory of Herodotus*. Translated by B[arnabe] R[iche]. London: Thomas Marshe, 1584.

———. *Herodoti Halicarnassei Historiae*. Translated by Lorenzo Valla and Henri Estienne. Edited by Henri Estienne. Geneva, 1566.

———. *The Histories* (*The Persian Wars*). Edited and translated by A.D. Godley. Cambridge, MA: Harvard University Press, 1926.

Longinus, *On the Sublime*. Translated by W.H. Fyfe. Edited by Jeffrey Henderson. In *Aristotle: Poetics. Longinus: On the Sublime. Demetrius: On Style*, 160–307. Loeb Classical Library 199. Cambridge, MA: Harvard University Press, 1995.

Longo, Susanna Gambino, ed. *Hérodote à la Renaissance*. Turnhout: Brepols, 2012.

Looney, Dennis. *Compromising the Classics*. Detroit: Wayne State University, 1996.

Momigliano, Arnaldo. "The Place of Herodotus in the History of Historiography." In *Herodotus and the Narrative of the Past*, edited by Rosaria Munson, 31–45. Oxford: Oxford University Press, 2013.

Montaigne, Michel de. "Of the Caniballes." In *Montaigne's Essayes. John Florio's Translation*, 160–71. New York: The Modern Library, 1933.

———. *Travel Journal*. In *Complete Works*, 867–1042. Edited by Donald Frame. Stanford: Stanford University Press, 1958.

Moryson, Fynes. *An Itinerary Containing His Ten Yeeres of Travell*, vol. 4. Glasgow: MacLehose, 1907.

Plutarch (or Pseudo-Plutarch). "On The Malice of Herodotus." In *Moralia*, vol. 11. Edited and translated by Lionel Pearson, 8–129. Cambridge, MA: Harvard University Press, 1965.

R.C. (Richard Carew?). "The Translator to the Reader." Henri Estienne. *A World of Wonders*, sig.5v.–A4v. London: John Norton, 1607.

Redfield, James. "Herodotus the Tourist." In *Greeks and Barbarians*, edited by Thomas Harrison, 24–49. Edinburgh: Edinburgh University Press, 2001.

Rich, Barnabe. *A New Description of Ireland*. London: for Thomas Adams, 1610.

Sextus Empiricus. *Sexti philosophi Pyrrhoniarum hypotyposeon*. Edited and translated by Henri Estienne. Geneva, 1562.

Shuger, Deborah. "Irishmen, Aristocrats, and Other White Barbarians." *Renaissance Quarterly* 50 (1997): 494–525.

Skinner, Joseph. *The Invention of Ethnography: From Homer to Herodotus*. Oxford: Oxford University Press, 2012.

Spenser, Edmund. *A View of the Present State of Ireland*. In *Edmund Spenser. Works*, vol. 10. Edited by Rudolf Gottfried, 43–231. Baltimore: Johns Hopkins University Press, 1949.

———. *The Faerie Queene. Works*, vols 1–6. Edited by Edwin Greenlaw et al. Baltimore: Johns Hopkins University Press, 1933–1938.

Thomas, Rosalind. *Herodotus in Context: Ethnography, Science, and the Art of Persuasion*. Cambridge: Cambridge University Press, 2000.

Van Es, Bart. *Spenser's Forms of History*. Oxford: Oxford University Press, 2002.

Ward, Ann. *Herodotus and the Philosophy of Empire*. Waco: Baylor University Press, 2008.

Ware, James. "Preface." In *Edmund Spenser. Works*, vol. 10. Edited by Rudolf Gottfried, 530–32. Baltimore: Johns Hopkins University Press, 1949.

6 Food, filth, and the foreign

Disgust in the seventeenth-century travelogue

Gitanjali Shahani

One day I went out by myself to fetch a walk . . . I saw some of those huts which the Hottentots dwell in. Upon sight of which, my curiosity led me to go and see what kind of life those people led. I went into one of 'em, and there I saw a parcel of 'em lying upon the ground like so many hogs, and fast asleep: But as soon as they awaked and saw me, they sprung up and came to me, making noises like turkies . . . I pulled out a piece of tobacco and gave it them: They were mightily pleased with that present . . . For no sooner had I given them this, but they all lifted up those flaps of sheep-skin which hang before their privy-parts to give me a sight of 'em. What with this beastly behavior, and what with the nasty stench of their kennels (as I think I may properly call 'em), I made all haste to be gone. Some of 'em I found at dinner, or rather eating, (for that is a word of too much order and decency for them). They had only a piece of cow-hide, laid upon the coals a broyling, and to make the carbonnade more pleasant, they had squeezed the dung out of the guts, and spread it finely on the hide to moisten it, and to give it relish; and this they take when it is broyl'd, and chop it, and so eat it. The very ordering of it in this manner, turn'd my stomach so, that I could not stay to see the eating of it: But I made all the haste I could to be gone.

—*Christopher Fryke,* A Relation of Two Several
Voyages Made into the East Indies

Disgust is a commonplace sentiment in the "Discourse of the Cape."[1] In this body of proto-ethnographic writing by seventeenth-century European travelers, halting at the Cape of Good Hope en route to the East Indies, disgust becomes a kind of generic convention. In particular, the dietary habits of the native inhabitants provoke the expression of unmitigated disgust. Traveler after traveler suspends his seemingly objective narrative voice to note the stench of raw entrails eaten by the Hottentots, the sight of excrement smeared on their food, or their ability to taste food "like dogs."[2] A series of anthropological observations regarding their dwelling, their dress, and their language inevitably culminates in commentary about the gross intermingling of food and filth.

Christopher Fryke's description of his travels, quoted at length above, is in many ways exemplary of this ethnographic disgust.[3] Traveling as a surgeon to the Dutch East India Company, Fryke begins his narrative as the prototype of what Mary Louis Pratt has called the "seeing-man."[4] He is drawn to the Hottentot dwellings by the traveler's objective curiosity to "see what kind of life these people led."[5] At this point he is simply what Pratt has called "the landscanning, self-effacing producer of information."[6] But as the Hottentots awaken, disgust intervenes with Fryke's inventory of the hut. The ritual offering of gifts – tobacco – is apparently greeted by the Hottentots' gratuitous display of their "privy-parts."

If the sight of such a ritual isn't enough to drive Fryke away, the smell of their food preparation is. As Silvan Tomkins writes, the physiological markers of disgust are evolutionarily designed to put as much distance between the self and the object of disgust:

> Although the face and nostrils and throat and even the stomach are unpleasantly involved in disgust and nausea . . . attention is most likely to be referred to the source, the object, rather than to the self or the face. This happens because the response intends to maximize the distance between the face and the object which disgusts the self. It is a literal pulling away from the object.[7]

Fryke's recorded response in his travelogue is a case study in disgust: "The very ordering of it in this manner, turn'd my stomach so, that I could not stay to see the eating of it: But I made all the haste I could to be gone," he writes. Per Tomkins, he must pull away from the object; he must distance himself from the very sight he set out to record; he must leave hastily. Disgust, it would seem, gets in the way of the proper ethnographic observation that the "seeing-man" sought out to begin with.

And yet it is entirely possible that Fryke felt no disgust at all. Perhaps he never saw raw entrails, or a dung relish, or a Hottentot partaking of this concoction. In the long tradition of travel writing, from Mandeville onwards, Fryke would hardly be the first to fabricate or exaggerate. For J.M. Coetzee, who examines the "Discourse of the Cape" in *White Writing: On the Culture of Letters in South Africa*, the historical veracity of Fryke's narrative is much to be doubted.[8] Shortly after the episode in the hut, Fryke describes the unlikely sight of a serpent eating a Hottentot, which for Coetzee is evidence enough of his proclivity to exaggerate throughout the travelogue.

But it is not any one improbable episode that renders Fryke's disgusting experience in the hut dubious. Rather, it is the routine expression of disgust at this particular juncture in the travelogue that suggests it is expected, rehearsed, and contrived as the "seeing-man" happens upon the native's food and filth. In writing about his physiological reaction to Hottentot food preparation, Fryke places himself in an evolving tradition of ethnographic observation seemingly interrupted by disgust or culminating in disgust, inscribing disgust itself as a textual convention of the travelogues and proto-ethnographies that proliferated in the seventeenth century. Disgust, as it were, lends an immediacy and authenticity to the very observations it interrupts. It anchors the traveler's narrative in an affective experience that seems to verify his act of seeing. In fact, it situates him as more than just the observer. He is one who feels, smells, and on occasion tastes. Its performance therefore becomes central to the very performance of credibility in the narrative.

It is in the disgusting moment that the travelogue becomes most acutely aware of the categories of sameness and difference through which it operates.

This staged moment of disgust, I want to argue, is unique to the cibarious experiences of the contact zone. As Fryke's observations suggest, Hottentot dwelling arrangements, sleeping habits, and sexual mores are all sources of disgust – but it is food preparation that clinches the sensation of disgust. Put another way, disgusting food is particularly disgusting. It is telling that Tomkins's explication of what he terms "contempt-disgust" centers on food:

> If the food about to be ingested activates disgust, the upper lip and the nose is raised and the head is drawn away from the apparent source of offending odor. If the substance has been taken into the mouth, it will be spit out and the head drawn away from it. If it has been swallowed, it will produce nausea and it will be vomited out either through the mouth or the nostrils.[9]

Here and elsewhere in Tomkins's work disgust is conceived in oral terms. While other orifices (the nostrils, for example) are involved, it is the mouth that most acutely registers disgust, whether in its consumption or expulsion of food.

According to Charles Darwin, "Disgust would have been shown at a very early period by movements round the mouth, like those of vomiting – that is, if the view which I have suggested respecting the source of expression is correct, namely that our progenitors had the power, and used it, of voluntarily and quickly rejecting any food from their stomachs which they disliked."[10] Evolutionarily speaking, the mouth as orifice must guard against the disgusting rather than consume it. But the act of disgusting food consumption inverts this logic, willingly allowing the polluting object into the mouth. Julia Kristeva reminds us that polluting objects "always relate to corporeal orifices." Schematically, for Kristeva, they fall into two types, "excremental and menstrual."[11] With regard to the former, Kristeva writes that "excrement and its equivalents (decay, infection, disease, corpse, etc.) stand for the danger to identity that comes from without: the ego threatened by the non-ego, society threatened by its outside."[12]

It is such a danger that the Hottentot seems to represent in the "Discourse of the Cape." The revolting image of excrement on Hottentot food – whether or not it is fabricated – arguably stems from fear: the mark of the outside threatening the inside, the other threatening the self. Its invocation at this point in the travel narrative is thus strategic. It is shorthand for describing the entire experience of Hottentot life as perverse and abject. The point is not so much to ascertain whether Fryke and his predecessors actually witnessed the comingling of food and filth. Rather, it is to examine what the repeated, lurid description of such a comingling in their narratives implies for the genre as a whole. If, as Mary Douglas notes in *Purity and Danger*, "There is no such thing as absolute dirt: it exists in the eye of the beholder," then the traveler as "seeing-man" reveals much in his vision of food, filth, and the foreign.[13]

In the contact zone, particularly, expressions of disgust with regard to food become part of a larger process of demarcating the self from the other. We might recall here Pratt's definition of the contact zone as "the space in which people geographically and historically separated come into contact with each other and establish ongoing relations, usually involving conditions of coercion, radical inequality, and intractable conflict."[14] In this space of encounter, food is frequently the object of disgust precisely because it is the marker of sameness and difference.

Fryke, for instance, records the Hottentots' food preparation along such an axis of sameness and difference. They are broiling, chopping, and seasoning, but they are broiling an animal's entrails, chopping up cowhide, and seasoning with dung. He comes close to describing their ritual as "dinner," but checks himself, "for that is a word of too much order and decency for them." It is this obvious difference that makes the episode worthy of ethnographic record, fascinating because disgusting. For without the elements that make the Hottenot "dinner" both same (insofar as it involves eating) and different (insofar as it entails eating dung-seasoned entrails), the acts of broiling, chopping, or seasoning would be simply banal routines, not particularly noteworthy for the traveler or his audience. Indeed, the travelogue as a genre revels in these very elements, even in its most recent incarnations. Shows like Andrew Zimmerman's *Bizarre Foods* or Anthony Bourdain's *Parts Unknown* come to mind as contemporary variants of this genre, unfolding in a culinary contact zone where intrepid hosts test the thresholds of the disgusting, the exotic, and the unfamiliar for the benefit of a stay-at-home audience.

Coetzee explains the process of recording the most obvious difference between the native and the European:

> While they are certainly differences, these items are perceived and conceived within a framework of sameness, a framework that derives from the generally accepted thesis . . . that although the Hottentots may seem to be no more than beasts, they are in fact men. Hottentot society being a human society, it must be amenable to description within a framework common to all human societies.[15]

Diet, along with categories such as dress, language, customs, trade, habitation, and recreation all belong to such a framework. Contempt-disgust is aroused in terms of this framework. The Hottentot diet is disgusting to the travel writer *because* the Hottentot is human rather than beast. But the Hottentot diet is also of interest to the travel writer *because* it shows the Hottentot as more beast-like than human. It is for this very reason worthy of observation, repetition, and – where necessary – fabrication in travelogue after travelogue.

Versions of Fryke's narrative abound in the "Discourse of the Cape." Travelers well after Fryke and in different parts of the globe tend to record some version of his disgust at the scene of bizarre foods. It is therefore worth contextualizing Fryke's "relation" in terms of the larger narrative at work in the genre. As Steve Clark has noted in his study of the travelogue, "its force is collective and incremental rather than singular and aesthetic. The tactic of singling out texts . . . as isolated masterpieces simply devalues the vast majority of these narratives"[16]

In what follows, I briefly consider this incremental effect in the narratives of the Cape. While an exhaustive consideration of disgusting foods across geographical regions and contact zones is beyond the scope of this chapter, I also examine a few travelers' culinary experiences beyond the Cape, as points of comparison. I then take up travelers' experiences in the culinary contact zones of the Ottoman and Mughal Court, where the sources of disgust become the hyper-civilized dietary customs of the Islamic East. Here, the experiences of disgust – and on occasion, pleasure – are more varied than those at the Cape and reveal much about the exigencies of early modern encounters in the East. Some of the authors considered here traveled to the Cape en route to their journey to the Mughal Court. Consequently, their travelogues present important comparative frameworks of disgust in their encounters with different cultural groups. The final travelogue examined in this chapter presents us with opportunities to look at the traveler himself as the potential object of disgust, an embodiment of all that is filthy and foreign to the peoples and cultures being observed and recorded in the travelogue, particularly in the culinary contact zone where issues of purity and danger become heightened through the ritual sharing of food. Collectively, these travelogues have much to tell us about the literal and symbolic importance of food and the affective responses to it in early modern cross-cultural encounters across the globe.

Among the earliest travel writers to note the Hottentot custom of eating raw animal entrails is the Dutch traveler Cornelis de Houtman, who commanded an expedition to the East in 1595. De Houtman's experience of disgust is established early in the narrative:

> They always stank greatly, since they besmeared themselves with fat and grease. We could find none of their dwellings, far less any of their women . . . When we killed any oxen they begged for the entrails, which they ate quite raw after shaking out most of the dung, or stretched it over the fire on four sticks, or warming up a little of the paunch ate it up . . . I could learn no more of them but that they speak very clumsily, like the folk in Germany . . . who suffer from goiter . . . Also they had some pieces of dried meat hanging round their necks.[17]

Here the traveler's ethnographic observations are general, charting the appearance (smeared with grease), language (clumsy like people with goiter), and diet (raw entrails) of his subjects, noting regret when information fails. Their dwellings and their women, for instance, were not to be found.

Disgust appears to be common to all categories in his case, evoked by the sights, sounds, smells, and tastes of Hottentot existence. This range of sensory experiences serves the interests of verisimilitude. To see, to hear, to smell, and to taste is to confirm the act of witnessing central to the genre itself. Jyotsna Singh argues in *Travel Knowledge*: "If witnessing was the primal act in the discourse of travel, it meant that travelers/writers could then attempt to record, objectify, and claim the world they encountered."[18] In the travelogues of early visitors to the Cape, like de Houtman, such an attempt to record and objectify is achieved by checking off each ethnographic category, which in turn records and objectifies difference through sameness.

By 1605, other travel writers reiterate de Houtman's observations about the Hottentots' eating of waste. The anonymous writer aboard Sir Edward Michelbourne's fleet brings little variation to de Houtman's narrative in his travelogue. However, Samuel Purchas's marginal notes near the journal entry on Hottentot nakedness add a point of interest to the anonymous writer's observations. Purchas states that their "women are well featured" but that "some of their men have but one stone."[19] This sexual attribute appears repeatedly in later travelogues, possibly reflecting what sociologist George Steinmentz suggests is a fascination with ritual circumcision among Hottentot men, to the point where it becomes a kind of fetish. According to Steinmetz, "Their partial 'self-castration' afforded the European male colonizer an opportunity to simultaneously acknowledge the threat of castration and to displace the anxieties associated with this threat onto a distant and exotic other, in an act of disavowal."[20] More generally, the repeated mention of ritualized castration bespeaks an obsession with projected lack in Hottentot society. They are without intact genitals just as they are without language, without law or government, and frequently without religion.

As a category, diet most obviously reflects this sense of lack. The Hottentots have no cuisine and subsist on the food scraps that English travelers throw away. For instance, the following is noted in the journal kept on Middlebourne's voyage:

> In all the time of our being there they lived upon the guts and filth of the meate which we did cast away feeding in most beastly fashion, for they would neither wash nor make cleane the guts, but take them and cover them with hote ashes, and before they were through hote, they pulled them out, shaking them a little in their hands, and so eate the guts the excrements and the ashes.[21]

This same scavenging habit is observed again by John Jourdain, captain on board an East India vessel in 1608. Jourdain claims to have seen the natives eating the waste that his crew could not bear to smell, fifteen days after it had begun to rot. It is their diet that confirms for him their uniquely disgusting status:

> And having brought our boates laden with these seals, we cutt the fatt from them for oyle, and the rest was throwne a good distance from the tents because of the noysomnes; upon which fish the Saldanians fed very heartily on, after it had lyen in a heape 15 daies, standing the loathsomnes of the smell, these people would eate of it as if it had bene better meate, and would not take of that which laye upon the top, which were the sweetest, but would search under for those which were the most rotte, and laye it on the coals without any ceremoneys of washinge; and beeinge a little scorched with the fire, would eate it with a good stomacke; in soe much that my opinion is, that if without danger they could come to eate mans flesh, they would not make any scruple of it, for I think the world doth not yield a more heathenish people and more beastlie.[22]

Perhaps the thing that disgusts Jourdain most is that the Hottentots feel no disgust. They seem not to smell the "loathsomnes" of rotting meat. They eat it with "good stomach" as if it were "better meate" and nothing was wrong with it. They seek out the festering parts and make no effort at washing. As with Fryke's travelogue, the Hottentots' disgusting diet becomes the culminating moment of ethnographic description in Jourdain's narrative. Since they are such a "heathenish" and "beast-lie" people, nothing further need be noted about them.

The point at which the author asserts his subjects' beastliness is, then, also where he situates the ethnographic record of those subjects beyond the categories of the recognizably human. In recording the Hottentots' beastliness, Jourdain also slips in, as it were, an ethnographic observation that appears to confirm the observations of those before him: "Off these kind of people and there behaviour I neede not to write, because it is sufficientlie knowne to many of our countrymen." Jourdain then immediately moves on to observations on the flora and fauna of the land. The Hottentots' cannibalistic tendencies, which Jourdain only speculates about, are offered with greater certainty by later travelers. Cornelis Claesz Van Purmerendt, who sailed to the Cape aboard the *Bantam* in 1609, writes that there was "good water" and "fine refreshing" to be had at the Cape, but its inhabitants, "As far as we could perceive . . . were cannibals . . . In a word, it is a beast-like people."[23]

Nicholas Downton, who sailed aboard the English vessel *Peppercorn* in 1610, lends a new perspective to the theme of disgusting consumption in Hottentot life, chronicling ways in which they smeared their bodies with food and filth. Like others before him, Downton interrupts his narrative of trade and exchange with an interjection about the particularly loathsome ways of the Hottentots:

> These people are the filthiest for the usage of there bodyes that I ever have heard of for besides the natural uncleanes (as by Sweat or otherwise) whereto all people are subject, which the most by washing cleare them selfes of, con-traryewise these people doe augment by anointing their bodyes with a filthy substance which I suppose to be the Juice of hearbes, which on there bodyes sheweth like Cow doung . . . [A]lso another most strange and filthy wearing, to what purpose I knowe not, as the guts of cattle about there neckes, which makes them smell like a Butchers slaughter house.[24]

For Downton, the Hottentots are disgusting precisely because they seek out the polluting objects that "all people" are supposed to shun. Cleansing rituals are reversed as they anoint themselves with herbs and dung, food and filth, rather than purge themselves of it. Thus it is that they are "the filthiest for the usage of there bodyes."

By around 1614 travel writers were noting a new kind of disgusting food consumption among the Hottentots. Travelers aboard Thomas Best's fleet to the East observed the peculiar Hottentot habit of adorning their necks with "fat guts" and "greasie Tripes, which sometimes they would pull off and eat raw."[25] They were frequently to be found "slavering" at the mouth as they ate off these adornments. "They will eat any garbage," concluded Nicholas Withington of this "miserable people."[26] For the French general Augustin de Beaulieu, who commanded an armed expedition to the East Indies in 1620, the Hottentots' extreme appetite might account for their revolting dietary habits: They always seemed to be "dying of hunger," he observed of their women.[27] Of the men, he wrote that "When they meet us, the first thing they do is to point to their stomach, which they so pull into their body that it seems as if they had a great cavity in their chest. But they do not eat human flesh."[28] While de Beaulieu, unlike his predecessors, didn't think the Hottentots were cannibals, it seemed that they could eat that "which neither the wolves nor other ravenous beasts would touch."[29]

While later nineteenth century medical and anthropological discourse would scrutinize the entire sexual anatomy of the female Hottenot, most notoriously in the case of the Hottentot Venus whose body was studied and displayed throughout European salons in the early 1800s, in early writings on the Cape it is the lactating female's body that draws particular attention.[30] Steinmetz notes that one of the standard symbols of Hottentot debasement – also frequently visually depicted in etchings accompanying the travelogues – was the Hottentot woman's distended breast slung over her shoulder to feed her child.[31] In the travelogue of Reverend Edward Terry, chaplain to English ambassador Sir Thomas Roe in the Mughal Court who stopped at the Cape in 1616, we see an early depiction of a Hottentot mother nursing her infant:

> God . . . they . . . acknowledge none . . . their speech it seemed to us inarticulate noise, rather than language, like the clucking of hens, or gabling of turkeys . . . Their ornaments and jewels [are] bullocks or sheeps guts, full of excrement, about their necks . . . and when they were hungry . . . [they] would gnaw and eat the raw guts. The women, as the men, are thus adorned, thus habited and thus dieted; only they wear more about their lower parts than the men; and . . . carry their sucking infants under their skins upon their backs, and their breasts, hanging down like bag-pipes, they put up with their hands to their children, that they may suck them over their shoulders. Both sexes make coverings to their heads like to skull-caps, with cow-dung . . . mingled with a little stinking grease, with which they likewise besmear their faces, which makes their company insufferable, if they get the wind of you . . . they would eat any refuse thing, as rotten and mouldy biskets.[32]

Diet hardly seems like a unified category for Terry, following quickly after his observations on the Hottentot religion or the lack thereof, Hottentot language or the lack thereof, and the Hottentot clothing or the lack thereof. Viewed carefully, though, Terry appears to suggest ways in which these categories merge. The Hottentots' habit is also their diet. They eat off their "clothes," which happen to be raw guts. Their headgear is smeared with waste, and their faces with grease. The overall effect is one that makes it "insufferable" to stand their presence if the wind blows out of their direction.

The Hottentot woman is casually mentioned among these other observations, when Terry notes that children suckle at her "bag-pipe" like breasts. That observation seems neither as disgusting as Hottentot diet, nor as revolting as Hottentot attire. But the general air of disgust that accrues to such an image is captured in an etching that accompanies Thomas Herbert's account to the Cape from 1627. Here, a partially clad Hottentot woman holds up animal entrails dripping with blood, while a child on her back suckles at a distorted breast thrown over her shoulder. A Hottentot male, naked but for the sheepskin on his loins, stands beside her, pointing his spear at the animal intestines as if to draw the readers' attention to the dismembered part. Hottentot feeding and Hottentot sexuality strangely merge in this tableau of the grotesque (see Figure 6.1).[33]

Figure 6.1 STC 13190, *A relation of some yeares trauaile, begunne anno 1626. Into Afrique and the greater Asia, especially the territories of the Persian monarchie: and some parts of the orientall Indies, and iles adiacent.* By permission of the Folger Shakespeare Library

One of the few relativized considerations of Hottentot diet occurs in an eighteenth-century travelogue by Peter Kolb, first published in German in 1719, and subsequently translated into English, French, and Dutch.[34] In addition to explaining Hottentot ideas of beauty as well as their advanced learning in medicine, surgery, and botany, Kolb attempts to understand their dietary preferences, arguing that while their food might appear "nauseous and uncleanly" to Europeans, it "agrees very well with their Constitutions."[35] Kolb points out that Africans would likely find butter inedible, raising a valid question: "Who are the barbarians, and who the civilized?"[36] Yet Kolb is the exception. In the "Discourse of the Cape," the general consensus is that the Hottentots are the "most savage and beastly people as ever . . . God created."[37]

In thus emphasizing disgust in the travelogue, this chapter might seem to contradict one of the most influential arguments about the genre that Stephen Greenblatt proposed in *Marvelous Possessions*. For Greenblatt, wonder is the defining experience of the early modern travelogue. He writes in his New Historicist work from 1991:

> Columbus's voyage initiated a century of intense wonder. European culture experienced something like the 'startle reflex' one can observe in infants: eyes widened, arms outstretched, breathing stilled, the whole body momentarily convulsed. But what does it mean to experience wonder? What are its origins, its uses, and its limits? Is it closer to pleasure or pain, longing or horror?[38]

And, we might ask, what room could disgust have in the experience of wonder? Perhaps it is accounted for in the sense of horror that Greenblatt includes within the spectrum of wonder. Conversely, it is possible that disgust takes the place of wonder in some travelogues. The myth of the New World as a terrestrial paradise allows for wonder in this body of travel narratives, whereas the myth of the Cape as degenerate only provokes disgust. Coetzee puts it succinctly: "Africa could never, in the European imagination, be the home of the earthly paradise because Africa was not a new world. The western Eden drew its power from a confluence of circumstances none of which would hold for a rival African paradise"[39]

It might be tempting then to suggest that wonder, like disgust, is geographically specific. Yet I want to propose the contrary. Disgust finds different modes of articulation in the different geographical terrains of the early modern travelogue, but it nevertheless does persist across geographical boundaries. Interestingly, Greenblatt's first mention of the ambiguities associated with wonder in the New World draws on Jean de Lery's *History of a Voyage to the Land of Brazil*, in which the Huguenot pastor is overcome with revulsion at the religious assembly of the Tupinamba in the Bay of Rio.[40] As he is sitting down to breakfast, de Lery hears their low murmuring, sees them alternately swaying and foaming at the mouth, and concludes that the devil had taken possession of their bodies. For Greenblatt it is in this moment that wonder manifests itself as a shudder of revulsion, before being transformed into ravishment at the harmony of their singing voices. Viewed as such, wonder need not preclude the experience of revulsion or disgust, allowing as it does an intense experience of the other. In the "Discourse of the Cape," ravishment rarely follows revulsion. But its interjections of disgust, as with de Lery's experience of an interrupted breakfast and a strange, apparently Satanic ritual, convey the writers' sense of the bizarre amid the banal.

If disgust is not confined to particular geographical regions, neither is it confined to the perceived savage or the primitive. In European travel writing about the highly civilized Mughal and Ottoman empires, disgust persists, albeit differently inflected. As Ania Loomba has pointed out, "Medieval notions of wealth, despotism, and power attaching to the East (and especially to the Islamic East) were . . . reworked to create an alternate version of savagery understood not as lack of civilization but as an excess of it, as decadence rather than primitivism."[41] George Sandys, who traveled to the Ottoman Court around 1610, dwells extensively on the disgusting food habits of Sultan Ahmet I.[42] This section of his travelogue reads like a blazon of disgust, moving from one body part to the next, each noting the Sultan's excess and corpulence:

> He is, in this yeare 1610, about the age of three and twenty, strongly limd, & of a just stature, yet greatly inclining to be fat: insomuch as sometimes he is ready to choke as he feeds, and some do purposely attend to free him from that danger . . . His aspect is as hauty as his Empire is large, he beginneth already to abstaine from exercise; yet are there pillars with inscriptions in his Seraglio, betweene which he threw a great iron mace, that memorise both his strength, and activity. Being on a time rebuked by his father Mahomet that he neglected so much his exercises and studies, he made this reply: that, Now he was too old to begin to learne . . . whereat the Sultan wept bitterly.[43]

Unlike the inhabitants of the Cape where Sandys' contemporaries traveled, the Sultan does not eat entrails or cow dung. Nevertheless, the description of his gastronomic rituals is intended to provoke disgust. Strangely tempered by awe, Sandys moves schizophrenically from one affect to the other. In this respect, his narrative embodies the many contradictions that Daniel Vitkus and others have shown typify the early modern English construction of Islamic power.[44] He notes the Sultan's "just stature," his well-proportioned face, and his extraordinary eyes. This admiring gaze, however, is interrupted by reference to the sultan's gluttony. He is "inclining to be fat," so much so that "sometimes he is ready to choke as he feeds." Sultan Ahmat I appears alternately as an omnipotent god-like figure and a helpless infantile creature. In likening his expansive body to his vastly impressive empire, Sandys grudgingly admires the larger-than-life monarch. Almost immediately, however, he reduces him to a stubborn child who, despite admonishments from his father, will exercise neither his mental nor his physical abilities.

Likewise, the Sultan's sexuality is evoked through opposing images of virility and emasculation. We are told of the many virgins and "choicest beauties of the Empire" that the Sultan keeps in his seraglio, apparently purged and dieted for several months in preparation for his pleasure. Despite his lascivious ways, however, the Sultan is only slightly more virile than his castrated eunuchs: "For all his multitude of women, he hath yet begotten but two sonnes and three daughters, though he be that way unsatiably given."[45] He even consumes "all sorts of foods that may inable performance," but they appear to do him little good.[46] Cast paradoxically in terms of excess and lack, the Sultan's rituals of sexual and gustatory consumption together become the locus of contempt-disgust.

If particular foodstuffs take on a disgusting character in travel narratives to the Ottoman Court, it is not because they are mired in filth as with the Hottentots, but because they come to be associated with filthy rituals. The lore of cucumbers and the illicit uses to which they could be put in the female seraglio is a case in point. Edward Grimestone's English translation of a French description of the Ottoman Court provides the salacious details of how food might be a source of sexual pleasure in the women's chambers, and the precautions taken against it:

> Fruits are sent unto them with circumspection: If their appetites demand any pompeons which are somewhat long, or cowcumbers, and such other fruits, they cut them at the Gate in slices, not suffering them to passe among them any slight occasion of doing evil, so bad an opinion they have of their continencie. It is (without doubt) a signe of the Turks violent jealousie: for who can in the like case hinder a vicious women from doing evill?[47]

Pleasure and disgust mingle in this writer's erotic speculation about food and female transgression in the Ottoman Court. Likewise, in writings on the Mughal Court the libidinal and the culinary are closely linked. Reverend Terry, whose encounter with the Hottentots is discussed above, had a very different perception of food and the foreign in the Islamic East. In a passage on the monarch's private realm he chronicles in detail the fine culinary preparations for which the court is renowned. But Terry's discussion of the culinary pleasures of the court is framed by his disgust at its sexual excesses:

> There lodge none in the Kings house but his women and eunuches, and some little boyes which hee keepes about him for a wicked use. Hee alwayes eates in private among his women upon great varietie of excellent dishes, which dressed and prooved by the taster are served in vessels of gold (as they say), covered and sealed up, and so by eunuchs brought to the King. He hath meate ready at all houres, and calls for it at pleasure. They feede not freely on full dishes of beefe and mutton (as we), but much on rice boyled with pieces of flesh or dressed many other ways. They have not many roast or baked meats, but stew most of their flesh. Among many dishes of this kinde he take notice but of one they call Deu Pario made of venison cut in slices, to which they put onions and herbs, some rootes, with a little spice and butter: the most savorie meate I ever tasted, and doe almost thinke it that very dish which Jacob made ready for his father, when he got the blessing.[48]

The dish in question, what Terry calls "Deu Pario," was in fact, *dupiyazah*, a dish that continues to be a staple of Mughlai cuisine on the Indian subcontinent.[49]

Terry's pleasure in partaking of it is apparent. He appears to relish the seasoning, the spices, and the meats, the extolling of which culminates in his description of "Deu Pario" as a preparation of biblical quality. But the general air of degenerate consumption in his description is unmistakable. The King's women, his eunuchs, and his boys kept about for "a wicked use" frame this vignette of culinary indulgence. If Terry's readers are to join in the pleasures of Mughal cuisine, they are also to deplore its sexual licentiousness. Terry's travelogue seems intent on presenting the culinary and the sexual together as evidence of a hedonistic regime.

Among the travelers most willing to partake of the bizarre foods of the Mughal Court and immerse himself in its unfamiliar food-related rituals is the Italian runaway Niccolao Manucci. As Jonathan Gil Harris puts it, Manucci's travelogue is a "foodie's dream."[50] In his characteristically playful tone, Manucci devotes long passages of his *Storia da Mogor* to his gastronomic experiences. Such passages offer a range of affective experiences from pleasure, to disgust, to shock. While traveling through Surat in the late seventeenth century, for instance, Manucci suddenly notices everyone spitting blood. When he enquires of a female English acquaintance whether the people of the town suffer from a malady or from broken teeth, she clarifies it is their habit of consuming the betel leaf and invites him to share one with her. Manucci gladly accepts the *paan*, but the taste has him in such shock that he swoons, faints, and has to be treated with smelling salts:

> Having taken them, my head swam to such an extent that I feared I was dying. It caused me to fall down; I lost my colour, and endured agonies; but she poured into my mouth a little salt, and brought me to my senses. The lady assured me that everyone who ate it for the first time felt the same effects.[51]

In the schema of contempt-disgust that we have seen at work in travel writing on the Hottentots and others, Manucci's physiological response here seems atypical. It appears to be neither contempt nor disgust, simply shock brought on by his distaste for *paan*. But as Natalie K. Eschenbaum and Barbara Correll point out in the introduction to this volume, the word "*Disgust* comes from the French, *desgoust* (modern *dégoût*), which in turn comes from the Latin *dis*- and *gustus* ("distaste") and refers to the physical sense of taste" (p. 4). This etymological connection signals to us the primacy of taste in the traveler's experience of both distaste and disgust. Foodstuffs and the rituals surrounding their consumption bear out the many valences of the phrase "good taste," both in a literal culinary sense and in a broader metaphorical sense of qualitative judgment. The travelers to the Cape, for instance, express distaste in an evaluative sense that links it to disgust. But as far as we know they did not risk tasting the dung-seasoned entrails they claimed to have seen, and in a literal culinary sense, they feel no distaste. That Manucci is among the few to readily take on the dangers of the culinary contact zone makes him an especially good candidate for a consideration of disgust as well as distaste.

Indeed, Manucci provides us with opportunities for the observation of both. Around April 1661, when an embassy from the province of Balkh in modern-day Afghanistan visited the Mughal Court and Manucci's services as physician were called upon, he felt an unmistakable sense of both distaste and disgust. While he appears to have been intrigued by the gifts they brought for the monarch, particularly the nuts, fruits, and aphrodisiacs made from a certain kind of fish spawn, in general Manucci was not impressed by the envoys' dirty, rustic habits. When prevailed upon to offer his medical expertise to one of the sick members of this entourage, Manucci confesses to his readers that he has little skill for the treatment but is anxious to see how "these savages" live.[52] When, however, he made it to their dwelling place, like Fryke in the Hottentot hut, he was overcome with revulsion by its odors. As a physician he could not flee the site of observation as Fryke did, so he feigned "great solemnity" but confesses his disgust to his readers: "When I had gone in I found the patient on a very dirty bed in a fetid sweat with the odour of very rotten cheese. I ordered his urine to be shown, and it, too, smelt the same."[53]

Manucci's distaste and disgust become most apparent when he is forced to dine with the envoys. In a particularly vivid passage he presents a scene of men with food-stained mustaches, digging into the flesh of camels with their bare hands, begging for more fat in their already greasy food, and ending the meal with their "eructations" as loud as bulls:

> Almost every day that I went there I was obliged to dine with the envoy, and I thus had the chance of observing their mode of eating . . . The food was flesh of camels and of horses cooked with salt in water, and some dishes of pulao of goat's flesh. The cloth, spread upon a carpet, was very dirty . . . It was disgusting to see how these Uzbak nobles ate, smearing their hands, lips, and faces with grease while eating, they having neither forks nor spoons . . . Mahomedans are accustomed after eating to wash their hands with pea-flour to remove grease, and most carefully clean their moustaches. But the Uzbak nobles do not stand on such ceremony. When they have done eating, they lick their fingers, so as not to lose a grain of rice; they rub one hand against the other to warm the fat, and then pass both hands over face, moustaches, and beard. He is most lovely who is the most greasy . . . The conversation hardly gets beyond talk of fat, with complaints that in the Mogul territory they cannot get anything fat to eat, and that the pulaos are deficient in butter. As a salute to their repletion, they emit loud eructations, just like the bellowing of bulls.[54]

What Manucci evinces here is distaste in the complex sense of a literal judgment about what the envoys eat, but also in a more metaphorical sense of an evaluative judgment about the way they eat. Perhaps his writings provide more opportunities for such a distinction since the medical practitioner more willingly ingests substances and is, in turn, more involved in what his subjects ingest. Manucci's experiences in the culinary contact zone, whether experimenting with *paan*, relishing a *pulao*, or sharing a greasy meal with a seemingly unmannerly group of visiting dignitaries, suggest ways in which the traveler is equally transformed by the experiences of pleasure and disgust.

But what of the subject being chronicled? In the many travelogues discussed above, we get few opportunities to observe their transformation, their affective responses to the foreign travelers in their domains, and their own sense of disgust at the outsiders' dietary practices. For the most part, as Singh observes of Reverend Terry's narrative, the traveler plays the part of ventriloquist, offering little by way of his subjects' motives, feelings, or reactions.[55] But it seems fitting to look at a rare moment in which the writer of the travelogue becomes aware of his subjects' disgust. Darwin reminds us of this in his own account of a Tierra del Fuego man touching his food and the mutual sense of disgust experienced by the traveler and the native: "In Tierra del Fuego a native touched with his finger some cold preserved meat which I was eating at our bivouac, and plainly showed utter disgust at its softness; whilst I felt utter disgust at my food being touched by a naked savage, though his hands did not appear dirty."[56] It is a moment in which the traveler is made conscious of his own status as a polluting object. And crucially, it is a moment during a ritualized meal.

The example I wish to consider here is a shared meal between an English traveler, Sir Thomas Roe, King James's ambassador to the court of Emperor Jahangir, and a Mughal official. An employee of the East India Company, Roe traveled to the Mughal Court from 1615 to 1619 to secure trading rights in the region. Stopping at the Cape of Good Hope, he reproduced almost verbatim much of what we have already encountered in the "Discourse of the Cape": the Hottentots are "the most barbarous in the world," they eat carrion, they wear the guts of sheep about their neck, and they rub their heads with dirt and the dung of beasts.[57] But in the Mughal Court, Roe encounters a slightly different sense of food, filth, and the foreign, particularly in an encounter recorded in August 1616.

For the most part, Roe found the many food-related rituals he encountered tiresome. In an irate journal entry he complains about the twenty melons that had been sent to him as a present by an official: "Doubtlesse they suppose our felicitye lyes in the palate, for all that ever I received was eatable and drinkable – yet no *aurum potabile*."[58] While the potable gold that Roe had wished for never comes his way, a much sought-after invitation to dine with Mir Jamal-uddin Husain finally arrives. Roe gladly accepts, hoping to benefit from the strategic alliance with an important official at court. The meal is planned in the King's gardens, an elaborate tent is erected, and a banquet is prepared. But after several warm exchanges, when dinner is brought, Jamal-uddin begins to retreat from the scene so he can eat with his own people. Roe becomes painfully aware that their rituals would not permit them to dine with him, "they houlding it a kind of uncleanness to mingle with us." He feebly objects: "Whereat I tould him hee promised wee should eate bread and salt together: that without his company I had little appetite. Soe hee rose and sate by mee, and wee fell roundly to our victuals."[59] After his host politely agrees to dine with him, Roe goes on to describe the many fruits and nuts that were served as part of the banquet, but reveals that another guest confessed his countrymen would take it amiss if they ate together.

Since we hear these voices only as Roe channels them, we never get the full range of their affective resonances. Yet it seems that Roe represents the polluting subject. The traveler, as outsider, perhaps poses the greatest danger to the rituals of purity associated with food preparation and food consumption. While this is only hinted at in Roe's travelogue, we might begin to imagine what such a potential for disgust from the object of disgust implies for other cultural encounters chronicled in the travelogue. We might think of how such lived experiences of disgust (and pleasure), possibly mutual, necessitated by the logistics of travel, shaped the genre as a whole. More generally, we might think of the implications of these cibarious experiences in the contact zone, where the food habits of diverse groups come into contact or conflict or confluence in ways that have not been adequately explored. As Kim Hall states, "While language and sex/desire do produce intimate points of convergence . . . food is in literary studies a less theorized way that societies mark cross-cultural encounters and articulate changing notions of difference"[60] It is in genres like the early modern travelogue that cross-cultural differences are constantly articulated and negotiated in the affective responses of the traveler and his subjects, most obviously so when they settle down to the simultaneously banal and bizarre routine of a meal.

Notes

1 The term is used by J.M. Coetzee in *White Writing*, 15.
2 See Nicholas Withington's travelogue in Raven-Hart, *Before Van Riebeeck*, 60.
3 Fryke, *Relation*, 211–12.
4 Pratt, *Imperial Eyes*, 7.
5 Fryke, *Relation*, 211.
6 Pratt, *Imperial Eyes*, 78.
7 Tomkins, *Shame*, 135.
8 Coetzee, *White Writing*, 16.
9 Tomkins, *Shame*, 135.
10 Qtd. in Tomkins, *Shame*, 135–6.
11 Kristeva, *Powers*, 71.
12 Kristeva, *Powers*, 71.
13 Douglas, *Purity and Danger*, 2.
14 Pratt, *Imperial Eyes*, 6.
15 Coetzee, *White Writing*, 13.
16 Clark, *Travel Writing*, 1.
17 With the exception of Fryke, all the travelers to the Cape cited here are from excerpts printed in Raven-Hart, *Before Van Riebeeck*. Here: 18.
18 Kamps and Singh, *Travel Knowledge*, 198.
19 Raven-Hart, *Before Van Riebeeck*, 33.
20 Steinmetz, *Devil's Handwriting*, 82, n. 34.
21 Raven-Hart, *Before Van Riebeeck*, 33.
22 Raven-Hart, *Before Van Riebeeck*, 42.
23 Raven-Hart, *Before Van Riebeeck*, 46.
24 Raven-Hart, *Before Van Riebeeck*, 48.
25 Raven-Hart, *Before Van Riebeeck*, 60, 59.
26 Raven-Hart, *Before Van Riebeeck*, 60.
27 Raven-Hart, *Before Van Riebeeck*, 100.
28 Raven-Hart, *Before Van Riebeeck*, 100–101.
29 Raven-Hart, *Before Van Riebeeck*, 100.
30 For an excellent discussion of the Hottentot Venus, see Gilman, "Black Bodies, White Bodies."
31 Steinmetz, *Devil's Handwriting*, 86.

32 Raven-Hart, *Before Van Riebeeck*, 83.
33 For an excellent discussion of this etching and other visual depictions of the Hotten-tots, see Steinmetz, *Devil's Handwriting*, 84–6.
34 I have drawn much of this information from Steinmetz, *Devil's Handwriting*, 91.
35 Qtd. in Steinmetz, *Devil's Handwriting*, 92.
36 Qtd. in Steinmetz, *Devil's Handwriting*, 92.
37 Qtd. in Steinmetz, *Devil's Handwriting*, 32.
38 Greenblatt, *Marvelous Possessions*, 14.
39 Coetzee, *White Writing*, 2.
40 Greenblatt, *Marvelous Possessions*, 16–20.
41 Loomba, *Colonialism/Postcolonialism*, 95.
42 Loomba, *Colonialism/Postcolonialism*, 109.
43 A section of Sandys' essay is excerpted in Kamps and Singh, *Travel Knowledge*, 23–4.
44 Vitkus, "Trafficking with the Turk."
45 Kamps and Singh, *Travel Knowledge*, 25.
46 Kamps and Singh, *Travel Knowledge*, 25.
47 Qtd. in Vitkus, "Trafficking with the Turk," 47.
48 Foster, *Early Travels*, 311.
49 Prasad, *Early English Travellers*, 301.
50 Harris, "Part V."
51 Manucci, *Storia do Mogor*, 62–3.
52 Manucci, *Storia do Mogor*, 39.
53 Manucci, *Storia do Mogor*, 39.
54 Manucci, *Storia do Mogor*, 40–41.
55 Kamps and Singh, *Travel Knowledge*, 204.
56 Qtd. in Miller, *Anatomy*, 1.
57 Foster, *Embassy*, 4.
58 Foster, *Embassy*, 152.
59 Foster, *Embassy*, 212.
60 Hall, "Extravagant Viciousness," 94.

References

Clark, Steve, ed. *Travel Writing and Empire: Postcolonial Theory in Transit*. London and New York: Zed Books, 1999.
Coetzee, J.M. *White Writing: On the Culture of Letters in South Africa*. New Haven: Yale University Press, 1988.
Douglas, Mary. *Purity and Danger: An Analysis of the Concepts of Pollution and Taboo*. London: Routledge, 1966.
Foster, William, ed. *Early Travels in India 1583–1619*. London: Oxford University Press, 1921.
——— ed. *The Embassy of Sir Thomas Roe to India: As Narrated in his Journal and Correspondence*. New Delhi: Munshiram Manoharlal, 1990.
Fryke, Christopher, and Christopher Schweitzer. *A Relation of Two Several Voyages Made into the East Indies*. London: D. Brown, 1700.
Gilman, Sander L. "Black Bodies, White Bodies: Toward an Iconography of Female Sexuality in Late Nineteenth-Century Art, Medicine, and Literature." *Critical Inquiry* 12, no. 1 (Autumn 1985): 204–42.
Greenblatt, Stephen. *Marvelous Possessions: The Wonder of the New World*. Chicago: University of Chicago Press, 1991.

Hall, Kim F. "'Extravagant Viciousness': Slavery and Gluttony in the Works of Thomas Tryon." In *Writing Race across the Atlantic World: Medieval to Modern*, edited by Philip D. Beidler and Gary Taylor, 93–111. New York: Palgrave Macmillan, 2005.

Harris, Jonathan Gil. "Part V: The Siddha Vaidya of Madras." *Hindustan Times*, December 10, 2011. Accessed August 4, 2014. http://www.hindustantimes.com/StoryPage/Print/780466.aspx.

Kamps, Ivo, and Jyotsna G. Singh, eds. *Travel Knowledge: European "Discoveries" in the Early Modern Period*. New York: Palgrave, 2001.

Kristeva, Julia. *Powers of Horror: An Essay on Abjection*. Translated by Leon S. Roudiez. New York: Columbia University Press, 1982.

Loomba, Ania. *Colonialism/Postcolonialism*. New York: Routledge, 1998.

Manucci, Niccolao. *Storia do Mogor; or, Mogul India 1653–1708*. Translated by William Irvine. 2 vols. London: Government of India, 1907.

Miller, William Ian. *The Anatomy of Disgust*. Cambridge, MA: Harvard University Press, 1997.

Prasad, Ram Chandra. *Early English Travellers in India: A Study of the Travel Literature of the Elizabethan and Jacobean Periods with Particular Reference to India*. Delhi: Motilal Banarsidass, 1965.

Pratt, Mary Louise. *Imperial Eyes: Travel Writing and Transculturation*. New York: Routledge, 1992.

Raven-Hart, Major R. *Before Van Riebeeck: Callers at South Africa from 1488 to 1652*. Cape Town: C. Struik, 1967.

Steinmetz, George. *Devil's Handwriting: Precoloniality and the German Colonial State in Qingdao, Samoa, and Southwest Africa*. Chicago: University of Chicago Press, 2007.

Tomkins, Silvan. *Shame and Its Sisters: A Silvan Tomkins Reader*. Edited by Eve Kosofsky Sedgwick and Adam Frank. Durham, NC: Duke University Press, 1995.

Vitkus, Daniel. "Trafficking with the Turk: English Travelers in the Ottoman Empire during the Early Seventeenth Century." In *Travel Knowledge: European "Discoveries" in the Early Modern Period*, edited by Ivo Kamps and Jyotsna G. Singh, 35–52. New York: Palgrave, 2001.

7 "Qualmish at the smell of leek"

Overcoming disgust and creating the nation-state in *Henry V*

Colleen E. Kennedy

As sensory historian Mark S.R. Jenner has argued, it is better to fully follow the whiff of a particular savor than to create a grand narrative that privileges sight as modern and evolved, relegating the lower senses of taste, touch, and smell to some uncivilized place in the past.[1] Jenner's study briefly follows the sensate history and reception of garlic in England. Beginning with "the English aversion to the smell of garlic [as] stereotypically one aspect of the Victorian repression of sensuality," Jenner notes that "there is considerable evidence of English aversion to the pungent herb in previous centuries."[2] While dislike of the smell of garlic is often simply xenophobic – garlic is usually represented as a French or Italian food – or even more prominently "a marker of social (and not just national) distinction throughout the early modern period," Jenner observes that garlic is also associated with religious austerity. Garlic was listed in herbals as having some medicinal qualities; and most importantly, despite all of the representations of the poor, foreign, reeking garlic-stench, "garlic *was* being cultivated and used."[3] By creating such a nuanced osmology and history of garlic odors in England, Jenner suggests how we must encounter the scents and sensibilities of the past. Unlike Jenner's garlic, however, the leek that features so prominently in Shakespeare's *Henry V* is not just a pungent vegetable. It is, rather, a cultural emblem of Wales, which further complicates both olfactory and literary representations.

In *Henry V*, the Welsh captain Fluellen's leek is introduced when the braggart English soldier Pistol tells Henry, disguised as a Welsh gentleman Harry Le Roy, that if "Harry" were to meet up with his captain, he should deliver a message from Pistol: "Tell him I'll knock his leek about his pate / Upon St. Davy's Day" (4.1.55–6).[4] Fluellen later recounts to the king the Welsh tradition of wearing "leeks on their Monmouth caps" as an "honorable badge" in remembrance of St David, the patron saint of Wales, for "the Welshman did good service in a garden where leeks did grow" (4.7.96–102). In Act V of the play, Fluellen again speaks of the Welsh leek – as well as his growing displeasure with Pistol – while conversing with the English Captain Gower. Joan Fitzpatrick claims, "Fluellen is insulted by Pistol's suggestion that he eat the leek because the object has been demoted from noble symbol of Welsh pride to a mere vegetable and, furthermore, one that will be consumed with basic foodstuffs as bread and salt."[5] The disrespected Fluellen later beats Pistol and forces him to eat the leek. Pistol's most quarrelsome words to

Fluellen – the catalyst for his beating – express his apparent disgust at Fluellen's leeky aroma: "Hence! I am qualmish at the smell of leek" (5.1.21).

The lowly leek has received a good deal of critical attention in recent scholarship.[6] The leek may be viewed as sacred or profane, a sign of national pride that may be reassuring or threatening. Allison M. Outland makes a convincing argument that "*feeding* the leek to Pistol opens up the possibility that he too could become part of the community by ingesting, embodying its symbolic representation." That is, the leek is part of "the cultural mystery of British national transubstantiation."[7] Patricia Parker, rather than reading this as a sort of forced communion, offers a more profane interpretation: the force-feeding is a type of sexualized violence, building upon a homophonic reading of "leek/leak" as representing "breaches/breeches" in the body politic of England.[8] Krystian Czerniecki plays with the puns of "di(s)gest/dis-jest," focusing on the theme of mockery. To Czerniecki, the recurring oral puns undermine the introjective project of staging a history play: "In a word, the play suggests to mock the past *is* to eat the past."[9] Ruben Espinosa reads the scene as enacting larger English anxieties over immigration and England's need to assert its superiority through cultural difference, but sees Fluellen's national pride as ennobling.[10] Megan S. Lloyd, however, reads Fluellen's muscular mastery over Pistol as demonstrating that "Fluellen still has not completely learned how to fit in."[11] Joan Fitzpatrick reads Shakespeare's leek through the lens of early modern dietaries to describe how early modern theatergoers would have known and thought of the leek not as a symbol of Wales, but as a potentially harmful herb.[12]

My own intervention in this conversation on the Welsh leek is to recover the importance of culinary memory, which begins before Shakespeare's famous food fight and afterward evolves into the national symbol of Wales. In the first Arden edition of *Henry V*, Herbert Arthur Evans claims, "For fact of service done by Welshmen in a garden of leeks . . . Fluellen remains our only authority."[13] Over one hundred years later, the source for Fluellen's leek remains undiscovered.[14] Patricia Parker reads Fluellen's speech on why the Welsh wear leeks on St David's Day as "simultaneous memorializing and strategic forgetting," claiming that Fluellen's patriotic narrative is "compounded by the fact that this passage itself is a fictive construction of Shakespeare's invention, with no corroboration from any independent history."[15] Unlike, say, the loftier, nationalistic, more overtly masculine, mythic, or patristic memories generated and shared in *Henry V*, the importance of the Welsh leek – if it is simultaneously Shakespeare's invention and yet Fluellen's (and Henry's) collective "memorable honour" (4.7.103) – belongs instead to a realm of culinary memories: lowlier, regionalized, feminized, folky, domestic, and potentially disgusting.[16] I suggest that the leek was common enough in gardens or growing uncultivated throughout Britain to be perceived as native to the kingdom as the Welsh, and it was smelly enough to signify that the Welsh were different from the English, yet not *too* different – not as malodorous, say, as garlic or onions. This signification holds true whether Fluellen and his Welsh leeks are Shakespeare's creations, or whether Shakespeare's play simply led to more common representations of the leek as distinctly Welsh.[17]

Reading the represented smell of the leek alongside early modern dietaries, herbals, and recipe books, ballads, broadsides, histories, and hagiographies, as well as contemporary theories on affect and disgust, I argue that the smell of the leek creates a loaded olfactory signifier and, when read as analogous to the smell of the Welshman's body, complicates the nationalistic readings of the play.[18] While the jingoist overtones of *Henry V* have been explored by many scholars, I offer a reading that focuses on the odor and sociocultural importance of leeks to understand issues of disgust, tolerance, and incorporation, all key issues in building a coherent nation-state. The scenes that focus on Fluellen's Welsh leek undermine ideals of national unity because ethnic difference is literally smelt out, yet perceived differences level out again as the Welsh leek is incorporated into the English body and the British garden. My argument thus is in line with other theories that attempt to recover the ambivalent status of Wales in early modern unification projects but it arrives at this conclusion through other routes – the nose and the stomach. I end by touching upon the larger implications of the leek as it acquires the status of odorous symbol of British assimilation and nation-building.

"Qualmishness": Recovering early modern disgust

Smell is a chief aspect of disgust and one of the more visceral and moralizing responses toward an ethnic other. Disgust remains an overlooked element in the larger arguments of nationalism and unification in this play. The insistence on the foreign Welsh aroma of the leek in contrast to the perceived representation of the inodorous – and dominant – English body incites disgust in Pistol. The leek reeks to Pistol because it is a Welsh odor, and Fluellen, despite his attempt to speak English, his loyalty to the English King Henry, and his bravery fighting for the English on the battlefield, smells distinctly not English. In the long run, this repugnance reveals more about Pistol's inability to properly assimilate to a unified and diverse Britain than it does about Fluellen as a potential foreigner. There is, however, nothing inherently disgusting about the leek, which is why it is such a complexly represented food and loaded signifier.

In *The Anatomy of Disgust*, William Ian Miller recovers a lexicon of Shakespeare's disgust-related terms in the tragedies, reminding us that Shakespeare "does not use the word *disgust*." Miller convincingly concludes from his survey, "The idiom of disgust constantly invokes the sensory experience."[19] Unlike other universal emotions such as happiness or anger, we indicate our disgust to others by employing vivid corporeal metaphors and sensory language. Pistol's "qualmishness" presents another example of Shakespeare's "specific vocabulary of disgust before the word disgust."[20] Furthermore, expressing disgust includes several almost universal physical characteristics: the wrinkled nose, the protruding tongue, the curled upper lip, and the head pulled away from the object of disgust, all expressions that we could imagine played on the early modern stage for great effect.[21] Likewise, Julia Kristeva introduces readers to her concept of the abject, the aversion of that which one does not wish to incorporate into the body or incorporeal self, with the simplest, most universal of responses: disgust toward a particular food – in her case, "that skin on the surface of milk." "Food loathing," Kristeva argues, "is perhaps the most elementary and most archaic form of abjection."[22]

Recoiling from a particular foodstuff is also highly indicative of ethnic difference. As the sensory psychologist Rachel Herz writes on contemporary issues of disgust, food odors, and the foreign threat:

> We learn which foods are disgusting and which are not through our cultural heritage. One reason why foods are so locally meaningful is because they come from the flora, fauna, and microbes of a given region, which can vary markedly between geographic areas. Another reason why culture is such an important determinant of the meaning of food is because we use food as a way of establishing brethren or foes, and as a mode of ethnic distinction. "I eat this thing and you don't. I am from here, and you are from there." Not only is the meaning of food learned through culture, food is used to establish cultural boundaries and borders.[23]

In *Henry V*, the leek operates as such "a mode of ethnic distinction," not between the warring French and English armies, but rather within the British army. Herz continues: "In every culture, 'foreigners' eat strange meals that have strange aromas, and their bodies reek of their strange food. These unfamiliar aromas are traditionally associated with the unwanted invasion of the foreigners and thus are considered unwelcome and repugnant."[24] The international war is comically inverted and replicated in the intra-national squabbles between English and Welsh soldiers' appreciation or disgust for the leek.

In Pistol's brief phrase – "Hence! I am qualmish at the smell of leek" – we have all the markers of disgust (5.1.21). "Hence" acts as imperative or demand, telling Fluellen to move away, and as interjection from the shock of the scent. If the smell of leek has entered Pistol's nostrils, the aitch of "hence" creates a strong and quick exhalation through the mouth to utter the command, which the exclamation mark stresses and augments. "Qualmish" – similar to our own "squeamish" or "queasy" – is synonymous with nausea. According to the *Oxford English Dictionary,* the adjective "qualmish" indicates "affected, or liable to be affected, with a qualm or qualms; (now esp.) affected with nausea, queasy."[25] Whether Pistol feels physical revulsion or merely uses such language to further insult Fluellen, he claims that either Fluellen's national pride or his bad breath moves him to the point of vomiting.

The English might note the toasted cheese and leek aromas of the Welshman, but wish to privilege themselves as inodorous.[26] Michel de Montaigne goes so far to state that "the best characteristic we can hope for is to smell of nothing,"[27] and even now in the modern Western world "groups in the centre – politicians, businessmen – are characterized by a symbolic lack of scent."[28] Holly Dugan argues, "A sixteenth-century stage devoid of smell is anachronistic."[29] A constant stinking threat within the theatre is the groundlings. Thomas Dekker seems to have had a particular aversion to garlic, as he often complained of the stenches of the lower classes and generally referred to the groundlings as "garlic-mouthed stinkards."[30] According to some editorial glosses, it is not the leek in Fluellen's hat that gives off the "noxious vapour," but maybe his breath.[31] Pistol claims to be "qualmish at the smell of the leek," and he speaks aloud to the "garlic-breathed stinkards" when Fluellen brandishes a leek, an "olfactive prop," that smells not unlike the odors of the closest audience members.[32]

Writing on the spatial relationship of actors and groundlings in the opening season offering of *Henry V* (1997, dir. Richard Olivier) at the reconstructed Globe Theatre, Pauline Kiernan offers this anecdote of the staging of Pistol's disgrace:

> In the 'leek scene' towards the end of *Henry V* much of the stage business involved the groundlings who were standing up against the stage. Llewllyn (David Fielder) kept beating Pistol (John McEnert) until the latter landed flat on his back on the stage, his head hanging over the edge of the stage platform right amongst the heads of the groundlings. When Llewellyn stuffed the leek into the mouth of the prone soldier, Pistol spat out the chewed pieces so that they were sprayed all over the nearest groundlings.[33]

When I viewed a recent Globe Theatre production (2012, dir. Dominic Dromgoole), Sam Cox's Pistol was cudgeled and sat far downstage as he gnawed the leek. The sharpness of the leek caused his mouth to water and he drooled, spitting chunks into his hand that Fluellen (Brendan O'Hara) forced him to re-ingest. While these are contemporary staging choices, many eighteenth- and nineteenth-century illustrations and photographs represent this scene of the indignant and choleric Fluellen forcing Pistol to "eat a leek." The physical comedy – two loud characters arguing, funny accents and dialects, scuffling, slapstick violence, and the defeated Pistol chewing away at a fresh leek on stage – must have been popular with early modern audience members as well, not unlike a Punch and Judy puppet show.[34]

Even if Pistol and Fluellen cannot speak the same English, they can partake of the same Welsh foods and emit the same Welsh aromas. Rachel Herz finds important links between overcoming repugnance at foreign foods and entering into the community: "[A] person can become more accepted by eating the right foods – not only because their body odor will no longer smell unfamiliar and 'unpleasant,' but because acceptance of food implies acceptance of the larger system of cultural values at hand."[35] Ingesting the odoriferous leek would indicate that English culture is now assimilated into Welsh culture. This contradicts the dominant narrative, which asserts that the English incorporated the Welsh. Pistol would have to grow accustomed to his own Welshed body and aromas.

The culinary memory of the leek (Part 1): Eating the leek

As Fluellen beats Pistol, he lists the medicinal qualities of the leek and how applying the leek can counteract the damage done with his cudgel: "It is good for your green wound and bloody coxcomb" (5.1.44–5). Philemon Holland's 1634 translation of Pliny the Elder's *History of the World* gives this same leek-based cure: "And a cataplasm therof cureth green wounds."[36] This brief example demonstrates that the culinary and therapeutic uses of the leek are complex, and turning to herbals and dietaries allows us to undertake the larger sociocultural importance of the leek.

Joan Fitzpatrick notes the dietaries' warnings against eating raw leeks and claims that these show the rather dark and homicidal implications of this otherwise comic food fight between Pistol and Fluellen. Eating a raw leek could cause a host of conditions: vomiting, thirst, provoking urine, headaches, inspiring bad dreams, triggering stomachaches, "even death."[37] She concludes that "the leek was not especially associated with Wales or the Welsh in the dietaries and its exotic signification in *Henry V* stems from Fluellen's characterization of the vegetable as a symbol of Welsh pride and the dangers of eating it raw."[38]

By focusing only on the harmful attributes of the raw leek, however, Fitzpatrick's otherwise persuasive argument of "Celtic acquaintance and alterity" becomes reductive.[39] The leek is a common panacea in many early modern herbals and dietaries. The noted herbalist and botanist John Parkinson lists the medicinal aspects of the leek in his *Theatre of Plants* (1640), along with those of onion and garlic, which he groups together based on olfactive similarities. Parkinson observes its many positive qualities: leek provokes the winds and flatulence, rouses the appetite, increases thirst, eases stomach pains, provokes urine and women's courses, "helpe[s] the biting of a mad Dog, and of other venomous creatures," increases sperm, kills worms in children, and helps with a cough, as "the juice being snuffed up into the Nostrills, purgeth the head."[40] While most remedies include boiling the leek, extracting the juice and mixing it with another element – often breast milk, vinegar, or oil – the leek may be eaten raw to cure a few complaints: drunkenness, counteracting poisonous mushrooms, curing an extreme cough with much phlegm, and restoring a lost voice.[41] Pistol, a frequent customer of the Boar's Head Tavern who is notorious for his histrionics and bombastic speeches, could very well appreciate a cure for drunkenness and a lost voice.

Pistol's "qualmishness" aptly expresses his repugnance to the odor of the leek, but like the leek itself, it also has medical connotations. The term "qualmish" often describes morning sickness, and several remedies involve leek aromatherapies. According to Jacques Guillemeau's *Child-birth or, The Happy Deliuerie of Women* (1612), to determine "whether a woman be with childe, or no," the observer should note the patient's qualmishness: "Againe, if within few dayes she falles a vomiting, and spitting, distasts her meate, groweth dull, carelesse, and *qualmish*, longeth after strange things, finding her belly fallen, and growne flat."[42] Rembert Doedens, in a *New Herball* (1578), offers bathing in leek water or sitting over a fume of leeks as a cure for several gynecological complaints: "A bath of Leekes made with salt sea water, prouoketh womens flowers, openeth the stoppings of the Matrix, and doth mollifie and soften all hardnesse of the same, if they sit ouer the fume thereof."[43]

While several scholars have noted the phallic shape of the leek and the sexualized assault of Pistol, the emasculating implication of "qualmishness" emphasizes

Pistol's true temperament as a braggart coward, regardless of his choleric temper and flinty name.[44] Fluellen does not need to debase Pistol. Pistol undermines his own masculinity by comparing himself with a delicate and queasy pregnant woman, rather than with a valiant soldier who has trained his body to overcome the threats of noxious odors. The image of the queasy and effeminate Pistol aligns his body with several female bodies in the play, and thus slips from being a subject who is disgusted into the role of an object of disgust. This may anticipate Henry VI's birth – and by extension, Katherine's missing pregnancy – in the Chorus' Epilogue; the vulnerability of the virgins, mothers, and infants that Henry threatens to kill and defile at the gates of Harfleur; or even the syphilitic and comically sexualized bodies of Mistress Quickly and Doll Tearsheet, Pistol's wife who dies of "malady of France" (5.1.83).[45]

If Pistol's masculinity is threatened or in flux, so too is his nationality. The English Captain Gower chides Pistol for "mock[ing] an ancient custom" and tells him that his beating and humiliation have taught him how to become a better Englishman: "And henceforth let a Welsh correction teach you a good English condition" (5.1.71, 78). While Gower's concept of "correction" maintains its meaning of chastisement or corporal punishment, the *Oxford English Dictionary* reminds us that "correction" also means "the counteracting or neutralizing of the ill effect of (something hurtful or unpleasant)" and cites Gerard's *Herbal* as a prime example of this usage.[46] That is, ingesting the Welsh leek can teach Pistol how to become English while healing his improper condition. This medicinal or alchemical alteration fails to change Pistol, however, and he vows to return to England, not in "good English condition," but rather as a battered and bruised, widowed and diseased pimp. Fluellen may beat and humiliate Pistol, but he also offers him the food of his people and teaches him to behave *and smell* like a good British soldier.

The culinary memory of the leek (Part 2):
Smelling the leek

The homeopathic and medicinal efficacy of the leek is due to its aromatic potency. John Floyer's *Pharmako-Basanos, or the Touchstone of Medicines. Discovering the Vertues of Vegetables, Minerals, and Animals by Their Tastes and Smells* (1687) creates a comprehensive taxonomy of the tastes and smells of most plants native to England. He places leeks in his chapter on "plants in gardens and shops," indicating that the leek was cultivated, purchased, and consumed regularly throughout Britain. He writes about the leek: "The Taste and Smell are strong and rank, like Garlick, abounding with a volatile salt."[47] In that same spirit, for the herbalist Thomas Parkinson, the medicinal qualities seem to outweigh the possibility of harm or the offensive stench. He suggests several ways to counter the leek's stink:

> But to alter the strong sent therof and cause it to be less offensive, divers have set downe divers things, as some to eat Rue, or herbe Grace, some to eate a raw Beane after it, others to take of a Beete roote roasted under the Embers and others say by eating a few Parsley leaves.[48]

Sir Thomas More composed a Latin epigram on the leek's odor (first printed in 1518), and the satirist Sir John Harington translates this hierarchy of stench in his compendium on the flush toilet, *A New Discourse of a Stale Subject Called the Metamorphosis of Ajax* (1596):

> If Leeks you leeke [like], and do the smell disleeke
> Eat Onyons, and you shall not smell the Leeke,
> Yf you of Onyons would the sent expell,
> Eat garlick, that shall drowne the onyons smell.
> But against garlick savour, at one word,
> I know but one receite [recipe]. what's that? Go looke.[49]

Harington rewrites More's last line in *Ajax* as the coy riddle "Go look:" as in, search out More's original Latin and follow his instructions. In More's poem, the only cure for leek-onion-garlic breath is engaging in coprophagia.[50] As Jason Scott-Warren argues in his study of Harington's epigram collections, the courtier coyly leaves only brackets in the inscribed copy to his wealthy mother-in-law and changes the last line to "Tobacco" for Prince Henry's copy, whose father King James I was notoriously anti-tobacco.[51]

For both More and Harington, the dietary itself becomes a genre worthy of mockery, and Harington later returns to the form when he creates comic translations of the medical advice poem *The School of Salerno* (1608). Reading these dietaries and the More/Harington epigram together, we can sniff out the degrees and varieties of stench associated with the leek; it is represented as "rank and strong" in smell, but ultimately not as offensively malodorous as garlic or onion. Leek, then, when compared to feces, both elides with such decidedly disgusting items and/or may be deemed as innocuous and appetizing in contrast to such nauseating fare. In *Henry V*, overcoming the disgust for leeks is essential to the unification project, especially as the leek is a potent plant with healing properties, and in Fluellen's estimation, an herb associated with the patron saint of Wales, St David.

To wear the leek and eat it, too: St David's leek

The myth of St David and the leek may be Shakespeare's invention. But after *Henry V* is performed and published, the leek becomes Welshed in the collective memory: established as a foodstuff loved by Welshmen and as the sacred symbol of St David. Later sources add the Welsh affinity for leeks as culinary memory transforms. Ben Jonson's Wasp in *Bartholomew Fair* (1614) calls the watchman Bristle a "Welsh cuckold" and complains that "You stinke of leeks, *Metheglyn* [mead], and cheese. You Rogue" (4.6.52).[52]

As Fitzpatrick observes, the leek is not mentioned as a particularly Welsh food in the dietaries that Shakespeare may have consulted. Pistol's mocking of Fluellen by bringing the Welshman salt and bread to eat with his leek, however, appears to have influenced later sources. For example, in *Paradisi in sole paradisus terrestri,* a work dedicated to Queen Henrietta Maria, herself quite the gardener, Thomas Parkinson offers the medicinal qualities of the plant (citing heavily from earlier herbals), and a brief history:

> The old World, as wee finde in Scripture, in the time of the children of Israels being in Egypt, and no doubt long before, fed much upon Leekes, Onions, and Garlicke boyled with flesh; and the antiquity of the gentiles relate the same manner of feeding on them, to be in all Countries the like, which howsoever our dainty age now refuseth wholly, in all sorts except the poorest; yet Muscovia and Russia use them, and the Turkes to this day, (as Bellonius writeth) observe to have them among their dishes at their tables, yea although they be *Bashas, Cades or Vaiuodas,* that is to say, Lords, Judges, or Governours of countries and places. *They are used with us also sometimes in Lent to make pottage, and is a great and general feeding in Wales with the vulgar gentleman.*[53]

For the leek, we see a biblical utility for the plant, but in "our dainty age" most people ("of all countries") refuse to eat the leek. The exceptions are the Russians and the Turks, which are both foreign threats, and the "poorest" of Britain. Both these groups recall Jenner's association of garlic with poverty and foreignness. The "dainty age" belies the general narrative that the Renaissance was a time of utter filth and stench if Parkinson differentiates his own times as having delicate palates. Nonetheless, the English "us" according to Parkinson consume the leek during Lent, a time of religious austerity, and as a popular ingredient for the "vulgar gentleman" – here, probably those who speak Welsh.[54] Parkinson's brief history creates a decidedly oxymoronic term for the Welsh leek eaters, who are both common and yet also landholding men of noble birth. The Welsh are likened to the exiled Israelites, the Russians, and the Turks, but they are only like the English during Lent. No longer a visual reminder of St David, Welsh martial valor, or the Welsh as the true and ancient Britons, the leek is problematically identified by Parkinson either with foreign threats or reduced to the lowliest form of sustenance.

By the mid-seventeenth century, the leek is firmly established as a symbol of Wales, yet it remains a problematic nationalistic or ethnic flora. Pistol and Fluellen's argument concerning whether the leek should be worn as a sacred symbol or eaten with salt and bread is revived in several brief hagiographies and histories about St David. Michael Drayton's poetic reconstruction of England and Wales, *Poly-Olbion* (1612, 1622), tells of how St David encouraged soldiers to wear leeks. Drayton began composing his work around 1598, contemporary with *Henry V.*[55] Drayton's "reverent British saint" lived an ascetic and contemplative life, subsisting only on river water and "fed upon the Leeks he gather'd in the fields."[56] In Drayton's account, the lowly vegetable becomes elevated to a "sacred herb," not eaten by David's followers but worn in "memory" of the saint.[57] In the 1630 ballad "*The praise of Saint David's day Shewing the reason why the Welshman honour the leeke on that day,*" the Welshmen wear – and do not eat – the leek commemorating a battle fought on St David's Day, when these "true Britons" descended into a garden and wore leeks in their hats to identify each other as friends on the battlefield.[58]

Even as late as 1642, the custom of the Welsh wearing leeks on St David's Day required explication. The "Gentleman" T. Morgan, in his *The Welchmens Jubilee to the honour of St. David*, writes "Yet one thing I cannot omit, viz. their custome in wearing a green Leek on their hats on that day likewise: and here (Gentle Reader) give me leave to expatiate my self a while, to see whether I can scrutably, and in a credible probability search out the meaning, and cause of the same."[59] Morgan cites a Pistolian culinary claim for the custom ("their general affection" for the leek), but dismisses it as a "fallible" etiology before choosing a Fluellenistic account instead. Morgan claims that St David was revived by the aroma of the leek:

> It is more credibly declared, that S. David when hee always went into the field, in Martiall exercise, he carried a Leek with him; and once being almost faint to death, he immediately remembered himself of the Leek, and by that means not onely preserved his life, but also became victorious: hence is the Mythologie of the Leek derived, and hence it was that they ever since continued respectively the investigation of the same, to the sempiternal.[60]

The leek here belongs to a martial version of St David, not the ascetic hermit of Drayton's account. Its rank odor restores the saint's vigor and is even lauded as the means by which he "became victorious." This Saint David becomes, like Fluellen, a leek-carrying Welsh soldier.[61]

Leeks and roses

I would like to end with what I believe is a relatively faithful adaptation of Shakespeare's intended treatment of British tolerance and unification. In Laurence Olivier's patriotic Technicolor extravaganza, *Henry V,* the four captains of the British Isles meet briefly.[62] Olivier boldly presented the captains as mid-twentieth-century ethnic stereotypes, retaining the particulars of their dialects and representing the Irish MacMorris as a black-haired, infantilized hothead, Jamy the Scot as a red-bearded, affable sort, Fluellen with bushy eyebrows, exaggerated whiskers, and a disconcerting stare, and Englishman Gower as the straight man. Each Captain's surcoat is emblazoned with the flora that signifies his British nation: the Irish clover, Scotch thistle, English red (or Lancaster) rose, and the Welsh leek. What Shakespeare creates in this meeting is a microcosmic British Isles.[63] Olivier's depiction plays with the recurring imagery of England as garden that is a significant trope of the *Second Henriad*.[64] All of these flora have distinctive scents as well, especially the contrasting leek and rose. Symbolic of Wales, the leek becomes metonymically linked to the Welsh body, just as the rose is linked to the aristocratic English body.[65]

Indeed, another Englishman accepts the Welsh leek, odors and all: King Henry V. Fluellen recounts the cultural significance to Henry, but unlike Pistol who mocks the tradition of the wearing of the leek, Henry admits that he knows and honors the tradition, too: "I wear it for a memorable honor; / For I am Welsh, you know, good countryman" (4.7.103–4). Henry V is Henry of Monmouth, born in Wales, made Prince of Wales upon his father's coronation. He helped his father defeat the last independent monarch of Wales, Owen Glendower, in the previous play. Henry is Welsh and English. His reaction shows not only tolerance, but also pride: He, too, wears the Welsh leek on St Davy's Day. Henry's acceptance, here, should not be surprising. When he disguised himself, he reassured his comrades: "I think the king is but a man, as I am. The violet smells to him as it doth to me . . . all his senses have but human conditions" (4.1.99–102). Henry's nose smells the same odors as other British men. He has not been taught to be disgusted by the leek, but has rather learned the complexity of the aromatic and cultural significance of this herb.

Leeks and roses do not grow side by side in early modern gardening practice, as the former belongs to the herb or kitchen garden ("for the many different scents that arise from the herbes, as Cabbages, Onions, &c. are scarce well pleasing to perfume the lodgings of any house") and the latter to the flower or pleasure garden.[66] But in literary and political gardens, both may flourish together. To create a unified nation-state, the ideal garden extolled in *Richard II*, the garden must be fruitful and well ordered, comprehensive and diverse.

It would be quite a stretch to correlate all of these aromatic plants to the perceived bodily odors of the corresponding British captains, but it is not difficult to see how, in the case of the Welsh leek, this bodily and national scent are conflated. In his St Davy's Day speech, Fluellen reminds Henry V, "The Welshmen did good service in a garden where leeks did grow" (4.7.97–8). Patricia Parker compellingly claims, "Welsh Fluellen's memorial garden of Welsh 'leeks,' which evokes simultaneously the figure of containment and its inverse, undermines the rhetoric of union."[67] But Parker's nuanced argument of problematic leaks/leeks does not consider how the odors of the garden's plants operate.

The ideal *hortus conclusus* might be represented as entirely self-contained and impermeable. Avery Gilbert uses the metaphor of boundaries in describing differing culinary and aromatic cultural signifiers: "At cultural boundaries the smell of food becomes an invisible, fragrant fence."[68] This, however, is not the model presented in *Henry V*. This garden is imagined with Welsh leeks and Lancaster roses. In other words, the British garden grows best because of its natural diversity, and the potentially disgusting is incorporated into the body politic and sublimated into a more cohesive and aromatic whole. Whether Fluellen's aroma of leeks is proudly accepted (Henry V), simply tolerated (Gower), or mocked as disgusting (Pistol), all of the Englishmen inhale his decidedly Welsh odor. By incorporating Fluellen's aroma (even if only around St Davy's Day), we can be certain that the smell of any Briton contains a whiff of leeks.

Notes

1 Jenner, "Civilization and Deodorization," 143–4.
2 Jenner, "Civilization and Deodorization," 138.
3 Jenner, "Civilization and Deodorization," 139, 144.

4 William Shakespeare, *King Henry V*, ed. T.W. Craik, The Arden Shakespeare, Third Series (London: Bloomsbury, 2013). All quotations and references from *Henry V* are from this edition unless otherwise noted.

5 Fitzpatrick, *Food*, 41. Fitzpatrick also notes that in their first disagreement, Pistol mentions the obscene Spanish gesture and phrase "fico" ("Spanish fig"), 38–9.

6 The best overview of recent trends in Shakespearean Welsh scholarship is Maley's "Let a Welsh correction teach you."

7 Outland, "Eat a Leek," 100.

8 Parker, "Uncertain Unions," 97. The pun on "breaches" refers to the "Once more unto the breach" speech.

9 Czerniecki, "The Jest Disgested," 76.

10 Espinosa, "Fluellen's Foreign Influence."

11 Lloyd, *Speak It in Welsh*, 85.

12 Fitzpatrick, *Food*, 6.

13 Evans, *Life*, 136.

14 Although Shakespeare's major sources for *Henry V* are Holinshed's *Chronicles* and the anonymous *The Famous Victories of Henry the fifth* (published 1598), Fluellen does not appear in them. Scholars have tried to link Fluellen to Welsh historical figures, whether from Henry V's time period, Henry VII's, or Elizabeth I's, even looking up the names of Stratford's residents. Richard Levin warns of the fruitlessness of such "literary Fluellenism," "find[ing] parallels that have been consciously employed by the author to affect our response to his work. Most often these parallels relate one of the characters in the work to an extraliterary personage." Levin, "On Fluellen's Figures," 303. I do not intend to engage in a reading that recounts the politics and place of Wales in late Elizabethan Britain or the actual lives of early modern Welsh but rather to adhere to broader readings of representations of the leek and its implied Welshness.

15 Parker, "Uncertain Unions," 90. Parker offers a reading that "undermines the rhetoric of unity, containment, and enclosure" by focusing on the destabilizing puns and verbal mockeries, especially of the homophones breach/breech and leek/leak, as well as Fluellen's comparison of Henry V as like "Alexander the Pig," 83. Parker emphasizes that wearing leeks to commemorate St David's Day is Shakespeare's fiction, his construction of a new history, yet she also mentions that "Essex was known to wear the leek on Saint David's Day as well as Elizabeth," 99, n. 8. This complicates her own readings of "simultaneous memorializing and strategic forgetting," as historical anecdote, folkloric tradition, and literary representation blur together. In my own myopic reading that focuses on the leek as key to the play – a severe case of Fluellenitis indeed – it does become – to paraphrase an old idiom – difficult to see the garden for the leeks.

16 As scholars have argued, the different critical interpretations of the play often hinge on the different types of "memory" within the play, from the collective memory inspired by Henry's St Crispin's Day speech, to the record of the English nobles killed in battle, and to a lesser extent, Fluellen's martial memories. Wilder states, "The past ten or fifteen years have produced a vast array of scholarship on this topic as well as a broad and varied sense of what 'memory' means. 'Memory' can describe repetition or reenactment, a mode of rhetoric, a way of thinking, a cultural pattern, or a material object or space. It can be dialectically opposed to history, record, forgetting, or reenactment." Wilder, "Shakespeare and Memory," 549. Baldo's recent work *Memory in Shakespeare's Histories* beautifully captures how Shakespeare captures the intricacies of "wars of memory," "how a nation remembers a momentous event like a war." Baldo, *Memory*, 102–3. In *Henry V*, such wars for creating collective memory attempt to accomplish many things at once: position Wales in opposition to France and Ireland, rewrite Elizabeth's loss at Calais through victory at Agincourt, and reinscribe the Tudor myth through the religious hagiographies of British saints. Baldo convincingly argues that Shakespeare can control and create collective memory through "remembering and forgetting," 2.

17 The staged Welsh are visually and aurally coded as foreign, and much work has covered these signs of difference. The scholarship on Fluellen's role, more generally Shakespeare's Welsh characters, and the nationalistic and patriotic readings of the play are recently receiving new attention. Joan Rhees in "Shakespeare's Welshmen" argues for a tossed salad rather than melting pot depiction of Fluellen as retaining his Welsh identity in the newly unified Britain. The leek – even if Fluellen insists on its status as visual symbol of Wales – indicates olfactory and gustatory difference as well, which is not as well covered. The staged Welshman sounds different than his English neighbor (replacing "p" for "b," "f" for "v," etc.). Lloyd's *Speak It in Welsh* may be the most comprehensive of the many pieces of scholarship on the marginalized Welsh voice, and Smith, *Acoustic World*, deftly captures English anxieties over languages spoken in England and its colonies. Lublin, *Costuming*, also writes on how they are visually represented as other through distinctive dress and accouterments: Monmouth caps, Welsh flannel friezes, Welsh hooks, and wearing the leek. Lublin cites a late Jacobean play, Thomas Randolph's *Hey for Honesty, Down with Knavery*, as such an example. Outland notes that while the staged Welshman, with his love of the harp, affinity for toasted cheese, and negative traits of laziness and theft, is grossly stereotyped and offensive, "at least the Welshman has some characteristics that add up to his identity; the Englishman remains less a normative model than a slightly ridiculous blank." Outland, "Goat," 306.

18 Fitzpatrick notes that in our own time, the leek has been so incorporated as symbolic of Wales and furthermore, as a green vegetable, would be considered a "healthy foodstuff," yet "it is only by considering the [early modern] dietaries that we can fully understand Fluellen's anger at Pistol's behavior and Fluellen's subsequent punishment of him." Fitzpatrick, *Food*, 38, 41. My own reading, while indebted to Fitzpatrick's refined attention to the role of dietaries and the importance of food to Shakespeare's themes, resituates these sources by attending to the sensate and affective properties of the leek. Pinnuck's "Regarding Henry" offers a deconstructive overview of the complicated critical reception of Henry, asserting that both positive and negative readings of the king are ultimately justified by literal or ironic readings of the Chorus' lines. This genealogy of critical reception begins with Rabkin's seminal essay "Rabbits, Ducks, and *Henry V*," which argues that the genius of the play is the ambivalent representation of Shakespeare's Henry as patriotic warrior king and/or Machiavellian colonizer.

19 Miller, *Anatomy*, 9.

20 Miller, *Anatomy*, 143, 144.

21 Ekman and Friesen, "Constants," studied the physical characteristics of disgust among the Fore people of Papua New Guinea. Galati, Scherer, and Ricci-Bitti, "Voluntary," recorded the expressions of disgust among the blind. Both groups found the same distinguishing characteristics as described above.

22 Kristeva, *Powers*, 2.

23 Herz, *That's Disgusting*, 7.

24 Herz, *That's Disgusting*, 8.

25 *Oxford English Dictionary Online*, s.v. "qualmish"; accessed June 15, 2014.

26 The culinary history of Welsh cheese is markedly different from and much older than that of the Welsh leek. Shakespeare may have invented the story of St David and the leek, but the Welsh love of cheese can be found in earlier sources. The English traveler and physician Andrew Boorde, in his poetic and comic descriptions of diverse people, wrote as early as 1542, "I am a Welshman, I do love cause boby [baked cheese], good roasted cheese." Furnivall, *Andrew Boorde's Introduction*, 126. Fitzpatrick states, "In Shakespeare's time, cheese was especially associated with the Welsh and, along with other dairy products, the Dutch . . . There are more references to cheese in *Merry Wives of Windsor* than in any other work by Shakespeare, which is not surprising since the play contains the Welshman, Sir Hugh Evans." Fitzpatrick, *Dictionary*, 84. Also see

Brennan's "The Cheese and the Welsh," which offers a few paragraphs on the titular "popular image in literature" of the "Welsh proclivity for toasted cheese," 53.

27 Montaigne, "On Smells," *Essays*, 352.
28 Classen, Howes, and Synott, *Aroma*, 161.
29 Dugan, "Scent of a Woman," 230.
30 Dekker, *Gull's Hornbook*, 9.
31 Craik offers the possibility of Fluellen's breath as source of the stench in his note, *King Henry V*, 339. The Oxford English Dictionary Online gives this note on the etymology of "qualmish": "the etymology although uncertain, may have always had an malodorous component, related to German qualm or 'noxious vapour or miasma'." OED, s.v. "qualmish," etymology.
32 I borrow the term "olfactive prop" from Dugan's essay, in which she lists Fluellen's leek as an example. Dugan, "Dirty as Smithfield," 195.
33 Kiernan, *Staging Shakespeare*, 19.
34 Fitzpatrick, *Food*, also notes the modern "pure slapstick" appeal of many productions, excepting Branagh's film, when he decided his very first cut would be the leek scene, "the more tortuous aspects of the Fluellen/Pistol antagonism, culminating in the resoundingly unfunny leek scene," 44.
35 Herz, *That's Disgusting*, 8.
36 Pliny the Elder, *Historie*, 43. For more on "green wounds," Gerard's *Herball*, Marvell's "Damon the Mower," and a compelling study of intertextual reading as (early) modern and scholarly practice, see Knight's *Reading Green*, especially 111–36.
37 Fitzpatrick, *Food*, 43. Eating cooked leeks, especially in a pottage, was recommended, which, of course, also lessens the strength of the flavor and aroma.
38 Fitzpatrick, *Food*, 44.
39 Fitzpatrick, *Food*, 37.
40 Parkinson, *Theatrum botanicum*, 873–4.
41 See, respectively, Thomas Hill's *Gardeners Labyrinth*, 86; Pliny the Elder's *Historie*, 43; and Parkinson's *Paradisi in sole paradisus terrestri*, 513.
42 Guillemeau, *Child-birth*, 5.
43 Dodoens, *A nievve herball*, 642.
44 For example, Jones suggests that the Welsh adopted the leek as their national flora due to its association with virility, sexual prowess, and military valor. Jones, "The Phallic Leek." See also Andrews, "Fluellen; or Speedwell," for a discussion of the efficacious application of the Welsh herb "Fluellen" (also called speedwell, veronica, or betony) and how the medicinal features of this plant act as a foil to Pistol's bombastic temperament.
45 See the Harfleur speech at 3.1.1–34. For related readings of the female body as object of disgust, Kristeva, *Powers*, focuses on the abject horror of the female body and menstruation, and Menninghaus offers an aesthetic reading of disgust in art, especially as it pertains to and obsesses over the "(masculine) imagination of the *vetula*, of the disgusting old woman." Menninghaus, *Disgust*, 7–8.
46 See under definition 6: "1597 J. Gerard *Herball* ii. 357. This strong medicine ought not to be giuen inwardly vnto delicate bodies without great correction." *OED Online,* s.v. "correction, n.," accessed June 15, 2014.
47 Floyer, *Pharmako-Basanos*, 252.
48 Parkinson, *Theatrum botanicum*, 874. Parkinson's amelioration of the leek's scent is common in many herbals and dietaries.
49 Harington, *New Discourse*, 99.
50 "Aut nihil, aut tantum, tollere merda potest" (cited in Harington, *New Discourse*, 99).
51 Scott-Warren, *John Harington*, 130–31.
52 Ben Jonson, *Bartholomew Fair*. Note that the leek now joins the more commonly depicted Welsh foods of cheese and mead.

53 Parkinson, *Paradisi in sole*, 513; emphasis added.
54 The Israelites during exile recalled the meats, spices, and sweets of their time in Egypt: "We remember the fish, which we did eat in Egypt freely; the cucumbers, and the melons, and the leeks, and the onions, and the garlick" (Numbers 11:5, *KJV*). Also see Keillor and Musselman, *Figs, Dates, Laurel, and Myrrh*.
55 Palmer laments that the lack of Celtic-Gaelic-Welsh scholarship and language studies in the works of Shakespeare's non-English contemporaries allows for lacunae in English-only representations. Palmer, "Missing Bodies." There is, of course, the possibility that St Davy's Welsh leeks are not Shakespeare's invention. There may have been a source for this tale that existed only as an oral or Welsh-language source, something lost to time, a source with which Shakespeare and Drayton may have both been familiar.
56 Drayton, *Chorographicall description*, 57.
57 Drayton, *Chorographicall description*, 58: "In memorie of whom, in the revolving yeere / The Welch-men on his day the sacred herbe do weare."
58 "*Praise of Saint Dauids Day*."
59 Morgan, *Welchmens iubilee*, A2r.
60 Morgan, *Welchmens iubilee*, 1.
61 For a political reading, see Highley's persuasive argument that "through association with Saint David the leek figures an autonomous, never dependent or homogenized, Welsh culture," but Fluellen's mythology erases the Welsh history of resistance, rebellion, and fighting invading forces. Highley, *Shakespeare, Spenser*, 148. Chapman argues that the focus is more on the Anglo-Welsh King Henry than the Welsh St David, a type of secularizing regional saint. Chapman, *Patrons*, 79–80.
62 Olivier, *Henry V*.
63 As Greenblatt argues, "By yoking together diverse peoples – represented in the play by the Welshman Fluellen, the Irishman Macmorris, and the Scotsman Jamy, who fight at Agincourt alongside the loyal Englishmen – Hal symbolically tames the last wild areas in the British isles, areas that in the sixteenth century represented, far more powerfully than any New World people, the doomed outposts of a vanishing tribalism." Greenblatt, *Shakespearean Negotiations*, 56.
64 Beginning with John of Gaunt's panegyric depiction of "this sceptered isle, / . . . this other Eden, demi-paradise" in *Richard II*, which continues in the garden scene as the discourse of pruning and maintaining the garden is contrasted with Richard's disordered kingdom, and into *Henry* as the new king's conversion is likened to sweet strawberries growing from the brambles; at the end of the play, France becomes a second garden, grown wild by war but fruitfully cultivated in peace.
65 Dugan beautifully reconstructs the olfactory iconography of the Tudor rose and recreates the rich bouquet of progression from the early importing of damask roses, the Catholic meanings of the rose as Mary's flower, Henry VIII's political, religious, and sexual denotations of scented rosewater, and Elizabeth I's reappropriation of the rose as dynastic and religious symbol. Dugan, *Ephemeral History*, 42–69.
66 Parkinson, *Paradisi in sole paradisus terrestris*, 461.
67 Parker, "Uncertain Unions," 85.
68 Gilbert, *What the Nose Knows*, 104.

References

Andrews, Michael Cameron. "Fluellen; or Speedwell." *Notes and Queries* 33, no. 3 (September 1986): 33–6.
Baldo, Jonathan. *Memory in Shakespeare's Histories: Stages of Forgetting in Early Modern England*. New York: Routledge, 2012.

Brennan, Gillian E. "The Cheese and the Welsh: Foreigners in Elizabethan Literature." *Renaissance Studies* 8, no. 1 (March 1994): 40–64.

Chapman, Alison. *Patrons and Patron Saints in Early Modern English Literature*. New York: Routledge, 2013.

Czerniecki, Krystian. "The Jest Disgested: Perspectives on History in Henry V." In *On Puns: The Foundation of Letters*, edited by Jonathan Culler, 62–82. Oxford: Blackwell, 1988.

Classen, Constance, David Howes, and Anthony Synott. *Aroma: The Cultural History of Smell*. London: Routledge, 1994.

Dekker, Thomas. *The Gull's Hornbook*. Edited by R.B. McKerrow. London: De La More Press, 1804.

Dodoens, Rembert. *A nievve herball, or historie of plantes wherin is contayned the vvhole discourse and perfect description of all sortes of herbes and plantes*. Translated by Henry Lyte Esquyer. London [i.e. Antwerp]: Henry Loë, 1578.

Drayton, Michael. *A chorographicall description of tracts, riuers, mountains, forests, and other parts of this renowned isle of Great Britain*. London: Printed for John Marriott, John Grismand, and Thomas Dewe, 1622.

Dugan, Holly. " 'As Dirty as Smithfield and Stinking Every Whit': The Smell of the Hope Theatre." In *Shakespeare's Theatres and the Effects of Performance*, edited by Farah Karim-Cooper and Tiffany Stern, 195–213. London: Arden Shakespeare, 2013.

———. *The Ephemeral History of Perfume: Scent and Sense in Early Modern England*. Baltimore: Johns Hopkins University Press, 2011.

———. "Scent of a Woman: Performing the Politics of Smell in Late Medieval and Early Modern England." *Journal of Early Modern Studies* 38, no. 2 (Spring 2008): 229–52.

Ekman, Paul, and Wallace Friesen. "Constants across Cultures in the Face of Emotion." *Journal of Personality and Social Psychology* 17 (1971): 124–9.

Espinosa, Ruben. "Fluellen's Foreign Influence and the Ill Neighborhood of King *Henry V*." In *Shakespeare and Immigration*, edited by Ruben Espinosa and David Ruiter, 73–90. Farnham: Ashgate, 2014.

Evans, Herbert Arthur, ed. *The Life of King Henry the Fifth*. London: Methuen, 1904.

Fitzpatrick, Joan. *Food in Shakespeare: Early Modern Dietaries and the Plays*. Aldershot and Burlington, VT: Ashgate, 2007.

———. *Shakespeare and the Language of Food: A Dictionary*. London: Continuum, 2011.

Floyer, John. *Pharmako-Basanos, or the Touchstone of Medicines. Discovering the Vertues of Vegetables, Minerals, and Animals by Their Tastes and Smells*. Stratfordshire: Printed for Michael Johnson, 1687.

Furnivall, F.J., ed. *Andrew Boorde's Introduction and Dyetary, with Barnes in the Defense of the Berde*. Early English Text Society. Extra Series X. London: Early English Text Society, 1870.

Galati, Dario, Klaus R. Scherer, and Pio E. Ricci-Bitti. "Voluntary Facial Expressions of Emotion: Comparing Congenitally Blind with Normally Sighted Encoders." *Journal of Personality and Social Psychology* 73 (1997): 1365–79.

Gilbert, Avery. *What the Nose Knows: The Science of Scent in Everyday Life*. New York: Crown, 2008.

Greenblatt, Stephen. *Shakespearean Negotiations: The Circulation of Social Energy in Renaissance England*. Berkeley: University of California Press, 1988.

Guillemeau, Jacques. *Child-birth or, The happy deliuerie of vvomen. Written in French by Iames Guillimeau the French Kings chirurgion*. London: A. Hatfield, 1612.

Harington, John. *A New Discourse of a Stale Subject Called the Metamorphosis of Ajax.* Edited by Elizabeth Story Donno. New York: Columbia University Press, 1962.

Herz, Rachel. *That's Disgusting: Unraveling the Mysteries of Repulsion.* New York: W.W. Norton, 2012.

Highley, Christopher. *Shakespeare, Spenser, and the Crisis in Ireland.* Cambridge: Cambridge University Press, 1997.

Hill, Thomas. *The Gardeners Labyrinth.* London: Henry Bynneman, 1577.

Jenner, Mark. "Civilization and Deodorization? Smell in Early Modern English Culture." In *Civil Histories: Essays Presented to Sir Keith Thomas*, edited by Peter Burke, Brian Harrison, and Paul Slack, 127–44. Oxford: Oxford University Press, 2000.

Jones, Lowanne E. "The Phallic Leek." In *Studies in Honor of Hans-Erich Keller: Medieval French and Occitan Literature and Romance Linguistics*, edited by Rupert T. Pickens, 419–26. Kalamazoo, MI: Medieval Institute Publications, 1993.

Jonson, Ben. *Bartholomew Fair.* Edited by Suzanne Gossett. New York: Manchester University Press, 2000.

Keillor, Garrison and Lytton John Musselman. *Figs, Dates, Laurel, and Myrrh: Plants of the Bible and the Quran.* Portland: Timber Press, 2007.

Kiernan, Pauline. *Staging Shakespeare at the New Globe.* New York: St. Martin's Press, 1999.

Knight, Leah. *Reading Green in Early Modern England.* Farnham and Burlington, VT: Ashgate, 2014.

Kristeva, Julia. *Powers of Horror: An Essay on Abjection.* Translated by Leon S. Roudiez. New York: Columbia University Press, 1992.

Levin, Richard. "On Fluellen's Figures, Christ Figures, and James Figures." *PMLA* 89, no. 2 (March 1974): 302–11.

Lloyd, Megan S. *Speak It in Welsh: Wales and the Welsh Language in Shakespeare.* Lanham, MD: Lexington Books, 2007.

Lublin, Robert L. *Costuming the Shakespearean Stage: Visual Codes of Representation in Early Modern Theatre and Culture.* Farnham: Ashgate, 2011.

Maley, Willy. "'Let a Welsh correction teach you a good English condition': Shakespeare, Wales, and the Critics." In *Shakespeare and Wales: From the Marches to the Assembly*, edited by Willy Maley and Philip Schwyzer, 177–90. Farnham: Ashgate, 2010.

Menninghaus, Winfried. *Disgust: Theory and History of a Strong Sensation.* Translated by Howard Eiland and Joel Golb. Albany: State University of New York Press, 2003.

Miller, William Ian. *The Anatomy of Disgust.* Cambridge and London: Harvard University Press, 1997.

Montaigne, Michel de. *Essays.* Translated by M.A. Screech. London: Penguin Classics, 1991.

Morgan, T. *The Welchmens Iubilee: to the honour of St. David. Shewing, the manner of that solemn celebration, which the Welshmen annually hold in honour of St. David. Describing, likewise the true and rea[ll] cause, why they wear that day a leek on their hats. With an excellent merry sonnet annexed unto it.* London: Printed for I. Harrison, 1642.

Olivier, Laurence. *Henry V.* Digitally remastered version. Directed by Laurence Olivier. 1944. DVD. Irvington, NY: Criterion Collection, 2006.

Outland, Allison M. "'Eat a Leek': Welsh Corrections, English Conditions, and British Cultural Communion." In *This England, That Shakespeare: New Angles on Englishness and the Bard*, edited by Willy Maley and Margaret Tudeau- Clayton, 87–103. Farnham: Ashgate, 2010.

———. "'Ridden with a Welsh goat': Parson Evan's Correction of Windsor's English Condition." *English Literary Renaissance* 41, no. 2 (June 2011): 301–31.

Palmer, Patricia. "Missing Bodies, Absent Bards: Spenser, Shakespeare, and a Crisis in Criticism." *English Literary Renaissance* 36, no. 3 (June 2006): 376–95.

Parker, Patricia. "Uncertain Unions: Welsh Leeks in *Henry V*." In *British Identities and English Renaissance Literature*, edited by David J. Baker and Willy Maley, 81–100. Cambridge: Cambridge University Press, 2002.

Parkinson, John. *Paradisi in sole paradisus terrestri, or, A choise garden of all sorts of rarest flowers*. London: Humfrey Lownes and Robert Young, 1629.

———. *Theatrum botanicum: The theater of plants*. London: Printed by Thomas Cotes, 1640.

Pinnuck, James. "Regarding Henry: The Good and the Bad in *Henry V*." *Critical Review* 41 (2001): 95–104.

Pliny the Elder. *The historie of the vvorld: commonly called, The naturall historie of C. Plinius Secundus*. Translated by Philemon Holland. London: Printed by Adam Islip, 1634.

The praise of Saint Dauids day. Shewing the reason why the Welshmen honour the leeke on that day. To the tune of When this old cap was new. London: s.n., c. 1630.

Rabkin, Norman. "Rabbits, Ducks, and *Henry V*." *Shakespeare Quarterly* 28, no. 3 (1977): 279–96.

Rhees, Joan. "Shakespeare's Welshman." In *Literature and Nationalism*, edited by Vincent Newy and Ann Thompson, 22–40. Liverpool: Liverpool University Press, 1991.

Scott-Warren, Jason. *Sir John Harington and the Book as Gift*. Oxford: Oxford University Press, 2001.

Shakespeare, William. *King Henry V*. The Arden Shakespeare. Third Series. Edited by T.W. Craik. London: Bloomsbury, 2013.

Smith, Bruce R. *The Acoustic World of Early Modern England: Attending to the O-Factor*. Chicago: University of Chicago Press, 1999.

Wilder, Lina Perkins. "Shakespeare and Memory." *Literature Compass* 9, no. 8 (August 2012): 549–59.

Part III
Textual encounters

8   The "Fairing of good counsel"

Allegory, disgust, and discretion in Jonson's *Bartholomew Fair*

Ineke Murakami

In an oft-cited passage from the last of Ben Jonson's great city comedies, *Bartholomew Fair*, two gallants encounter Ursula, "a fine oily pig-woman" (ind.91–92), who has paused outside her booth to cool off after scolding her tapster:[1]

> QUARLOUS Body o' the Fair! What's this? Mother o' the bawds?
> KNOCKEM No, she's mother o' the pigs, sir, mother o' the pigs.
> WINWIFE Mother o' the Furies, I think, by her firebrand.
> QUARLOUS Nay, she is too fat to be a Fury! Sure some walking sow of tallow.
> WINWIFE An inspired vessel of kitchen-stuff!
> QUARLOUS She'll make excellent gear for the coachmakers here in Smithfield, to anoint wheels and axel trees with. (2.5.56–62)

The gamesters adopt a familiar satirical pose: an amused distance from the object of their derision. Their scorn marks a number of characters in the play as disgusting, but I am less interested in the branding power of disgust than in its constructive function through a textual technique that lies at the heart of Jonson's civilizing endeavor. I refer here to allegory, the device that connects the high-velocity transformations of the passage above to the play's larger exploration of "discretion" (1.5.9).

In just six lines, the dialogue transforms Ursula from a gross emblem of the fair, to a genetrix of bawds and furies, to an uncanny tallow sculpture, before dispersing her into lubricant for the moving parts of coaches. In her final reduction to grease, Ursula becomes a facilitator for *things that bear*. Coaches bear bodies; so do sex workers. This submerged pun brings Ursula's greasy metamorphosis full circle to the "bawd" of line 56, a joke that makes her a "pander to any evil design."[2] But the quip's full impact emerges only when we draw on all the play asks us to associate with "Ursula." Her name, which means "she-bear" (2.3.1), links her metatheatrically to the new Hope playhouse, which "stink[s]" (ind.119), as the Scrivener admits, from its secondary function as a bear baiting pit, an allusion that sets the tone for the imminent mock-baiting in which Ursula is bested by the insults of the "dog's-head" gallants (2.5.94).[3] The occupational reference with which Knockem good-naturedly corrects Quarlous connects Ursula to the play's earliest reference to her as a "pig-woman": a designation some read as emblematic of the repugnant hybridity that characterizes the fair (ind.91).[4] Meanwhile, Win-wife's fury analogy returns us to the materiality of theater, to the sight of Ursula gripping her "firebrand" (2.5.58) before a booth that occupies the conventional position of hell-mouth, laying ground, through staging, for her later identification with the "three enemies of man" (3.6.28). Literature on the play brims with such associations: evidence, I suggest, of the extraordinary polysemy at the command of one of the period's most stunning allegorists.[5]

In the latter assertion, I depart from a critical tradition that considers neither Jonson nor his city comedies particularly allegorical. Some very fine readers have found *Bartholomew Fair*'s apparent invitation to allegory through conventions like personifying character names somewhat disingenuous. Suzanne Gossett notes that attempts to read "methodological religious allegory into *Bartholomew Fair* tend to fall of their own weight and inappropriateness," while Debora Shuger writes that "Jonson is not working out a consistent allegory" in the play.[6] Such declarations seem connected to a hermeneutic known as "allegoresis": the search for a single, stable code that unlocks a text by locating one-to-one correspond-ences between a signifier on one semantic level and its apparent signified on a higher, more "truthful" level. As allegory specialists like Maureen Quilligan note, allegoresis almost never works because complex allegory, from Dante to Pynchon, functions very differently than this vertical match-game. Allegory invites readers to track a signifier as we tracked "Ursula," above, through *multiple* dynamic con-texts (or discursive registers) within a comprehensive but flexible gestalt, like Jonson's fair. The reader of allegory moves horizontally, more often than verti-cally. In terms of our opening example, Ursula's qualities as a bear dominate a scene's semantic sense only as long as its other elements—like her deployment of canine slurs to fend off the gallants, or the spectators' participatory cry, "to 'em, Urs" (2.5.67), associated with animal fights—resonate with ursinity.[7]

Jonson states in *Timber* that he is loath to draw out "allegory too long, lest either we make ourselves obscure, or fall into affectation, which is childish."[8] Thus, he derides the "inspired ignorance" of allegoresis in the Induction to *Bartholomew Fair*, where he dissuades us from "search[ing] out who was meant by the gingerbread-woman, who by the hobby-horse-man, who by the costermonger, nay, who by their wares" (ind.104–5). Likewise, the absurdity of Reverend Busy's allegoresis, which reduces the fair's trinkets to their ostensibly true diabolical significance – a toy drum is the "broken belly of the Beast"; bottle-ale is Satan's "diet-drink" (3.6.53, 24) – persuades us to resist such closure. We are expected, rather, to hold in ten-sion a sense of the ways Ursula is a bear *and* a bawd *and* a/the (B)east *and* grease, within the interpretive framework of the play. Complex allegory confounds, in other words, the simple decoding and premature closure allegoresis demands.

In dwelling on this particular conception of allegory, I signal my sense of the vital role it plays in Jonson's solution for dealing with a materiality he finds both repugnant and indispensable. Ambivalence toward the sensual world has been a common theme in Jonson scholarship, at least since Katharine Eisaman Maus's influential statement on Jonson's satiric and ideal economies. Of the readers exploring how this ambivalence shapes his poetics, however, few have connected

Jonson's use of allegory to his larger endeavor to provide "Good Counsel" (2.4.15).[9] As a technique of the body long valued for its pedagogical efficacy, allegory fits Jonson's bill. When taken in a culture whose anxieties about differentiating kinds of literature often echo concerns about distinguishing kinds of people (gender, class, ethnicity), allegory is disgusting. It has an intrinsic propensity, as we shall see, for combining high with low forms, goading readers to distinguish between wholesome and dangerous mixture. My contention, stated most simply, is that Jonson deploys allegory to evoke disgust as an occasion on which to exercise his audience in the self-regulatory discipline of discretion.[10]

By discretion, I mean the capacity for sound judgment in the face of London's burgeoning consumer culture, a judgment that manifests itself as something like good "taste."[11] I use the term advisedly. Taste's modern, post-Kantian sense as a metaphor for evaluating artifacts in an ostensibly disinterested and isolated aesthetic sphere does not fully emerge until the eighteenth century.[12] Jonson's taste is decidedly un-Kantian. It does not divorce objects from their economic, religious, moral, or political uses but remains unabashedly interested in them. Taste, for Jonson, is the external expression of an inner distinction. One of the few worth cultivating: discretion.[13]

The assumption that poetry performs political work gives Jonson's discretion its potency. As an acquired attribute detached from both traditional social rank and the power of new money, Jonson's discretion is ultimately – as is the case with any aesthetic – an ethos, implicated in the period's larger process of culture-wide embourgeoisement. The discretion staged in *Bartholomew Fair* thus constitutes a flashpoint in something we have come to associate with the "civilizing" expansion of collective "threshold[s] of repugnance" that accelerated in the early modern period. It continues today in ways some theorists warn are less than salubrious. In the final moments of this chapter, I will suggest ways Jonsonian discretion might add to work being done by those exploring the political value of disgust in the ongoing work of civilization.[14]

Before proceeding, I want to clarify one final point. To say that discretion is, in *Bartholomew Fair*, a technique of self-regulation is to affirm what both period scholars and theorists of many stripes agree is the interpretive work that gives rise to acts of aesthetic and other forms of judgment.[15] When we consume or in other ways appropriate an object – and I follow Bourdieu in assuming that the exercise of critical judgment is a kind of consumption, even when it results in an object's rejection—we accomplish not only the immediate aim of enjoyment, but the secondary one of communicating our "elective distance" from "necessity." The *way* we consume signals to others the extent to which we can afford to prefer form, a "pleasure purified of pleasure," over function.[16] This self-classifying work depends on a kind of internalized law that sets a proper distance between the self and sensual pleasure, a law that fuses individual custom to communal morality in a way that bears the trace of a particular class position. This is why Terry Eagleton considers the aesthetic a "mediatory category."[17] To make judgments about the commercialized world's commodities is to exercise a discretion that constitutes both the self and its relation to others.

Allegory's vocation

That allegorical tropes populate Jonson's work, from his plays to his epigrams to the settings of his masques, should not be surprising. Allegory was a significant part of the Tudor schoolboy's education, and by the time Jonson was old enough to read, allegory's pedagogical efficacy was already associated with its ability to disgust. For centuries, schoolmasters relied on allegory's generation of mnemonically useful affect: the stronger, the better. As Mary Carruthers demonstrates in her study on medieval mnemonics, the infamous battle imagery that concludes Prudentius's fifth-century allegorical poem the *Psychomachia* was *"designedly disgusting and morbid because it is those qualities that ma[k]e it memorable."*[18] Cognitive science has subsequently confirmed what ecclesiastical educators once intuited: disgust affects long-term memory.[19] The image of Chastity smashing in Lust's mouth with a rock, causing the Vice to vomit up clots of her own blood, teeth and shattered bone, provokes a powerful affective response. This response was believed to produce an emotional "phantasm" in the soul, a memorial impression to which one could return long after an initial reading to recall the vile end of Lust. Disgust was thus instrumental in the acquisition of virtue through *habitus* – habit of mind and intellectual practice – fortifying and recalibrating the reader or listener's moral compass through memory.[20] Not surprisingly, Prudentius's descriptions of mangled Vices, a staple for centuries of medieval curricula, remained a valued supplement to the more prestigious texts of the Tudor classroom. Jonson's humanist masters may have emphasized the *Psychomachia*'s adaptation of epic conventions, but they would also have valued its appeal to the puerile delight in the disgusting. The *Psychomachia*'s allegory continued, in this way, to set mnemonic hooks that inspired centuries of visual and poetic art.[21]

Inheritors of this tradition include the moral drama that infuses Jonson's city comedy with such vigor. To touch on the morality play connection to Jonson's work, details of which are elaborated in any number of critical accounts, is not to insist that Jonson, for whom humanist knowledge is a point of pride, developed his allegorical technique independently of classical models. We cannot ignore, for example, Jonson's choice of the stately Horace to function as his alter ego in *Poetaster* (1601), or his insistence, through the erudite Cordatus, in *Every Man Out of His Humour* (1600), that his comedies resemble the *"vetus comedia"* (ind.28), a claim Jonson repeats in later conversations with Drummond.[22] My point is not that Jonson learned allegory from the moral drama of his youth, but that such drama bore a quotidian witness to allegory's power to reconcile humanist didactic aspirations with the pleasure of popular entertainment. This was because, from Bale's *Kyng Johan* (c. 1538) to Wilson's *Three Ladies of London* (1584), Tudor interludes secured allegory's didactic vocation in post-Reformation England.[23]

Consequently, with its mimetic pretension to represent spiritual – we might say "psychological" – truths through the materiality of things, allegory was only conditionally respectable. It bears repeating that the "Protestant dodge," whereby early moderns attempted to cleanse Protestant poetics of licentious allegory by redefining it as historical typology, sought to address real anxieties.[24] Nor were these entirely doctrinal. Allegory's improprieties became increasingly apparent with the circulation of English rhetorical manuals like Thomas Wilson's *Arte of Rhetorique* (1553), Henry Peacham's *Garden of Eloquence* (1577), and George Puttenham's *Art of English Poesy* (1589). Puttenham's fascination with allegory seems especially pronounced in the way he enlivens a section on figures of speech by rendering them prosopopoeiae, led by the bizarre, courtly False Semblant or "allegoria."[25] Even "the most noble and wisest prince," Puttenham claims, relies on False Semblant to "thrive and prosper in the world." Subsequent examples depict French kings and English aristocrats deploying allegory's powers of dissimulation. Yet, like the magus of an allegorical romance, False Semblant proves slippery even for his patrons, shape-shifting in a manner that "trespasses" against the ostensibly honorable intentions of his superiors. Puttenham describes, by way of example, the "reprobate" sense some "naughty body" once gleaned from a gentlewoman's ostensibly innocent riddle about a furred glove. It begins: "I have a thing and rough it is / And in the midst a hole iwis." Deploring the bawdy association with pudendum, Puttenham notes how easily "guileful" allegory falls into "foul speech."[26]

Perhaps it is this disquieting tendency to collapse high into low that motivates Puttenham's attempt to straighten allegory out, to set it to work, as it were, as "captain" of all figures. But even here allegory proves problematic, for the "soldiers" who "fight under [his] banner of dissimulation," from "Privy Nip" to the "Fleering Frump," prove to be "lying" knaves all, licensed by the noble speakers who employ them.[27] Puttenham's silent assertion of allegory's ambiguity seems precisely the point. Dress it as you will: allegory is properly improper. As we saw in our opening discussion of the passage in which the gallants encounter Ursula, allegory rewards the challenging work of associative thought with comically outrageous transformations. More than simple wordplay, allegory's associations tap the loose, allegorical substructure of the pleasure fair through which Jonson decries the lack of discretion that enables a disgusting erosion of boundaries between theater, market, and social relations.[28]

Such boundaries, Jonson seems to suggest, are socially constructed for all their apparent permanence. And if the play's allegorical troping provides occasion to practice discretion, to identify behaviors and objects proper to one realm or another, the pleasure fair setting underscores the degree to which such sorting depends on self-regulation. Bourdieu describes this contingency in terms of the educational and familial background that trains one to consume objects with greater or lesser "detachment."[29] But in light of Jonson's more *ante*-aesthetic approach to consumption, I want to turn briefly to a model that enables us to think about the way our internalized hierarchies appear to us from without, as the ostensibly natural order that organizes a culture's objects within spheres of exchange. This seemingly objective structure permits us to trace how Jonson's allegory disrupts the morality of exchange to arouse disgust.

Market morality and self-regulation

Jonson's late sixteenth- and early seventeenth-century moment is of special interest to social anthropologists as a transitional stage between a culture that maintains status systems through the overt restriction of exchange in a "stable universe of commodities," and the modern "fashion system," in which "an ever-changing universe of commodities" dependent on the "illusion of complete interchangeability and unrestricted access," is controlled by taste.[30] The fashion system's apparent freedom—anyone may buy anything—occludes what is actually a highly effective method of social stratification. In this regime, taste-makers and their "affiliated experts who dwell at the top of society," set the rapidly changing guidelines for the best to be worn, eaten, or seen in a given moment. What we consume distinguishes the high (i.e., those with the disposable income to bankroll and keep up with fashion's high-velocity turn-over) from the low. That the consistent appearance of good taste is mistaken for a sign of discretion, rather than a reflection of access to resources that allow the elite to stay on trend, is typical of the system's mystification.

Discretion also does the crucial work of sorting commercialized culture's objects into moralized spheres of exchange: a "high" sphere for the circulation of singular and sacred things, like rights in people, ideas, or beliefs; a "prestige" sphere for things that solidify status, like clothing or public office; and a "low" sphere for subsistence commodities. By the moral economy that structures these spheres, objects within a sphere may be exchanged for one another, but traffic *between* spheres is discouraged by a clash of moral codes.[31] We often register this disjuncture as humorous, a humor Jonson trades on as early as the Scrivener's reading of the "Articles of Agreement" in the Induction to *Bartholomew Fair*:

> SCRIVENER It shall be lawful for any man to judge his six penn'orth, his twelve penn'orth, so to his eighteen pence, two shillings, half a crown, to the value of his place – provided always his place get not above his wit. (ind.49, 66–8)

Our amusement derives from the diversion of judgment from the high, theologically inflected sphere of human faculties, to the low, commodity-based sphere of public entertainment. This device encourages us to appraise our "place," literally but also figuratively, in relation to our "wit."[32] The shameful possibility that we are seated better than we deserve gestures to its more infuriating opposite as well. The Articles thus provoke the socially and intellectually aspirant to return to the Hope another day and buy up the best seats in order to exercise what the Scrivener calls our "free-will of censure" (ind.64). The passage makes place an index of discretion: an outward sign of our inner ability to judge. And while our knowledge of market morality tells us that one can't purchase a particular amount of censure, it suggests that our movement to a better seat, like the movement of a commodity to a higher sphere of exchange, may read as audacious but movement downward would be utterly shameful.

The Articles thus sensitize us to down-market conversion in preparation for the play's densest piece of allegory: the puppet show of the final act. The unseemliness of this entertainment begins at the extradramatic level, with Littlewit's scurrilous translation of *Hero and Leander*, Marlowe's "learned and poetical" epyllion (5.3.84). Rendering the tragic poem "a little easy and modern for the times," Littlewit's update translocates *Hero and Leander* from the high sphere of humanist poetics to the low "familiar strain" of puppet theater (5.3.92, 89). Heroic couplets give way to tumbling iambic tetrameter, and Marlowe's exquisite, god-enticing couple is reduced to a dyer's son and his promiscuous Bankside "drab" (5.4.203). Exacerbating these faults, Littlewit's arbitrary insertion of characters from an old university play, *Damon and Pythias*, transforms the eponymous para-gons of friendship into belligerent alehouse louts. Their fight for Hero's favors shatters the puppet play's frame on more than one occasion, spilling out into the space the puppeteer shares with his audience. Whether he is worse beset by these slapstick brawls or by the barrage of inquiries from the distracted Bartholomew Cokes is beside the point: all of the seemingly improvised curses, blows, and interruptions remind us that the disturbances belong to a fictive second world whose exaggerated collapse of exchange spheres has something to teach us about our own. Through this metatheatrical flourish, Jonson invites us to read the puppet show as an allegory of discretion.

The set-up begins a scene earlier when, having asked to meet the actors before the play, the foolish young Cokes is handed a basketful of puppets:

> COKES Do you call these players?
> LEATHERHEAD They are actors, sir, and as good as any . . . for dumb- shows –
>   indeed, I am the mouth of 'em all!
> COKES Thy mouth will hold 'em all. I think one tailor would go near to beat
>   all this company with a hand bound behind him. (5.3.58–62)

The last line's three-fold allusion is to the proverbial timidity of tailors, the water poet, John Taylor's, recent contest of wit at the Hope, and one-time boy player, Joseph Taylor, who now appears in *Bartholomew Fair*. This touches off a prolif-eration of quips on the names of ex-boy players, like Ostler and Field, evidently present on stage, evoking recent theater history to make a scurrilous analogy: boy players are to adult players as puppets are to boy players; that is, simply small ver-sions of the larger thing. Cokes adds an additional layer of meaning by adopting the puppets as his own, personal "fairings" (5.3.102). The transformation of actors into souvenirs sets the stage for an even more absurd level of analogy that ends in Zeal-of-the-Land Busy's denouncing the wooden toys as idolatrous "beam[s] . . . in the eye[s] of the Brethren" (5.5.7).

The puppet show strikes at several targets simultaneously: actors who voice other men's words as their own; managers who treat players like puppets; gallants who treat actors as personal playthings; and Puritans who treat toys as enormities.[33] In attacking this lack of discretion the puppet show also parodies the exchange value driving the pleasure fair. As Jean-Joseph Goux suggests in his reading of Marx, exchange value functions very much like allegory by rendering things apparently unlike fungible, which is to say, alike at the abstract level of potential exchange.[34] In Jonson's increasingly commercialized culture, both "your punk and your pig" (2.5.33) may be had for a particular sum of the money, which standardizes their value, enables their circulation, and renders them virtually the same.

Against the background of the fair, this leveling of people, animals, and subsistence commodities effaces difference in providers as well as in their ware. Jonson invites us to compare popular playwrights like Littlewit, who waters down classical texts for mass consumption, to producers like Ursula or Joan Trash, who adulterate their ale and gingerbread to profit at the expense of the apparently indiscriminate. Jonson thus discovers a lack of discretion at the scene of production as well as at the site of consumption. Blame is assigned unilaterally, as Jonson goads producers and consumers alike to step up their game: to make production and purchase a more exclusive, thoughtful process.

Yet, the cultivation of boundaries may also go too far. By the time he writes *Bartholomew Fair*, Jonson understands that the discreet individual can ill afford to draw absolute lines between himself and the world. Discretion is a kind of gate-minding, a vigilance to exclude when necessary but also to admit what may be of moral or other profit. It is generally agreed that the play's three authority figures, Zeal-of-the-Land Busy, Justice Adam Overdo, and Henry Wasp, fail because of an overly rigid identification with some type of law: respectively, Puritan doctrine, common law, and the government of youth.[35] Their excessive outrage at the smallest infraction resembles nothing so much as an overdeveloped sense of disgust, and for this they are punished. Stocked together, they are charged with "quarrelling" (4.6.87), a word which, in addition to meaning violent disagreement, includes at this time the more rhetorical sense of attempting "to move [others to] act, change, etc. by force of argument."[36] For all their railing, the three are such transparent hypocrites that they fail to persuade. That they are stocked together is significant, for in the world of early modern allegory, character similarity is often suggested through proximity and posture, as Theresa Krier argues.[37] The economy of allegory suggests that we need to meditate on only one would-be authority to understand the way hyper-vigilance and poor judgment precipitate all three downfalls.

The new civility

If, as the play suggests, traditional mores have grown risible in England's increasingly cosmopolitan center, the need for an up-to-date model of civility is urgent. Jonson depicts civility as mastery of discretion in two ways: emblematically, through the team of Cokes and Wasp, and characterologically, through the enigmatic Quarlous.

Neither Cokes nor Wasp are sufficient in themselves to navigate commercialized London, but tellingly, Quarlous, who is the closest thing to a spokesman for the play, alludes to the team's practical potential through the figure "cross and pile" (1.4.71). In an attempt to gain sympathy from the gallants, Wasp has just finished a lengthy lament about his young charge, depicting his behavior in conventional terms of a fool. The gentlemen converse in an aside:

> QUARLOUS Well, methinks this is a fine fellow!
> WINWIFE He has made his master a finer by this description, I should think.

QUARLOUS Faith, much about one; it's cross and pile, whether for a new farthing. (1.4.69–71)

Most editors gloss the phrase "cross and pile" as "it's heads or tails," meaning it is
all the same, or it's doubtful Wasp's criticism could make Cokes appear any more
foolish. Heads or tails touches nicely on the line's "farthing," but misses the early
modern sense of the word "whether" as meaning "which of the two" (characters
are worse). In my reading, "whether" underscores the heads or tails difference of
the two.[38] I suggest that, within the allegorical frame of the play, "cross and pile"
yokes the opposing drives of Cokes and Wasp to the same setting by way of the
audience's familiarity with textile terminology. "Cross," or "pile," an orientation
in a fabric's weave contrary to "warp" threads, are those treated to produce luxury
fabrics like velvet.[39] As matter of great value, "cross and pile" fleetingly points,
through the fair's oddest couple, to the contrary forces at both the commercial and
the libidinal core of the historical Bartholomew Fair.[40]

If Ursula is the body of the fair, Cokes and Wasp are its soul. The characters
metaphorize the conflicting but potentially productive drives cultural anthropologists identify as constitutive of most commercial societies: an erotic drive toward
commodification and consumption, and an opposing impulse to restrict exchange.
In *Bartholomew Fair*, the commodifying impulse inspires Dan Knockem's equation
of city wives with horses in an equine blazon that slides from Win's "delicate dark
chestnut" head to her "smooth hoofs" (4.5.17–21). But the character most closely
associated with commodification is Cokes.[41] To the indiscriminate squire, "in love
with" all he sees and "allied to" all he consumes, everything is for sale (5.3.100–101).
His possessions are so deeply incorporated into his sense of identity that the loss of
an item throws him into crisis. Relieved of his two purses, cloak, hat, and sword,
Cokes complains, "I ha' lost myself," "do you know who I am?" (4.2.65–6, 64).

The opposing force, an enclaving impulse, is seen in a culture's attempt to set
some items apart as too "sacred" or singular to be commodified. We contribute to
enclaving as individuals and in groups by negating, often for social reasons, the
desire to consume. This is crucial distinction-making, but in Wasp's repudiation
and negation of everything, ultimately no more discriminating than the appetite
of his young charge, we locate the restrictive urge's extreme thanatic edge. Were
every Cokes-like urge suppressed by a Wasp's scorn, there would be no circulation, no "truck" (2.6.13) with one's fellows, no erotic or any other exchange. It
is the tension between warp and weft that enables something like the Freudian
formula for judgment: "I should like to take this into me and keep that out of me."
For Freud, judgment's first and most interminable task is self-regulation, or the
management of erotic energy which rushes not only after pleasure, but also, as he
argues in *Beyond the Pleasure Principle*, toward the negation of all stimuli.[42] Bartholomew Fair makes an ideal testing ground for these difficult, internal negotiations. Without limits, Cokes's erotically-charged drive to consume runs profligate
into self-destructive excess, while without interest in something beyond its own
limiting power, Wasp's negativism dissolves into the entropic discord which ends
the game of Vapors.

Appreciation of the distinctions that loosely govern London's spheres of exchange restrains those who would make indecorous equivalents of puppets and actors; doggerel and poetry; "fill[ies]" and city wives (4.4.178). At the same time, recognition of similarities reminds us that we are all "but Adam, flesh and blood" (5.6.80). The civilized citizen in early seventeenth-century London cannot afford the hermetic distance of the traditional saint, for an excess of piety buys into difference to an antisocial degree. To imagine, with Busy, that religious zeal sets one above others is only slightly less foolish than Mistress Overdo's belief in the elevating power of her French hood (4.4.115–16). The play penalizes such blinkered judgment without exception: Busy is converted by a puppet, Overdo is beaten by Wasp, and Wasp is humiliated by Cokes. Even Winwife, a mild social snob, is deprived of his elegant new wife's inheritance. Discretion, as a gatekeeping faculty, is the key to fashioning the civil self, because it controls necessary flows between internal and external worlds, from individual to commonwealth and back.

In his commonplace book *Timber*, Jonson describes this civilizing process in a way that illuminates early modern understandings of disgust's centrality to identity formation. Jonson advises the would-be poet to subject his sources to meticulous intellectual rumination, turning over a likely text in order to absorb only the best and most rigorously processed morsels. We are encouraged to incorporate models "[n]ot, as a creature, that swallows, what it takes in crude, raw, or indigested; but that feeds with an *appetite*, and hath a stomach to concoct, divide, and turn all into nourishment."[43] In addition to appetite's usual connotations of hunger, desire, and inclination, Jonson's usage brings the rarer, emergent meaning, "so as to suit one's tastes," to the fore as he advocates for a more scrupulous "imitation," the method by which writers turn "the best, and choicest" matter of others into their own work. This process culminates in the incorporation of sources in such a way that they seem a natural part of the "comely" new body, like muscle accrued through what will one day be extolled as a regime of diet and exercise. Significantly, even before chewing, good *imitatio* demands ante-aesthetic evaluation, an "appetite" for what is suitable to put in one's mouth and what to spit out.[44] Disgust warns us away from choking down great gobs of "indigested" matter. Without discretion, as is the case with Justice Overdo in *Bartholomew Fair*—purged of his hyperbolic *sententiae* through displacement to the drunken "green madam" who turns out to be his wife—the only remedy is purging (5.6.37). And purging, in Jonson, flags shameful indiscretion.

Yet, the play's paragon of discretion is characterized not by continence, but by engagement. Jonson's identification of him as "a gamester" in the list of "Persons of the Play" (7, 6) reveals something about the new civility we find repeated in the fact that Quarlous often seems to have more in common with Ezekiel Edgworth, the "civil cutpurse," than with his gentle friend Winwife (2.2.48). Like Edgworth, Quarlous views even entertaining spectacle with an eye to its utility. When the gallants see Edgworth's theft of Cokes's purse, for example, Quarlous leverages this information into a deal. To secure their silence, Edgworth must steal Cokes's marriage license, a document Quarlous admits seems at first "nothing to me without other circumstances concur" (4.6.25). A good speculator, Quarlous secures a commodity for its potential value, but is thwarted in his first plan to marry Grace Wellborn, and her inheritance, after an encounter with the fair's madman, Troubleall. Rebounding nimbly, Quarlous invents "another use" for Troubleall, and disguising himself in the madman's clothes, he sets out to trick Overdo out of what amounts to a blank check: the Judge's official warrant (4.6.126). Before he can secure it, however, Dame Purecraft, formerly the target of Winwife's fortune hunting, accosts him. Believing she is fated to marry a madman, Purecraft throws herself at the disguised gamester. When he rebuffs her, she reveals the wealth she has accrued as a matchmaker for Puritans. Quarlous assesses the opportunity, the widow-winning for which he once mocked Winwife in terms of "currying a carcass that thou hast bound thyself to alive" (1.3.54):

> QUARLOUS Why should not I marry this six thousand pound . . . And a good
> trade, too, that she has beside . . . there's the question. It is money that
> I want; why should I not marry the money, when 'tis offered me? I have
> a licence and all: it is but razing out one name and putting in another.
> There's no playing with a man's fortune! (5.2.62–8)

Discretion demands an openness to even the mildly sordid proposition: one never knows which opportunity will make one's fortune. Sometimes, occasion demands the embrace of the unsavory; at other times, it requires the negative work of rejection.

The problem, as Quarlous recognizes, is that iniquity effaces social distinction, placing the burden on the tainted to distinguish himself anew ("*Facinus quos inquinat, aequat,*" 4.6.23–4).[45] Once Quarlous releases Edgworth from his bond, the grateful young cutpurse invites him to partake in a "moiety," half of a "silken gown," at Ursula's (4.6.17, 16). In the play's metonymic language, Edgworth has asked Quarlous to share a prostitute, an offer Quarlous rejects sharply with the words, "Keep it for your companions in beastliness." He adds, "If I had not already forgiven you a greater trespass, or thought you yet worth my beating, I would instruct your manners to whom you made your offers" (4.6.18–20). Quarlous's opprobrium marks Edgworth's pleasure as too base for gentle consideration. Thus, distaste distinguishes the slumming gamester from the indigenous flock of "Barthol'mew-birds" (ind.10).

That disgust separates in this way seems less surprising than its function as a "political poetics" that builds community.[46] Analyzing the typical reaction to a disgusting object encountered in public space, affect theorist Sianne Ngai concludes that the performed rejection—pointing, a guttural phatic utterance of grunting or retching, turning away—is actually a form of sociability which solicits others to find the object disgusting as well. We might reframe this observation in terms of our earlier discussion of market and drives by noting how the act of articulating disgust performs a kind of negation, a form of distinction by which exclusion itself becomes the ground for inclusion in an exclusive club of the appalled.[47]

Like Quarlous's rejection of Edgworth's proffered moiety, repudiation classifies the disgusted as a group: people who find the sharing of a prostitute loathsome.

Audience members who find themselves affiliated in this way may now recall other ways Quarlous's civility differs from that of the cutpurse. The most striking difference, which recalls us to the early modern sense of "quarrel," is that Quarlous's expected fractiousness is mated to a Sidneyian virtue, for, like Sidney's poet, the adept quarreller has the power and inclination to move others to moral improvement.[48] By the play's end, Quarlous's schemes support the humanist belief in theater's social utility, for in addition to exercising the discretion of Jonson's audience, Quarlous's machinations reform a bad magistrate, secure a love-match for Winwife, free a Wellborn lady from an ill-conceived match, and provide dinner for all.[49] His ungentle behavior results in a civil justice that fortifies community and potentially reproduces the narrative's deserving gentry, few though they may be. Quarlous's playful immersion instructs, in the words of the chastened Overdo, "*ad correctionem, non ad destructionem*" of the rest, fostering community, but hardly at the expense of all distinction (5.6.93).[50]

For Jonson, unconcerned that noting difference might be deemed discriminatory, the idea that some things are, for reasons particular to educated judgment, superior to others, makes disgust a useful gauge. From his vantage point prior to "pure" aesthetics, Jonson apprehends how the things we consume or incorporate do not remain separate from us, but color us, implicate us, and "ally" themselves to us, like toys to a Cokes. He cautions us, therefore, to attend to the alarm of disgust, the sign to which our polite, postmodern disinterest now so often inures us.

The danger of ignoring disgust's warning, as cultural critics Wendy Brown and Ellen Rooney join Sianne Ngai in pointing out, is that a refusal to be moved by or even to acknowledge what strikes us as potentially dangerous or contaminating is an error that enervates our political relations. Cultural artifacts once recognized as a site for social contest in their production and consumption have been depoliticized in recent decades by a bland, aesthetic pluralism that punishes critical rhetoric.[51] This is not to diminish the laudable gains of aesthetic and political inclusivity but to recognize that, taken to an extreme, even pluralism can be counterintuitively repressive. Extending Herbert Marcuse's insights in this regard, Ngai notes how a pluralistic ethos urges the polite – we might say "civilized" – classes to habitually suppress their objections to people and things that seem offensive, a practice that has, over time, encouraged the form of sociopolitical impotence Marcuse called "repressive tolerance." From a distance, such tolerance resembles an ahistorical tact, but Ngai intriguingly locates its early modern correlative in Thomas Hobbes's description of "contempt."[52]

In *Leviathan*, contempt bears the distinctive features of an aristocratic *noblesse oblige* that, in common with pity or scorn, deigns to tolerate the disgusting because they are ultimately deemed harmless.[53] For Hobbes, contempt is a kind of willful immobility that emerges when "the Heart is already moved otherwise, by other more potent objects." "Appetite" for or "aversion" to a potent object moves Hobbes's individual, but contempt for the impotent makes us "resist" all movement in a manner Ngai associates with the "tolerance" of repressed disgust. Once aversion can be managed in this way, the objects of our culture, as well as the criticism that developed to assess them, are rendered harmless and politically inconsequential.

Repressive tolerance, like Hobbesian contempt, exempts the civilized from being moved to act, even as it indexes the "sociopolitical ineffectuality" of classes of people and things considered unworthy of sustained or serious attention.[54]

If Ngai is correct, it seems almost inevitable that tolerance in its postmodern form would, on occasion, serve as an ethos to diffuse the class conflict that might otherwise threaten the status quo. But I want to suggest that this ethos needn't have developed along these lines. Jonson's early modern tolerance, significantly different than Hobbes's, does not sunder political function from form, so it takes all of its potential objects seriously until they prove unworthy. In Hobbes, contempt for certain kinds of objects plants an immediate "contumacy," or stubborn resistance to movement in "the heart," whereas in Jonson, the slow, internal eddy of decision-making may *appear* still but is actually a pooling of forces in which the "free flow of clear fluids in the brain" responsible for "clear judgment" remain vulnerable to the influx of darkening, action-inducing passions.[55] To tarry in the temporary eddy of the decision, like the thwarted Quarlous who turns over possibilities in the example above, is to be "judicious," not contemptuous (ind.57). As Quarlous demonstrates, the pause for judgment initiates action that may very well involve an embrace or violent rejection of things neither Hobbes nor his royalist friends would find worthy of affective engagement: a cutpurse's services, a game of Vapors, a swindler's love. Indeed, Jonsonian tolerance, like Jonsonian contempt, is whole-hearted when expressed: the articulation of a decision no more subdued than Quarlous's rejection of Edgworth's moiety.

Jonsonian discretion answers Ngai's call for a politics of disgust, and demystifies the ostensibly sophisticated disavowal of disgust that vindicates apathy as tolerance. Warp and weft, the allegorical fabric of discretion, connects *all* fair goers, whether visitor or denizen, high or low, in a ceaseless process of incorporation and negation that configures individual and collective civil identities. Only flexible wits, who operate from the civilized vantage of comprehending the values that structure transactions without sacralizing them as absolute law, will thrive. Quarlous's triumph communicates the counterintuitive wisdom that willing immersion in the world, glutted as it is with inferior, down-market trash, strengthens our ability to recognize the good and renders visible the taste of the discreet. Discretion, materialized in what one buys and passes by, what one assimilates and rejects, is reflected back to us through our social interactions, our politics. If concerns about the threat of repressive tolerance are warranted, then Jonson's allegorical pleasure fair proffers an even more useful "fairing" (2.4.15) for those encouraged to tolerate the intolerable, quash their objections, and repress their disgust: be more Quarlous.

Notes

1 Jonson's plays *Bartholomew Fair* and *Every Man Out of His Humour* both begin with "inductions" preceding Act I. Some play citations in this chapter reflect this. Unless otherwise noted, Jonson quotations in this chapter are cited from the following sources: *Bartholomew Fair*, in *The Cambridge Edition of the Works of Ben Jonson*, vol. 4, ed.

John Creaser (Cambridge: Cambridge University Press, 2012); *Every Man Out of His Humour*, ed. Helen Ostovich (Manchester: Manchester University Press, 2001); *Timber: or Discoveries*, in *Ben Jonson: The Complete Poems*, ed. George Parfitt (New York: Penguin Books, 1975).

2 *Oxford English Dictionary*, 2nd ed., s.v. "bawd."

3 For more on this stink's olfactory evocation of memory and the temporal dislocations of smell, see Harris, "The Smell of Macbeth." Holly Dugan's subsequent "As Dirty as Smithfield and Stinking Every Whit," explores the site specificity of this odor.

4 For example, Jay Zysk connects Ursula's hybridity to the play's generic conflation of city comedy and cookbook. Zysk, "What You Eat," 70–1.

5 Space prohibits more than a mention of perhaps the predominant vein of commentary on Ursula, which reads her as a figure for the promiscuous and multiplying market. See Miller, "Consuming Mothers/Consuming Merchants"; Paster, "Leaky Vessels"; and Haynes, "Festivity."

6 See Suzanne Gossett's introduction to her edition of the play, 10. Debora Shuger's "good medieval allegory" depends on a "biblical passage provid[ing] a key to unlock the moral significance of its analogue." Shuger, "Hypocrites," 71–2. More broadly, in his book on premodern allegory, Jeremy Tambling insists that Jonson "implicitly opposed allegory" for its thwarting of "perspicuity." Tambling, *Allegory*, 57. It is likewise noteworthy that despite its refreshing materialist emphasis, which touches on Jonson's interest in the embodiment of language and materiality of figures, the recent Cambridge collection *Ben Jonson in Context* contains not a single entry for "allegory" in its index.

7 I subscribe to Maureen Quilligan's understanding of allegory in *Language of Allegory*, 26–33, and to Walter Benjamin's in *Allegory and Trauerspiel*, in which he describes a similar dynamism. Daniel Boyarin's sense of allegory as a "technique . . . of the body" that relies on readers' sensual understanding of the world's objects, including the sound of language and materiality of the text, has been influential, as well. Boyarin, *Radical Jew*, 14.

8 Jonson, *Timber*, 2500–503.

9 Maus, "Facts." Laurie Ellinghausen does some of this work, reading the allegorical figure of Vulcan to locate Jonson's "anti-materialism within a broader social context," but she does not discuss allegory per se. Ellinghausen, *Labor and Writing*, 64. Critics who treat the disgusting in Jonson's city comedies generally frame it in terms of the carnivalesque, or "festive," which tends to preclude much focus on literary form. For an overview of this criticism, see Gossett's introduction to *Bartholomew Fair*, 23–4.

10 A number of studies explore Jonson's interest in the nearly synonymous "judgment" in relation to the new market economy. Strong examples, most of which adopt a more historicist approach than the present study, include Dutton, *Ben Jonson*; McLuskie, "Making and Buying"; Salingar, "Jacobean Playwrights"; Agnew, *Worlds Apart*, 119–21; and Wayne, "Pox," 72, who comes closest to my interests in his argument that Jonson makes judgment visible as a "guarantor of social distinction." Wayne, in "Drama and Society," 122–3, also anticipates my understanding of Jonson's creative approach to morality but does not explore how Jonson seeks to reorient morality through allegory or by evoking disgust. On the early modern understanding of occasion as an intellectual and ethical test, see Berger, "Narrative as Rhetoric."

11 "Discretion" in Jonson's period retains both the sense of "sound judgement" and "distinction," *OED*, s.v. "distinction"; in the century after Jonson, it will also come to mean "civility," another key term in the play.

12 There is consensus that Kant's *Critique of Judgment* represents the foundational modern statement of aesthetics as a sphere of the beautiful in fine art, isolated from economics and politics, to be contemplated disinterestedly, which is to say, free from obfuscating passions and practical interests. See Gigante, *Taste*, and Ross, *Aesthetic Paths*.

13 See Whitney's insight into early moderns' "ante-aesthetic" approach to drama. I depart only in my conviction that dramatists were very aware of drama's ability to elude attempts to "measure and control" meaning. Whitney, "Ante-aesthetics," 50.

14 See Elias' much debated but still generative pioneering statement on "the civilizing process." Elias, *Civilizing Process*, 51, 99. Jonson's interest in civility is suggested by the play's thirteen variations on the word.

15 Paster describes the fair as a kind of "laboratory" for "self-management." Paster, "Humoral Body," 263. See Paster's earlier book for more on the way Jonson imagined humors shaping both individual and social identity. Paster, *Humoring the Body*, 238–40.

16 Bourdieu's analysis of the "lifestyle" choices of his study's participants reveals how "taste classifies." Bourdieu, *Distinction*, 5–6. The higher one's status, the more stylized one's taste in everything from food to artwork tends to be because elite taste eschews sensual delight for more abstract pleasures.

17 Eagleton, *Ideology*, 7.

18 Carruthers, *Craft of Thought*, 144. The *Psychomachia*, with its symmetrical opposition between Virtues and Vices, may seem a perverse choice for a discussion of complex allegory, but see Paxson's persuasive poststructuralist reading of the poem in *Poetics of Personification*.

19 See Carruthers on the "neuropsychology" of memory in *Book of Memory*, 46–79.

20 Carruthers, *Book of Memory*, 68–9.

21 Taylor, *Thomas Middleton*, 34, confirms that Tudor grammar schools relied on Prudentius and other "Christian poets." On Jonson's debt to moral drama, see Dessen, *Jonson's Moral Comedy*, and the fifth chapter of Murakami, *Moral Play*.

22 While many readers, like Vickers in "Ben Jonson's Classicism," reaffirm Jonson's self-identification with classical texts, others, like Shapiro, call attention to Jonson's repression of his debt to less prestigious sources that are nevertheless echoed in his work. Shapiro, *Rival Playwrights*, 40, 62.

23 White provides ample evidence in *Theater and Reformation*. And certainly, poets like Spenser contributed to allegory's reformation in a manner that attests, as Barbara Correll suggests in "Guyon's Blush," to allegory's "unsettling" deterritorializing potential (see Chapter 2 in this volume).

24 Luxon, *Literal Figures*, 40–50.

25 Puttenham, *Art of English Poesy*, 270–71.

26 Puttenham, *Art of English Poesy*, 238, 271–2.

27 Puttenham, *Art of English Poesy*, 270–76.

28 As Quilligan notes, wordplay is "generically basic to allegory." Quilligan, *Language of Allegory*, 42.

29 Bourdieu, *Distinction*, 1–5, 229.

30 Appadurai, *Social Life of Things*, 25.

31 While allowing for the cultural specificity of items in particular exchange spheres, Kopytoff persuasively defends the relevance of this model for describing moral exchange economies in non- or pre-commercial as well as commercial societies. Kopytoff, "Cultural Biography of Things," 71–2, 77.

32 By the early seventeenth century, the double sense of "place" as both geographical locale and rank in traditional social hierarchy makes it a fraught term, as in John Bulwer's complaint that all creatures but man "keep their ranks, their places and natures in the world," qtd. in Agnew's *Worlds Apart*, 96. On the role of "place" in maintaining social harmony, see Hindle, "A Sense of Place?"

33 McLuskie describes how the exploitation of boy players opened the door for increasingly abusive capitalist relations between theater impresarios like Henslowe and adult players. McLuskie, "Making and Buying," 147–9.

34 See Goux's discussion of the "totally imaginary" relationship of commodities to gold. Gold's superfluous qualities foster exchange as the "general equivalent" by which all other commodities may be measured. Goux, *Symbolic Economies*, 19–20. "[A]lphabetic writing" also serves this purpose, argues Goux, because of its tendency to "overflow" with significance, by which Goux seems to have in mind techniques like allegory. Goux, *Symbolic Economies*, 42, 31.

35 For Marcus, the play suggests that "communal vitality" "depend[s] on the ... breaking of legalism itself." Marcus, "Mire and Authorship," 175. See also Knapp, "Publicke Riot," 589.
36 *OED*, 2nd ed., s.v. "quarrel."
37 Krier, "Form and Gait," 73.
38 *OED*, 2nd ed., s.v. "whether."
39 Gossett's gloss reads: "*cross and pile*] technically, across or with the nap of cloth; either way." Jonson, *Bartholomew Fair*, ed. Gossett, 1.4, n. 92–3.
40 It is well known that Bartholomew Fair began as an annual cloth fair linked to St. Bartholomew's feast day. For more on the "deep making" of clothing, see Stallybrass and Jones, *Renaissance Clothing*.
41 This discussion draws on Kopytoff's reading of the social life of the Marxian commodity. Kopytoff, "Cultural Biography of Things," 71–3.
42 Freud, "On Negation," 215. Freud first introduced his controversial theory that the pleasure principle serves both Eros and Thanatos in *Beyond the Pleasure Principle*, 77.
43 Jonson, *Timber*, 3063–7; emphasis mine.
44 Jonson, *Timber*, 3069–70. *OED*, s.v. "appetite."
45 "Whom crime pollutes, it makes level," Lucan, *Civil War*, 5.290, qtd. in Jonson, *Bartholomew Fair*, John Creaser, ed., 4.6.23, n. 23.
46 Ngai, "Raw Matter," 167.
47 Ngai, "Raw Matter," 172, 185. Ngai draws felicitously on post-structural and psychoanalytic theory to consider affect's political function. This method allows her to perceive, for example, that the "real" object of disgust is not an ontological object, per se, but that object's exclusion, which builds community through abjection of an other. Ngai, "Raw Matter," 186. Her thinking about disgust's potential in the face of the current moment of depoliticizing repressive tolerance led me to ponder Jonson's discretion, at home with disgust and more embodied than the Hobbes-Kant variety, as the road to a civility not taken.
48 *OED*, 2nd ed., s.v. "quarrel." Sidney famously argued that poetry is the highest knowledge in "moving [men] to well doing." Sidney, *Defence*, 18.
49 See Tylus, "Par Accident," on continental and English humanist debates concerning theater's capacity to promote the public good.
50 "[T]o correct, not to destroy." Latin Vulgate text of the Bible, 2 Corinthians 13:10. Qtd. in Jonson, *Bartholomew Fair*, John Creaser, ed., 5.6.93, n. 93–4.
51 See Brown for the ways "tolerance" can consolidate the dominance of the hegemony, in *Regulating Aversion*, 4–18; also Rooney in *Seductive Reasoning*, 27.
52 Ngai, *Ugly Feelings*, 336.
53 Ngai, *Ugly Feelings*, 341, 336–7. I extend Ngai's reading of Hobbes on contempt, *Leviathan*, 34–5.
54 Ngai, *Ugly Feelings*, 342. The articulation of things like racism, homophobia, and misogyny are contaminating, Ngai maintains, and not to be shrugged off in service to maintaining a peace that fosters affluence, 341.
55 Jonson seems especially invested in the "changeable currents of feeling" found in the hydraulic model of humoral theory Paster describes in *Humoring the Body*, 198. The heart, as she notes, functioned in this model as both a receptacle and a font for the flowing mixture of humors, thoughts, and feelings that inundate the body. Paster, *Humoring the Body*, 69.

References

Agnew, Jean-Christophe. *Worlds Apart: The Market and the Theater in Anglo-American Thought, 1550–1750*. Cambridge: Cambridge University Press, 1986.
Appadurai, Arjun, ed. *The Social Life of Things: Commodities in Cultural Perspective*. Cambridge: Cambridge University Press, 1986.

Benjamin, Walter. *Allegory and Trauerspiel: The Origin of German Tragic Drama*. Translated by John Osborne. New York: Verso, 1998.

Berger, Harry, Jr. "Narrative as Rhetoric in the *Faerie Queene*." *English Literary Renaissance* 21, no. 1 (1991): 3–48.

Bourdieu, Pierre. *Distinction: A Social Critique of the Judgement of Taste*. Translated by Richard Nice. Cambridge, MA: Harvard University Press, 1984.

Boyarin, Daniel. *A Radical Jew: Paul and the Politics of Identity*. Berkeley: University of California Press, 1997.

Brown, Wendy. *Regulating Aversion: Tolerance in the Age of Identity and Empire*. Princeton: Princeton University Press, 2006.

Carruthers, Mary. *The Book of Memory: A Study of Memory in Medieval Culture*. Cambridge: Cambridge University Press, 1990.

———. *The Craft of Thought: Meditation, Rhetoric, and the Making of Images, 400–1200*. Cambridge: Cambridge University Press, 1998.

Dessen, Alan C. *Jonson's Moral Comedy*. Evanston, IL: Northwestern University Press, 1971.

Dugan, Holly. "'As Dirty as Smithfield and Stinking Every Whit': The Smell of the Hope Theatre." In *Shakespeare's Theatres and the Effects of Performance*, edited by Farah Karim-Cooper and Tiffany Stern, 195–213. London: Bloomsbury, 2013.

Dutton, Richard. *Ben Jonson: To the First Folio*. Cambridge: Cambridge University Press, 1983.

Eagleton, Terry. *The Ideology of the Aesthetic*. New York: Blackwell, 1990.

Elias, Norbert. *The Civilizing Process: Sociogenetic and Psychogenetic Investigations*. Translated by Edmund Jephcott. Rev. ed. 1994. Edited by Eric Dunning, Johan Goudsblom and Stephen Mennell. Oxford: Blackwell, 2000.

Ellinghausen, Laurie. *Labor and Writing in Early Modern England, 1567–1667*. Farnham: Ashgate, 2008.

Freud, Sigmund. *Beyond the Pleasure Principle*. Translated and edited by James Strachey. The Standard Edition. New York: W.W. Norton, 1961.

———. "On Negation" (1925). In *General Psychological Theory: Papers on Metapsychology*. Edited by Philip Rieff, 213–17. New York: Simon & Schuster, 1963.

Gigante, Denise. *Taste: A Literary History*. New Haven: Yale University Press, 2005.

Goux, Jean-Joseph. *Symbolic Economies: After Marx and Freud*. Translated by Jennifer Curtis Gage. Ithaca: Cornell University Press, 1990.

Harris, Jonathan Gil. "The Smell of *Macbeth*." *Shakespeare Quarterly* 58, no. 4 (Winter 2007): 465–86.

Haynes, Jonathan. "Festivity and the Dramatic Economy of Jonson's *Bartholomew Fair*." *English Literary History* 51, no. 4 (Winter 1984): 645–68.

Hindle, Steve. "A Sense of Place? Becoming and Belonging in the Rural Parish, 1550–1650." In *Communities in Early Modern England: Networks, Place, Rhetoric*, edited by Alexandra Shepard and Phil Withington, 96–114. Manchester: Manchester University Press, 2001.

Hobbes, Thomas. *Leviathan, or The Matter, Forme, & Power of a Common-Wealth Ecclesiasticall and Civill*. Edited and introduced by Ian Shapiro. Rethinking the Western Tradition. New Haven: Yale University Press, 2010.

Jonson, Ben. *Bartholomew Fair*. Edited by John Creaser. *The Cambridge Edition of the Works of Ben Jonson*, vol. 4. Edited by David Bevington, Martin Butler, and Ian Donaldson. Cambridge: Cambridge University Press, 2012.

———. *Bartholomew Fair*. Edited by Suzanne Gossett. Revels Student Editions. Manchester: Manchester University Press, 2000.

————. *Every Man Out of His Humour*. Edited by Helen Ostovich. The Revels Plays. Manchester: Manchester University Press, 2001.

————. *Timber: or Discoveries*. Edited by George Parfitt. *Ben Jonson: The Complete Poems*. New York: Penguin Books, 1975.

Knapp, Peggy. "Ben Jonson and the Publicke Riot." *English Literary History* 26 (1979): 577–94.

Kopytoff, Igor. "The Cultural Biography of Things: Commoditization as Process." In *The Social Life of Things: Commodities in Cultural Perspective*, edited by Arjun Appadurai, 64–91. Cambridge: Cambridge University Press, 1986.

Krier, Theresa M. "The Form and Gait of the Body: Physical Carriage, Genre and Spenserian Allegory." In *Approaches to Teaching Spenser's* Faerie Queene, edited by David Lee Miller and Alexander Dunlop, 72–81. New York: Modern Language Association, 1994.

Luxon, Thomas. *Literal Figures: Puritan Allegory and the Reformation Crisis in Representation*. Chicago: University of Chicago Press, 1995.

McLuskie, Kate. "Making and Buying: Ben Jonson and the Commercial Theatre Audience." In *Refashioning Ben Jonson: Gender, Politics and the Jonsonian Canon*, edited by Julie Sanders et al., 134–54. New York: St. Martin's Press, 1998.

Marcus, S. Leah. "Ben Jonson's Bartholomew Fair: Of Mire and Authorship." In *The Theatrical City: Culture, Theatre, and Politics in London, 1576–1649*, edited by David L. Smith, Richard Strier, and David Bevington, 170–81. Cambridge: Cambridge University Press, 1995.

Maus, Katharine Eisaman. "Facts of the Matter: Satiric and Ideal Economies in the Jonsonian Imagination." In *Ben Jonson's 1616 Folio*, edited by Jennifer Brady and W.H. Herendeen, 64–89. Newark: University of Delaware Press, 1991.

Miller, Shannon. "Consuming Mothers/Consuming Merchants: The Carnivalesque Economy of Jacobean City Comedy." *Modern Language Studies* 26, no. 2 (1996): 73–97.

Murakami, Ineke. *Moral Play and Counterpublic: Transformations in Moral Drama, 1465–1599*. New York: Routledge, 2011.

Ngai, Sianne. "Raw Matter: A Poetics of Disgust." In *Telling It Slant: Avant-Garde Poetics of the 1990s*, edited by Mark Wallace and Steven Marks, 161–90. Tuscaloosa: University of Alabama Press, 2002.

————. *Ugly Feelings*. Cambridge, MA: Harvard University Press, 2005.

Paster, Gail Kern. "*Bartholomew Fair* and the Humoral Body." In *Early Modern English Drama: a Critical Companion*, edited by Garrett A. Sullivan, Jr., Patrick Cheney, and Andrew Hadfield, 260–71. Oxford: Oxford University Press, 2006.

————. *Humoring the Body: Emotions and the Shakespearean Stage*. Chicago: University of Chicago Press, 2004.

————. "Leaky Vessels: The Incontinent Women of City Comedy," *Renaissance Drama* 18 (1987): 43–65.

Paxson, James. *The Poetics of Personification*. Cambridge: Cambridge University Press, 1994.

Peacham, Henry. *The Garden of Eloquence. English Linguistics 1500–1800: A Collection of Facsimile Reprints*. Edited by R.C. Alston. Menston: Scolar Press, 1971.

Puttenham, George. *The Art of English Poesy by George Puttenham: A Critical Edition*. Edited by Frank Whigham and Wayne A. Rebhorn. Ithaca: Cornell University Press, 2007.

Quilligan, Maureen. *The Language of Allegory: Defining the Genre*. Ithaca: Cornell University Press, 1979.

Rooney, Ellen. *Seductive Reasoning: Pluralism as the Problematic of Contemporary Theory*. Ithaca: Cornell University Press, 1989.

Ross, Alison. *The Aesthetic Paths of Philosophy: Presentation in Kant, Heidegger, Lacaoue-Labarthe, and Nancy*. Redwood City, CA: Stanford University Press, 2007.

Salingar, Leo. "Jacobean Playwrights and 'Judicious Spectators'." *Renaissance Drama* 22 (1991): 209–34.

Sanders, Julie, ed. *Ben Jonson in Context*. Cambridge: Cambridge University Press, 2010.

Shapiro, James. *Rival Playwrights: Marlowe, Jonson, Shakespeare*. New York: Columbia University Press, 1991.

Shuger, Debora. "Hypocrites and Puppets in *Bartholomew Fair*." *Modern Philology* 82 (1984): 70–73.

Sidney, Sir Philip. *The Defence of Poesie, Political Discourses, Correspondence, Translation*, vol. 3. Edited by Albert Feuillerat. Cambridge: Cambridge University Press, 1962.

Stallybrass, Peter, and Ann Rosalind Jones. *Renaissance Clothing and the Materials of Memory*. Cambridge: Cambridge University Press, 2000.

Tambling, Jeremy. *Allegory*. The New Critical Idiom. New York: Routledge, 2009.

Taylor, Gary. Introduction to *Thomas Middleton: The Collected Works*. Edited by Gary Taylor and John Lavagnino. Oxford: Oxford University Press, 2010.

Tylus, Jane. "'Par Accident': The Public Work of Early Modern Theater." In *Reading the Early Modern Passions: Essays in the Cultural History of Emotion*, edited by Gail Kern Paster, Katherine Rowe, and Mary Floyd-Wilson, 253–71. Philadelphia: University of Pennsylvania Press, 2004.

Vickers, Brian. "Ben Jonson's Classicism Revisited," *Ben Jonson Journal* 21, no. 2 (2014): 153–202.

Wayne, Don E. "Drama and Society in the Age of Jonson: An Alternative View." *Renaissance Drama* 13 (1982): 103–29.

———. "'Pox on Your Distinction!' Humanist Reformation and Deformations of the Everyday in *The Staple of News*." In *Renaissance Culture and the Everyday*, edited by Patricia Fumerton and Simon Hunt, 67–91. Philadelphia: University of Pennsylvania Press, 1999.

White, Paul Whitfield. *Theater and Reformation: Protestantism, Patronage and Playing in Tudor England*. Cambridge: Cambridge University Press, 1993.

Whitney, Charles. "Ante-aesthetics: Towards a Theory of Early Modern Audience Response." In *Shakespeare and Modernity: Early Modern to Millennium*, edited by Hugh Grady, 40–60. New York: Routledge, 2000.

Zysk, Jay. "You Are What You Eat: Cooking and Writing Across the Species Barrier in Ben Jonson's *Bartholomew Fair*." In *The Indistinct Human in Renaissance Literature*, edited by Jean E. Feerick and Vin Nardizzi, 9–84. New York: Palgrave Macmillan, 2012.

9 Jonson's old age

The force of disgust

Laura Kolb

To call Ben Jonson a deliberately disgusting writer is neither an insult nor an overstatement. Throughout his long career, in lyric poems and dramatic works, Jonson analyzes the complex dynamics of revulsion, aversion, and abhorrence. In two of his best-known plays, for example, Jonson calls attention to the border between delicious and disgusting foodstuffs, in speeches linking materialistic greed to physical appetite, and both to an expansive, enumerative poetic mode.[1] *The Alchemist*'s (1610) Epicure Mammon dreams of "the tongues of carps, dormice and camels' heels" (2.2.75) and "the beards of barbels, served, instead of salads" (2.2.82), while the title character of *Volpone* (1606) imagines a meal concocted entirely of birds' brains and tongues (3.7.201–2).[2]

Mammon and Volpone are not trying to disgust their onstage audiences. Indeed, their speeches are intended to elicit desire, and, in Volpone's case, to inflame it. Nevertheless, Jonson may well be trying to disgust *us*. His vivid gustatory and tactile "inventions" may conjure in our mouths as much as in our minds the prickliness of "barbels' beards," the slipperiness of bird brains, the cartilaginous toughness of a camel's heel.[3] In these speeches disgust emerges as an involuntary response to the imagined ingestion of animal parts that, for all their status as exotic luxuries, "challenge the boundary between food and not food."[4] Elsewhere, Jonson takes up differently disgusting matter to different effect. The poet's interest in the scatological is well documented and much discussed. In *Sejanus* (1603), for instance, the emperor notes that Eudemus, the court physician, could tell him ladies' most intimate secrets: whose urine smells most of violets, whose "siege is best," and "who makes the hardest faces on her stool" (1.1.305–6).[5] Jonson does not limit his exploration of disgust to the foods we put in the body or its excrement. In his poetry, he considers the flesh itself – his own flesh, no less – as the stuff of a comically revolting spectacle: "Unprofitable chattel, fat and old / Laden with belly and doth hardly approach / His friends, but to break chairs, or crack a coach."[6]

What is immediately striking about these brief passages is their persuasiveness, the way they compel and hold attention, and the way they invite imaginative supplementation on the part of the reader.[7] We cannot look away from Jonson's unflattering self-portrait in "To My Lady Covell" any more than we can help involuntarily feeling Mammon's "barbel's beards" on our tongues or imagining the look (and feel and smell) of the objects of Eudemus's scrutiny. Nor, perhaps, do we want to. In the *Poetics* Aristotle observes, "We enjoy looking at the most exact portrayals of things we do not like to see in real life, the lowest animals for instance, or corpses."[8] Aristotle attributes the allure of such images to basic, human enjoyment of artful representation, but as these scattered examples from Jonson's work suggest, the effect of "disgusting" text – repulsive subject matter irresistibly conjured in the mind's eye by means of vivid language (*enargeia*) – involves something in excess of pleasure in mimetic accuracy.

In Jonson's work the disgusting compels attention alongside aversion and gives rise to the conflicting impulses to look away and to look more. The paradox, that disgust involves attraction as well as revulsion, emerges in myriad accounts of the affect, in literary studies and the social sciences.[9] Here, I want to suggest that in Jonson's work the double response invited by disgusting objects and artworks relates to the poet's own "double attitude" toward presenting work to audiences and readers.[10] In conjuring images of disgusting things and in amplifying their effects with grossly material language, Jonson isolates and explores one problematic aspect of the reception of his own work: the efficacy of poetic texts whose power derives from unpleasantness and ugliness and from the capacity to disgust as well as to delight.

Jonson's exploration of disgust as an allegory for textual relations has an important counterpart in a theory of beauty articulated by writers ranging from the Renaissance poet Sir Philip Sidney to the twentieth-century art critic Dave Hickey. This line of thinking holds that beauty is rhetorical. That is, beauty can be measured in terms of its effects, which are analogous to the workings of artful speech. The sisters Philoclea and Pamela in Sidney's *Arcadia*, one characterized by "sweetness" and the other by "majesty," illustrate the point.[11] Sidney writes that "Philoclea's beauty only persuaded, but so persuaded as all hearts must yield; Pamela's beauty used violence, and such violence as no heart could resist."[12] Two styles of beauty map onto two modes of rhetoric, the one gently persuasive, the other irresistibly so.

Writing on Renaissance painting, Hickey describes immediate "visual pleasure" as a precondition to ongoing engagement.[13] Overtly "beautiful" works of art, in his account, first make claims on the viewer's attention and then address her intellect and ideological commitments:

> Throughout this period, a loose, protean collection of tropes and figures signifying "beauty" functions as the *pathos* that recommends the *logos* and *ethos* of visual argumentation to our attention. The task of beauty is to enfranchise the audience and acknowledge its power – to designate a territory of shared values between the image and its beholder and then, in this territory, to advance an argument by valorizing the picture's problematic content.[14]

According to Hickey, beauty is efficacy: a source of immediate pleasure and fascination that enables persuasion. It offers sensory and experiential excitement that recruits the beholder to grapple with the argumentative content of that which is beheld.

I would like to suggest that Ben Jonson understands disgust in similar terms. His work posits that *disgustingness* is rhetorical: it commands attention, and it compels a response. Moments of disgust in Jonson consistently ask us to think about the relationship between text and reader and, in particular, about the forms of control texts exert over their audiences. For Aristotle depictions of repulsive objects were a test case for the appeal of mimesis itself. For Jonson they are a test case for his and his works' power to enthrall an audience, especially that Jonsonian bugbear, the unresponsive or misapprehending audience made up of those who are not "understanders."[15]

Studies that delve into Jonson's treatment of disgusting subject matter, especially on stage, have centered on matters of food, digestion, and excretion. Jonson, the poet of the belly, linked the alimentary tract to everything from the creative processes of *imitatio* to theories of gender to the allure and danger of giving rein to the lower bodily orders.[16] Here I turn away from issues of consumption, digestion, and excretion toward images of the aging or dying body, which, I argue, operates simultaneously as an object of disgust and as site for reflection on the effect of poetry and drama on their audiences. The psychologist Paul Rozin and his collaborators distinguish "core disgust," which relates to issues of food, eating, and contamination, from "animal-reminder" disgust, revulsion at the body, death, and decay.[17] Hamlet's repeated return to the paradox of mankind – at once "like an angel" yet grossly embodied, earthbound, food for worms – exemplifies this type of disgust, mixing fascination with horror at the fact that, as Rozin puts it, "humans must eat, excrete, and have sex, just like other animals."[18] And, Hamlet might add, die like other animals. Rozin cites violations of our "fragile body envelopes" as particularly "disgusting . . . reminders of our animal vulnerability."[19] For Hamlet almost everything to do with bodies – eating, drinking, kissing, dying – operates as a reminder of the grossness and impermanence of flesh, of death and decay.

For Jonson, signs of aging seem to have been particularly disgusting.[20] This chapter focuses on two texts that present states in which "human being" and "dead thing" are proximate, and where that proximity produces or is made to produce revulsion in an audience. In *Volpone* this happens in the outrageous exchange in which Mosca coaches and collaborates with Corvino on a grotesque, descriptive blazon of his "dying" master's face. In the late "self-portrait" poems it happens when Jonson imagines his own body as an object of disgust in the eyes of an other. In both texts disgust has a strongly rhetorical dimension, operating as a means through which an author seeks to control both his text and its reception.

Old age, death, and disgust in *Volpone*

At the end of *Volpone*'s second scene, Volpone begins a transformation from evidently robust middle age to elderly infirmity.[21] The first step in his metamorphosis is sartorial: "Fetch me my gown, / My furs, and night-caps" (1.2.84–6), he commands, donning the costume of a sick old man. Next he conjures the bodily ailments of age:

> Now, my feigned cough, my phthisic, and my gout,
> My apoplexy, palsy, and catarrhs,

Help, with your forced functions, this my posture,
Wherein this three year I have milked their hopes. (1.2.124–7)

Volpone calls upon sickness as a poet might call upon his muse.[22] Indeed his performance as a whole invites a parallel with Jonson's work as a poet and dramatist. Volpone "counterfeits" and "feigns," and in so doing he creates an illusory, fictional world.[23] As he conjures his diseases his language is copious, proliferative, and sonically thick; heavily alliterative and clogged with consonants; fat with sounds.

Elsewhere in *Volpone* Jonson links the pleasures of words in profusion both to the glittering allure of material plenitude and to the delights of the flesh.[24] Here he associates *copia verborum* with a more repulsive form of materiality, the phlegm and fluids that build up in and issue forth from a sick body, and the coughs and palsies that shake it. Yet these words, too, enact a kind of enchantment. In *Volpone*, disgust – or characters' (highly variable) capacity to be disgusted by repulsive objects, language, imagery – works as an index of poetic efficacy, measured in terms of audience affect. Through Mosca's grotesque blazons of his master's face and body especially, Jonson articulates a poetics of disgust in which the paradoxical allure of repulsive objects allegorizes the irresistible force of images conjured through heightened speech and the pleasures of artful language.

The first of the hopeful heirs to visit, the lawyer Voltore, encounters Volpone in what appears to be poor physical health but relatively sound mind. This is his least disgusting "sick" guise, which he later presents to Lady Would-Be. The *magnifico* coughs and complains, "Mine eyes are bad" (1.3.17). Yet he speaks clearly to his visitor and expresses sad acceptance of his supposed fate: "I feel me going – uh! uh! uh! uh! – / I am sailing to my port – uh! uh! uh! uh!– / And I am glad I am so near my haven" (1.3.28–30). Here Volpone plays one actively preparing for death, mentally and spiritually. In the following scene, however, Corbaccio encounters Volpone wordless and inert. To Corbaccio, himself advanced in years and plagued by the diseases Volpone only counterfeits (see 1.5.147–59), Mosca describes his master almost entirely in terms of bodily decline: "His eyes are set, / His face drawn longer than 'twas wont" (1.4.39–40); "His mouth / Is ever gaping and his eyelids hang" (1.4.41–2); "A freezing numbness stiffens all his joints, / And makes the colour of his flesh like lead" (1.4.42–3); "His pulse beats slow and dull" (1.4.44). When Corbaccio asks whether Volpone still experiences "the swimming of his head" (1.4.51), Mosca responds that he is "past the scotomy" (that is, dizziness) having "lost his feeling" altogether (1.4.53). This is a far cry from the previous scene's articulate sufferer whose world-weariness signaled the persistence of an inner life. The Volpone presented here is incapable of thought, language, and perhaps even sensation. He is scarcely more person than thing. Only the involuntary excretions of the eyes, nose, and mouth signal that his body is still alive.[25] Volpone himself later discusses age in similar terms, scornfully emphasizing the "subhuman" quality of the elderly: "Their limbs faint, / Their senses dull, their seeing, hearing, going, / All dead before them . . . Yet this is reckoned life!" (1.5.147–51).

On stage Volpone probably looks much the same to the second visitor as he did to the first. Yet Mosca's words overlay his master's appearance with new significance. For one thing, they ensure attention to his ointment-daubed eyes and sickly demeanor, the costume and posture that make up Volpone's part of the performance. For another, Mosca's description of his master's face has a kind of force of its own. The materiality of his abundant, proliferative language mimics the insistent, uncontrolled materiality of Volpone's body – or rather, creates it – since even "in costume" Volpone provides only the basic ground for the lavishly grotesque figure Mosca describes. Volpone makes himself look old and ill, and Mosca in turn makes Volpone disgusting. His words amplify and supplement the on-stage visitor's encounter with the "dying" man and conjure repulsive details in the theater audience's imagination.

Some of the most effectively "disgusting" description focuses on Volpone's face and head. "From his brain" (1.4.46), Mosca reports, "flows a cold sweat, with a continual rheum / Forth the resolved corners of his eyes" (1.4.48–9). The head, the seat of reason and the site of thought, imagination, and creative power, is reduced to its physical components, and even these are breaking down. As Mosca presents him, Volpone has become mere matter. A living corpse, both stiff and liquefying, his dying body points simultaneously to both the grossness and the impermanence of flesh.

If it is fairly obvious *that* Mosca makes Volpone disgusting – in our eyes if not in Corbaccio's, a distinction to which I'll return. *Why* he chooses to do so is less immediately clear. In his *History of Old Age*, Georges Minois argues that Renaissance attitudes toward the elderly were often deeply negative: "Old age and death constituted the greatest of scandals for the two went together: one announced the other; old people's faces were henceforth to be viewed above all as death masks."[26] In Minois's account, the aging face functions as a *memento mori* and the body's "decline [and] decrepitude" foreshadow the transformation of living person to corpse.[27] Minois's argument resonates strongly with the themes concentrated in Volpone's sickbed scenes: the reduction of self to body, and the Jonsonian mixture of horror and fascination at the fact that, as Alexander Leggatt puts it, "a human being can become a dead thing."[28]

Volpone's Act One transformation not only proleptically transports him between middle and old age; it also turns him into a symbol of the even more fragile temporal boundary between the end of life and death itself. A familiar school of critical thought on the play holds that Volpone seeks to cheat death by his acquisitiveness and scheming.[29] His possessive enthusiasm for the world's variety and plenitude coupled with an insatiable desire for more (more money and stuff, but also more variety, experience, sensation, fantasy) can be seen as a way of stopping time, of creating a dilated temporality in which worldly pleasures expand infinitely. Yet it is equally true that the character and the play as a whole have a tendency to speed up time as well as to slow it down, making the middle-aged *magnifico* into a sick old man (with Voltore) and then making that sick old man into a near-corpse (with Corbaccio). In fact, the inheritance trick on which the plot hinges depends on this kind of proleptic knitting-up of *soon* into *now*. The heirs repeatedly receive assurance that Volpone's wealth essentially already belongs to them since he is so near death. Mosca directs his question, "Is not all here yours?" (1.5.77) at Corvino, the third of the legacy hunters, quietly eliding present and future, and expectation with possession.

A reading of the play influenced by Minois, then, might suggest that when Mosca's rhetoric amplifies the vileness of his master's body he makes Volpone into a token of his own, supposedly imminent death, thereby heightening the heirs' mood of greedy "expectation" (5.2.67). At the same time, however, Mosca's grotesque inventory of his master's parts does seem to slow down time, though with the close attention commanded by disgusting rather than desirable matter. Even as it conflates present – illness, old age – with the near future – death – Mosca's vivid portrait of the dying man dilates the present moment – the gap between *now* and *soon* – as it forces us to attend, in minute detail conjured through heightened language, to a lavishly realized object of disgust. His words call for an almost erotic appreciation of the minutiae of Volpone's oozing, stiffening body.

Indeed, disgust and desire skim close to one another throughout the play. Most obviously perhaps, Mosca's portrait of the "dying" Volpone to the legacy hunters resembles his later enumeration of Celia's charms to Volpone: "A beauty, ripe as harvest! / Whose skin is whiter than a swan all, over! / Than silver, snow, or lilies" (1.5.110–11). Here he offers a version of a conventional lyric blazon, idealizing and objectifying Celia: "Bright as your gold! Lovely as your gold!" (1.1.14). Yet his Celia portrait differs primarily in effect, not in method, from the Volpone portrait, which recreates Volpone's body as an *anti*-ideal, an object of disgust rather than desire.

Desire and disgust resemble each other experientially as well as mechanically, sharing a dilatory temporality and a kind of open-ended, proliferative, non-teleological structure. As Boehrer has argued, desire in the play "flows . . . multiply, on various levels, in headlong sequences of enumeration, without settling within a single function or organ."[30] It is easy to see how energetic, copious language gives shape to and replenishes desire. The play's myriad lists of goods, foods, and sexual delights produce and prolong the desire, or lack – the gap between *wanting* and *having* – that causes characters to produce fantastic thoughts and effulgent language. Boehrer argues that such language creates an erotically charged atmosphere in which consummation is finally "beside the point"; what matters instead are the "remarkable enumerative and transformative energies" of the simulacrum world compounded of ever-shifting configurations of abundant things, bodies, words, and images.[31]

Deliberately disgusting language, I would argue, is equally important. The play's visions of material abundance and sexual variety are entangled with the grotesque illusion of "sick" Volpone's hanging lids, gaping mouth, and rheumy eyes. The play's lavish fantasies of wealth and sex are predicated on the fiction of the *magnifico*'s disgusting body and its nearness to death.[32] When Mosca conjures it with the full force of his linguistic abilities, that body is as arresting as any fantasy of gold or sex. Celia's "soft lip / Would tempt you to eternity of kissing" (1.5.111–12), but Volpone's slack cheeks and rheumy eyes also remove their beholder from the ordinary flow of time.

Heather Dubrow has argued that Renaissance lyric poems frequently encode and address multiple audiences, both diegetic and external.[33] In so doing they anticipate the multiple, shifting possibilities of their own reception.[34] In *Volpone*, I would like to suggest, Jonson similarly imagines a variety of audiences encountering his theatrical work with a range of responses.[35] The play's prefatory material famously acknowledges both "good" and "bad" potential audiences. Its prologue condemns vulgar pleasure-seekers who come to the theater looking for "monstrous and forced action" (25), and who care more for recycled "jests" (27) than for "quick comedy refined" (29). The prefatory epistle dedicates the play to Oxford and Cambridge, thanking university audiences for "love and acceptance shown" to *Volpone* in performance and implicitly hailing readers of the printed play among the more discerning, learned, appreciative sort.

Jonson stages myriad moments of reception in the play: Mosca's quietly deflating, mock-appreciative interruption of Volpone's extraordinary opening speech; his more forthright praise of the Scoto performance; Volpone's delight in his servants' Pythagoras masque and his pained impatience at Lady Would-Be's word-floods; the courtroom response to Voltore's speeches. Mosca's attempts to arouse disgust in his on-stage audiences present a special case, allegorizing Jonson's multifaceted relation to his own readers and spectators. Though a reader or theatergoer might find Mosca's disgusting portrait of his master irresistible, the elderly and impatient Corbaccio evidently does not, responding merely "good" (1.4.42) and "good symptoms still" (1.4.45), and at times failing to follow along. Mosca says, "no amends" (1.4.7), and Corbacco mishears, "Mends he?" (1.4.7); Mosca says, "I have often / Heard him protest that your physician / Should never be his heir" (1.4.22–4), at which a dismayed Corbaccio cries, "Not I his heir?" (1.4.24). Not only are Mosca's artful verbal productions and vivid images wasted on such an audience, but even his basic message, that Volpone is near death and Corbaccio stands to inherit, risks getting lost. Corbaccio is like those audience members who fail to unwind the "skein" of a dramatic narrative, as Jonson would later complain.[36]

Voltore potentially presents a livelier, more intelligent audience, but his vanity makes him an unfit audience for subject matter other than himself. Mosca accordingly presents the lawyer with a flattering – if faintly foreboding – portrait of his future, swimming "in golden lard, / Up to th' arms in honey, that your chin, / Is borne up stiff with fatness of the flood" (1.3.70–72). Drawing together images of wealth, food, and the body, these lines do work similarly to the Volpone portraits, but from a different angle. Turning gold into a flood of honey-thick lard, they implicitly claim that even the loveliest, richest form of matter participates in a kind of horrifying grossness, a sticky materiality that is fundamentally a trap (just as, elsewhere, Mosca's portrait of the most grotesque of bodies, seen or described the right way, becomes an emblem of the endlessly fascinating, ebulliently material world). Materiality itself is always at issue, always double: grotesque and gorgeous, a type of death and a vision of vibrating, various, sublunary life.

In the third of the would-be heirs Mosca finds a very different kind of audience, one that is not only receptive but also collaborative. Demonstrating to Corvino that his master cannot overhear them, Mosca shouts, "The pox approach and add to your diseases, / If it would send you hence the sooner, sir" (1.5.52–3), reiterating Volpone's invocation as a curse. He goes on:

> Would you would once close
> Those filthy eyes of yours that flow with slime
> Like two frog-pits, and those same hanging cheeks
> Covered with hide instead of skin – Nay, help sir –
> That look like frozen dishclouts set on end. (1.5.57–60)

Corvino joins in at Mosca's urging, at first reluctantly and then with gusto:

> CORVINO Or like an old smoked wall on which the rain
> Ran down in streaks!
> MOSCA Excellent, sir, speak out.
> You must be louder yet; a culverin
> Dischargèd in his ear would hardly bore it.
> CORVINO His nose is like a common sewer, still running.
> MOSCA 'Tis good! And what his mouth?
> CORVINO A very draught. (1.5.61–6)

Corvino's additions demonstrate mastery of the material and bring out the scatological dimension implicit in Mosca's imagery of sliminess and leaks. Together the pair convert Volpone's body into something that disgusts in multiple ways; it is once more a living corpse, but now it is also a kind of human sewer flowing with excremental slime. Their Volpone is repulsively open, involuntarily emitting what should be kept inside and at the same time vulnerable to invasion from without.[37] When Corvino calls his mouth a "draught" (1.5.66), a word that could mean "privy" or "cesspool," Mosca briskly advises, "Oh, stop it up" (1.5.70).

In Corvino, Mosca has found "an understander." Writing on *The Alchemist* Ann Barton notes that Subtle and Face do not simply sell false hope to the greedy; rather, they peddle increased imaginative horizons, improving on the fantasies brought to them by giving them grander scope and more abundant, various content.[38] The same dynamic is at work here. Corvino is obsessed with bodies, especially bodies as tokens of the *mere* materiality of persons. In a later scene he imagines disfiguring his wife: "I will . . . rip up / Thy mouth unto thine ears; and slit thy nose / Like a raw rotchet" (3.7.96–9). In the next breath, he articulates an even more grotesque fantasy of degradation, threatening to tie her living body to that of a dead slave, with a description of "some monstrous crime" (3.7.103), etched into her breast with "*aquafortis* and burning corsives" (3.7.104–5).

Corvino's misogyny and sadism shade into a broader fascination with inflicting and observing pain, and an ability to take active pleasure in the reduction of person to "subhuman thing." As his imagined punishments for Celia reveal, he is adept at turning the body into a symbol, in this case of sexual impropriety. He imagines Celia's face and body not as signs of her selfhood – outward badges of her particularity, her status as an other, a subject, a mind – but as manipulable surfaces that can be made to signify according to his will. Thus his projected disfiguring of his wife works like the parasite's verbal disfiguring of his master. Though Mosca turns Volpone into a symbol of death, not sex, both focus on the "disgusting" animal nature of the other, reducing that other from person to thing. Egging the merchant on by Volpone's sickbed, Mosca augments and expands Corvino's imaginative capacity and his ability to give expression to the products of his grotesque fancy.

The disgusting imagery that Mosca and Corvino produce together is profoundly involved in the pleasure induced by copious language, the "free floating satisfaction" of "sheer syllables" piled together. It is this pleasure that makes this scene and others like it so troubling and so compelling.[39] Here as elsewhere in Jonson's plays and poems the pleasure of verbal heaping up evokes the pleasures of material goods and of the body. Lists of foodstuffs, scatological insults, and catalogues of medicines and cosmetics, for example, tend to unfold in this copious, enumerative style. In such moments Jonson's words conjure the material world in images and are themselves "halfway to being matter."[40] For Jonson there is a particular kind of creative or poetic energy generated by abundant, proliferative stuff, and this energy creates copious, corpulent, language. In this "copious" poetic mode the word responds to the world and replicates its allure.

Such language is double-edged, inviting us to lose ourselves in the enchantments of abundant words and things, multiply and mutually signifying, while tempting us to find pleasure in moral depravity, bodily impropriety, excessive consumption, and Corvino-like perversity. In the *Discoveries* Jonson describes "vicious language" as "vast, and gaping, swelling, and irregular," adding "that which is high and lofty, declaring excellent matter, becomes vast and tumorous, speaking of petty and inferior things."[41] Mosca and Corvino's description of Volpone fits the bill; their language is "vicious," "vast," and "swelling," and their subject, the beslimed body of an old charlatan, is certainly not "excellent matter" in any sense of the word. And yet the pleasures of free-flowing, indecorous language can threaten to overwhelm the "proper" moral response to a text.[42] These pleasures cannot easily be reconciled to virtue, but neither can they be discounted out of hand. Jonson effectively puts his readers in a bind: if they fail to respond to "disgusting" passages, if they avert their eyes, then they are insufficiently receptive, or a dull, vulgar, "bad" audience. Yet if they are overly drawn to these passages, as the Corvino scene suggests, they are "bad" in a different way, relishing the grotesque and depraved, their imaginations as "swelling" and "tumorous" as the language that inflames them.

In *Volpone*'s "Epistle" Jonson famously claims "the impossibility of any man's being a good poet without first being a good man." As his treatment of the disgusting in the play suggests, however, effective poetry is not necessarily identical with "good" poetry and, when it comes to reception, susceptibility to poetic efficacy is decidedly not the same as goodness in a moral sense. If art that presents disgusting matter is a test case for the efficacy of that art, the success of its claims on our attention, then Jonson's disgusting passages in *Volpone* and elsewhere operate as double and seemingly incompatible tests: both of our susceptibility to effective verbal production (necessary in an audience) and of our immunity to (morally) bad ones. It's a quandary to which Jonson poses no solution. His moralizing prefatory material is forever in tension with a play whose language "appeals so engagingly to our lower natures."[43]

One final aspect of Jonson's handling of disgust in *Volpone* deserves mention. Above I suggested that, as an avatar for the play's author, Mosca exerts varying degrees of control over his on-stage audiences as he creates a forcefully "disgusting" portrait of Volpone. Here I want to draw attention to the way in which this portrait also functions as a form of control over Volpone himself. At this early stage of the action the parasite and *magnifico* are brilliant collaborators, seamlessly coordinating both their backstage preparations for and their onstage roles during each "visitation" (1.2.88). They are also each other's best, most receptive audience. Mosca praises Volpone's turn as the mountebank Scoto of Mantua (see 2.5.31–8) and much later, his appearance in the "public" (5.1.4) stage of the courtroom. In the scenes discussed above, as his own role proceeds from that of a vocally suffering old man to that of insensible semi-corpse, Volpone remains alert to Mosca's performances, exclaiming, "Excellent, Mosca! / Come hither let me kiss thee" (1.3.78–9) after Voltore's departure, and, after Corbaccio's, crying, "O, I shall burst, / Let out my sides, let out my sides – " (1.4.133–4). Throughout, Mosca subtly undermines Volpone, suggesting that he is "out of control," both as audience and actor. "Contain / Your flux of laughter, sir" (1.4.133–4), he commands in response to his master's exuberant delight and, later, comments "'t seemed to me you sweat sir" (5.2.37) in the courtroom.

As Mosca glosses it Volpone's is a body that cannot control itself. It is distressingly open and "leaky," involuntarily emitting real laughter and sweat in addition to illusory phlegm, spit, and rheum. According to Gail Kern Paster, in Jonson's work, "the question of who defines as voluntary or involuntary any particular moment of bodily or psychic exposure is crucial in instantiating power relations."[44] Mosca gains mastery over his master first by defining his bodily motions and, especially, effluvia as involuntary. He emphasizes, in earnest as well as in game, Volpone's failure to control the boundaries of his own body. In so doing he points quietly but insistently at the animal nature of the old fox and to his inevitable participation in the way of all flesh, turning the robust, wily figure before us into one that is sweating, excreting, aging, and dying – if not now, not long from now. Mosca's exertion of power over his master derives from his ability to redescribe him, and Volpone's metamorphosis from person to "dead thing" is a function of Mosca's transformation of his master into ground for verbal inventions.

In the final act Volpone receives his sentence from the court, "To lie in prison, cramped with irons, / Till thou be'st sick and lame indeed" (5.12.123–4). He comments sardonically, effectively renaming the play, "This is called the mortifying of a Fox" (5.12.125). Mosca's aggressive objectification of his master may not have the physical effects of the magistrates' sentence. Yet it offers a parallel kind of mortification. Mosca textualizes Volpone, simultaneously making him an object of disgust and bringing him closer to death.

"My picture left in Scotland"

The attractive force of disgusting objects and the rhetorical power of disgusting language re-emerge as central concerns of Jonson's brief lyric "My Picture Left in Scotland," the ninth poem of *The Underwood*. Like *Volpone*, "My Picture Left in Scotland" considers disgust in terms of the power dynamics that come into play at the site of reception. But whereas *Volpone* acknowledges a great variety of audience responses to effectively disgusting language, ranging from true "understanders" to those who lack ears to hear, and from the "vulgar" audience at the public theater to the learned university spectators and the print reader, "My Picture" imagines lyric reception in simpler terms. The poem points toward two distinct audiences and two separate scenes of reception.[45] It explicitly describes the unreceptive "she" to whom the poet has, it seems, offered earlier lyrics, and it implicitly acknowledges the unspecified, external reader of "My Picture" itself, to whom Jonson's speaker makes privy his complaint.[46] In so doing the lyric brings to the fore the issue of the difference between an object of disgust – a figure defined by the disgusted gaze of an other – and a disgusting text, a rhetorical artifact that actively recruits and seeks to hold that gaze.

The poem begins with a scenario familiar to students of Renaissance love lyric: the speaker laments that his beloved has failed to understand his poems. The project of wooing, intimately bound up in the project of writing, has come to an impasse:

> I now think, Love is rather deaf, than blind,
>   For else it could not be,
>   That she,
> ·   Whom I adore so much, should so slight me,
>   And cast my love behind:
> I'm sure my language to her, was as sweet,
>   And every close did meet
>   In sentence, of as subtle feet,
>   As hath the youngest he,
> That sits in shadow of Apollo's tree. (1–10)

As the complaint unfolds it becomes clear that the beloved's unreceptiveness has two crucial dimensions: inattention to his verses and attention to his aged face and form. Considered in terms of poetic agility, the speaker can compete with and perhaps outdo any younger poet. In the comparison between his verses and those of "the youngest he," Jonson presents his verse as agile and in motion. His previous "language to her" moved nimbly, dancing on "subtle feet," as does the language in this poem, a little masterpiece of metrical flexibility and control. The "subtle feet" of the imagined younger poet, Jonson slyly suggests, are rather less active. While Jonson's language dances, "the youngest he" sits in the shade.

Comparing his own language to the imagined rival poet's body, Jonson articulates a distinction between the inward self revealed in poetry and the outward, physical self. The poem's complaint is that the Lady gives her attention to the wrong one. The poem's opening conjecture, that love is "deaf not blind," might be translated into interpersonal, dramatic terms as follows: Since she sees only my aging, imperfect body, my mistress is incapable of being moved by my poems – despite their skill and beauty, which in a different audience might translate to powerful poetic efficacy. The poem continues:

> Oh, but my conscious fears,
>> That fly my thoughts between,
>> Tell me that she hath seen
> My hundreds of grey hairs,
> Told seven and forty years
> Read so much waste, as she cannot embrace
> My mountain belly, and my rocky face,
> And all these through her eyes, have stopped her ears. (11–18)

As in *Volpone* the symptoms of aging elicit – or, in this case, are thought to have elicited – disgust.

Mosca insists that Volpone cannot control his laughter, sweat, and rheum. Jonson's speaker here says that, in the beloved's eyes, he too appears out of control, albeit less grotesquely. The *waist/waste* pun conjures both vastness and desolation.[47] And as it calls attention to the body's excessive size, it presents it as the sign of a self that has, in some sense, been squandered; the mistress sees his "waist" and reads into it "waste."[48] The immobile solidity of the "mountain belly" and "rocky face" adds to the sense of monumental size and weight. The beloved not only looks at this body, she takes stock of it, inventorying its parts and assessing their value, reckoning up his years and his "hundreds of grey hairs."[49] The images here do not add up to a *memento mori*, but they do signal an unstoppable decline: the last vestiges of youth are gone; the best is past. In the beloved's eyes, Jonson's speaker conjectures, he appears as a body that is big and getting bigger, old and getting older. Even the sparest, slenderest, nimblest verse cannot shake this image.[50]

John Lemley notes that "My Picture Left in Scotland" is of a piece with other late-career "self-portrait" poems in which the poet's "personality increasingly intrudes upon his art with an almost corporeal impact."[51] Frequently these works distinguish Jonson's body from Jonson's verse; they ask us to look from surface to substance, from his "repulsive appearance" and "hulking appearance" to "ever-youthful, graceful poetry."[52] In the "Epistle to My Lady Covell," for instance, Jonson entreats his addressee to reject his corpulent, embodied self if she must, but not his poems: "Although you fancy not the man, / Accept his muse."[53] Even more clearly, in "My Picture" Jonson lays out the problem of being "a Bigg fatt man, that spake in Ryme."[54] His verses are one kind of text, his body another (see Figure 9.1).

Yet to read the poem primarily as a tacit admonition to readers to differentiate between surface and substance – or picture and poem, image and word – would, I think, be missing the point. The external reader is granted access to an entirely different experience than the unreceptive "she" of the first stanza, and he is given

Ben: Johnson

Figure 9.1 STC 14771, *[Execration against Vulcan] Ben: Ionson's execration against Vulcan VVith divers epigrams by the same author to severall noble personages in this kingdome. Never published before.* By permission of the Folger Shakespeare Library

a different set of tasks: to integrate, rather than to differentiate, the body from the text. This poem is, after all, not actually part of the thwarted exchange of writing and love but a commentary on it, after the fact, and one that takes up the poet's age and corpulence as its subject matter.[55] In the poem's second stanza, quoted above, Jonson restages the initial moment of disgust but to his own advantage, seeking to control rather than to be controlled. His physical body, he claims, recently produced an insurmountable reaction in a potential lover. Converting that body into text, he invites his audience to see it both as a repulsive object and as a virtuosic poem, the machine that produces that object, irresistibly, before the mind's eye, forcing the beholder to look more rather than away. Receptive readers are left – not unlike the unreceptive lady, it must be said – with heads full of Ben Jonson: eyes filled with the image of his rocky face and mountain belly, and ears with his verse.

In the late 1620s Jonson suffered a stroke that left him confined to his chamber and unable to attend the single performance of his final finished stage play, *The Magnetic Lady*, in 1632. Prior to this disappointing theatrical event, one observer commented that the play was by "Ben Jonson (who I thought had been dead)."[56] As Ian Donaldson has recently remarked, Jonson's fascination with aging began long before this, when he himself was still relatively young.[57] He was in his thirties when he wrote *Volpone* and about a decade older when he published *The Forest*, whose opening verse ends with the declaration, "Love is fled, and I grow old" ("Why I write not of love," 1.12). In "My Picture Left in Scotland" he puts himself at 47, close to Volpone's age, somewhere between the middle and final phase of life. Elsewhere in *The Underwood* he writes disparagingly of a far older figure: "Here's one out-lived his peers / And told forth fourscore years . . . What did this stirrer but die late?"[58]

It may be tempting to see in Jonson's fate a version of Volpone's: trapped in becoming the thing he played, old and immobile, reduced in the last instance to the body, the belly, the bed. Indeed, the poet-playwright may well have felt himself to be a mind increasingly imprisoned in a big body, an object for others' indifference, scorn, or disgust. Yet at least in *The Underwood* he retains a sense of the ability to disgust as agential and authorial. A quality of his body appropriated to his verses rather than expelled from them, *disgustingness* becomes, for Jonson, a technology of control that works from within the structures – embodiment, old age, textualization – that can reduce person to thing in the eyes of an other.

Notes

1 On list-making and other forms of verbal copiousness in Ben Jonson, and on the meaningful connection between linguistic *copia* and worldly, material, bodily, expansive subject matter in his works, see (among others) Marotti, "All About"; Prescott, *Imagining Rabelais*, 116–23; and Boehrer, *Fury*, esp. 147–9.

2 Ben Jonson, *The Alchemist*, in *Volpone and Other Plays*, ed. Michael Jamieson (London: Penguin Classics, 2004), 185–320, and *Volpone, or the Fox*, ed. Brian Parker, The Revels Plays (Manchester: Manchester University Press, 1999). Parenthetical references are to act, scene, and line.

3 Jonson's main source for grotesque luxury foodstuffs is *The Life of Elagabalus*, in which Aelius Lampridius reports that the emperor, "frequently ate camels-heels and also cocks-combs taken from the living birds, and the tongues of peacocks and night-ingales." To others, he served, "huge platters heaped up with the viscera of mullets, and flamingo-brains, partridge-eggs, thrush-brains, and the heads of parrots, pheasants, and peacocks. And the beards of the mullets that he ordered to be served were so large that they were brought on, in place of cress or parsley or pickled beans or fenugreek, in well-filled bowls and disk-shaped platters." Lampridius, *Historia Augusta*, 147. In Jonson, as in Lampridius, exotic foodstuffs signal extravagance, and the "magi-cal" power of money to bring the faraway near, for consumption. Jonson, as Boehrer argues, is also interested in such items' status as ambiguously edible. Boehrer, *Fury*, 81, 106–7. On Jonson, food, digestion, and morality see also Loewenstein, "Jonsonian Corpulence," esp. 508–10. On cultural associations of "disgustingness" with eating strange animals and "novel foods," see Rozin, Haidt, and McCauley, "Disgust," 760.

4 Boehrer, *Fury*, 81, 106–7.

5 On Jonsonian scatology, see Boehrer, *Fury*, 147–75. On cultural perceptions of female "leakiness," see Paster, *Body Embarrassed*, 23–63, esp. 34–50 for a reading of Jon-son's *Bartholomew Fair*, and 41–3 for medical investigations of urine, of the kind Eudemus presumably practices in *Sejanus*.

6 Ben Jonson, "Epistle. To My Lady Covell" (8–10), in *Complete Poems*, 201–2.

7 Preston notes that certain vivid but suggestive descriptions demand that readers (or listeners) import further details, supplementing the text itself with their own imagina-tions. Preston, "Ekphrasis," 117.

8 Aristotle, *Poetics*, 86.

9 As Korsmeyer writes, disgusting things often seem, paradoxically, to have an "allur-ing, enthralling" magnetism, while works of art that represent the disgusting are fre-quently aesthetically riveting, commanding attention rather than compelling aversion. Korsmeyer, *Savoring*, 38. For a succinct account of the tradition linking disgust to pleasure, see Menninghaus, *Disgust*, 103–7. The essays in the present volume together make a compelling case that a mixture of relish and repugnance was characteristic of many "disgusting" encounters in the English Renaissance.

10 The phrase "double attitude" is from Leggatt, *Ben Jonson*, 44.

11 Sidney, *Arcadia*, 76.

12 Sidney, *Arcadia*, 76.

13 Hickey, "Enter the Dragon," 1.

14 Hickey, "Enter the Dragon," 11.

15 In his letter "To the Reader" in *The Alchemist* (London, 1612), Jonson calls his ideal reader an "understander." See also *Epigrams* 1, "To the Reader": "Pray thee, take care, that tak'st my Book in hand, / To read it well: that is, to understand."

16 See especially Boehrer, *Fury*; Loewenstein, "Jonsonian Corpulence"; and Paster, *Body Embarrassed*, 23–39, 143–62. All three works suggest that disgust is an intentional Jonsonian effect.

17 "Anything that reminds us that we are animals elicits disgust." Rozin, Haidt, and McCauley, "Disgust," 761.

18 Rozin, Haidt, and McCauley, "Disgust," 761.

19 Rozin, Haidt, and McCauley, "Disgust," 761.

20 On Jonson's life-long obsession with aging, see Donaldson, *Ben Jonson*, 386: "While still a young man [Jonson] had worried about the pains of growing old . . . While still in his thirties, he had seen himself as already ancient."

21 Scodel places Volpone in his mid-forties: "He claims to have triumphantly played 'young Antinous' (emperor Hadrian's youthful beloved) at a Venetian festivity of 1574 (3.7.157–62, *HS* 9:718) which, since Volpone was first performed around 1606 and alludes to events of that year, would suggest that around thirty-two years earlier

Volpone played a beautiful youth, presumably when he was at least around 12-years old, the youngest age for boy actors on the Renaissance English stage." Scodel, "Making Literary History." This would, as Scodel notes, make Volpone roughly the same age as other Jonsonian "old lovers," including the speaker of "My Picture Left in Scotland," discussed below. According to some period systems, the mid-to-late forties were the first flush of old age ("green" old age), but according to others, this was still middle age. See Taunton, *Fictions of Old Age*, 1.

22 See Kernan's notes to these lines in his edition of *Volpone*.

23 This is true not only for Volpone, but for other Jonsonian "makers," who use money, power, or deceit to create elaborate fictional worlds around themselves. Leggatt finds "a natural analogy between their activities and Jonson's business as a dramatist." Leggatt, *Ben Jonson*, 3.

24 On critical and poetic traditions that emphasize the worldly allure of the poetic word, see, among others, Prescott, *Imagining Rabelais*, esp. 42–85 and 116–23, and Nirenberg, *Anti-Judaism*, 231–7.

25 Such effluvia were understood to be a symptom of great age. The French physician Andre du Laurens observes, "The eyes of these old men [are] alwaies distilling teares, their nose alwaies running, there commeth out of their mouth evermore great store of water, yea, they doe nothing but cough and spet." Laurens, *A Discourse*, 174. Du Laurens and other medical professionals attributed increased excretions to humoral imbalance. Paster argues in her discussion of specifically feminine "leakiness" (also linked to the humors) that an inability to control bodily effluvia was considered a sign of a debased, lesser humanity in the Renaissance. Paster, *Body Embarrassed*, 23–63.

26 Minois, *History of Old Age*, 250. Minois's claim that abhorrence was the dominant attitude toward the elderly in the Renaissance has been challenged by recent scholarship on the complexities of aging and its representations. See Skenazi, *Aging Gracefully*; Martin, *Constituting Old Age*; Campbell, *Growing Old*; Thane, *Old Age*, esp. 55–70; and Taunton, *Fictions of Old Age*.

27 Minois, *History of Old Age*, 249.

28 Leggatt, *Ben Jonson*, 48.

29 See for example Greenblatt, "False Ending," and Maus, "Idol and Gift."

30 Boehrer, *Fury*, 109.

31 Boehrer, *Fury*, 105.

32 On gaping mouths as a site of disgust, see Menninghaus, *Disgust*, 60–64.

33 Dubrow, "Domain of Echo."

34 Dubrow, "Domain of Echo," 56.

35 This occurs in other plays as well, especially those including "chorus" figures (*Every Man Out of His Humour, The Magnetic Lady*) and lengthy inductions (*Bartholomew Fair*). "Jonson includes the reception of the work as part of the work's vision, so that we are to reflect not just on our own view of it but on how a work of art relates to its public in general – what it can achieve and how it is liable to be frustrated . . . The drama within the play is thus extended to include what happens when the play enters the world." Leggatt, *Ben Jonson*, 242.

36 "A good play is like a skein of silk: which, if you take by the right end, you may wind off, at pleasure, on the bottome, or card of your discourse in a tale or so, how you will: but if you light on the wrong end, you will pull all into a knot, or elf-lock." Jonson, *Magnetic Lady*, Induction, lines 142–7.

37 On openness as a feature of the grotesque body in the Renaissance, see Paster, *Body Embarrassed*, 16. Douglas's classic formulation that disgust arises in response to fears of contamination by "matter out of place" is also relevant. Douglas notes the potential for defilement inherent to "matter issuing from" and traversing the body's boundaries, including "spittle, blood, milk, urine, faeces, or tears" and "bodily parings, skin, nails, hair clippings, and sweat." Douglas, *Purity and Danger*, 150.

38 Barton, *Ben Jonson*, 273.
39 Boehrer, *Fury*, 148–9.
40 Prescott, *Imagining*, 117.
41 Ben Jonson, *Explorata: or Discoveries*, in *Complete Poems*, 375–458, 435.
42 See Boehrer, *Fury*, 148–9; Prescott, *Imagining*, 116.
43 Leggatt, *Ben Jonson*, 226.
44 Paster, *Body Embarrassed*, 144.
45 Writing on the Petrarchan tradition with which "My Picture" is in dialogue, Wall notes that, in the case of many lyric poems, the text's "anticipated moment of reception" is frequently analogous to the anticipated, or at least hoped-for, fulfillment of his erotic desires. Wall, *Imprint of Gender*, 42. Here, however, Jonson separates this poem's anticipated reception (by an unspecified reader) from the unsatisfactory reception previous verses delivered to the lady.
46 Jonson, "My Picture Left in Scotland," *Complete Poems*, 140. Donaldson notes that at least one of this poem's early audiences was a specific individual. Jonson sent a manuscript version to his Scottish host and interlocutor William Drummond of Hawthornden. Donaldson, *Ben Jonson*, 50–51.
47 A "waste," in the period, could be either an unbroken expanse of land or sea, or a "devastated region." "Waste," n., 1b and 3, "waste, n.," *OED Online*.
48 "Waste," n., 5. *OED Online*.
49 In *Twelfth Night*, Olivia even more pointedly links the conventional listing strategy of a lyric blazon to a household inventory: "Item, two lips, indifferent red; item, two grey eyes, with lids to them; item, one neck, one chin, and so forth" (1.5.250–52).
50 Leggatt writes, "Normally a love poet will not describe his own appearance, but he may describe the lady's in lavish (if conventional) detail. Jonson turns that device on its head: the lady disappears, and the blazon becomes a point-by-point description of his own gross body." Leggatt, *Ben Jonson*, 218. Jonson's playful subversion of convention has another dimension, as well. Petrarchan poets often claimed to hold an image of the beloved in their hearts, which refreshed both love and the desire to write. Here, the image is in the *lady's* heart, and instead of aiding the flow of emotion and of language, it stops it short.
51 Lemley, "Masks and Self-Portraits," 248.
52 Lemley, "Masks and Self-Portraits," 250.
53 Jonson, "Epistle," lines 25–6.
54 Cited in Loewenstein, "Jonsonian Corpulence," 516: "From a poem by Francis Andrewes in the Newcastle MS (Harley 4955 f. 166b)."
55 Loewenstein comments that, though the speaker's "age and girth . . . threaten to obstruct his erotic appeal," they simultaneously signal gravity and seriousness, granting him ethical as well as physical weight. "Jonsonian Corpulence," 506. Jonson takes himself seriously, even as he describes himself as a comically pathetic figure. On the "old lover" tradition and this poem's place within it, see Martin, *Constituting Old Age*, 100–136, and Achilleos, "Youth, Old Age."
56 Donaldson, *Ben Jonson*, 417. See also Happé's "Introduction" to *The Magnetic Lady*, 1.
57 Donaldson, *Ben Jonson*, 386.
58 Jonson, "To the Immortal Memory and Friendship of that Noble Pair, Sir Lucius Cary and Sir H. Morison" (25–30), in *Complete Poems*, 212. Of this octogenarian figure Leggatt writes, "The sheer length of his life is what undid him," making him a subhuman thing. Leggatt, *Ben Jonson*, 47. See also Donaldson's discussion of this figure in *Ben Jonson*, 425–6.

References

Achilleos, Stella. "Youth, Old Age, and Male Self-Fashioning: The Appropriation of the Anacreontic Figure of the Old Man by Jonson and his 'Sons.'" In *Growing Old in Early*

Modern Europe: Cultural Representations, edited by Erin Campbell, 39–53. Burlington, VT: Ashgate, 2006.

Aristotle. *Poetics. Ancient Literary Criticism: The Principal Texts in New Translations*. Edited by D.A. Russell and M. Winterbottom, 85–132. Oxford: Clarendon, 1957.

Barton, Ann. *Ben Jonson: Dramatist*. Cambridge: Cambridge University Press, 1984.

Boehrer, Bruce Thomas. *The Fury of Men's Gullets: Ben Jonson and the Digestive Canal*. Philadelphia: University of Pennsylvania Press, 1997.

Campbell, Erin, ed. *Growing Old in Early Modern Europe: Cultural Representations*. Burlington, VT: Ashgate, 2006.

Donaldson, Ian. *Ben Jonson: A Life*. Oxford: Oxford University Press, 2011.

Douglas, Mary. *Purity and Danger: An Analysis of Concepts of Pollution and Taboo* (1966). New York: Routledge, 2002.

Dubrow, Heather. "The Domain of Echo: Lyric Audiences." In *The Challenges of Orpheus: Lyric Poetry and Early Modern England*, 54–105. Baltimore: Johns Hopkins University Press, 2008.

Greenblatt, Stephen J. "The False Ending in Volpone." *Journal of English and Germanic Philology* 75, no. 1/2 (1976): 90–104.

Hickey, Dave. "Enter the Dragon." In *The Invisible Dragon: Essays on Beauty*, 1–18. Chicago: University of Chicago Press, 2009.

Jonson, Ben. *The Alchemist*. In *Volpone and Other Plays*. Edited by Michael Jamieson, 185–320. London: Penguin Classics, 2004.

———. *The Complete Poems*. Edited by George Parfitt. London: Penguin Books, 1996.

———. *The Magnetic Lady*. Edited by Peter Happé. The Revels Plays. Manchester: Manchester University Press, 2000.

———. *Sejanus his Fall*. Edited by W.F. Bolton. New Mermaids. New York: Hill and Wang, 1966.

———. *Volpone, or the Fox*. Edited by Alvin Kernan. New Haven: Yale University Press, 1962.

———. *Volpone, or the Fox*. Edited by Brian Parker. The Revels Plays. Manchester: Manchester University Press, 1999.

Korsmeyer, Carolyn. *Savoring Disgust: The Foul and the Fair in Aesthetics*. Oxford: Oxford University Press, 2011.

Lampridius, Aelius. "Antoninus Elagabalus." *Historia Augusta*. Translated by David Magie, 105–77. Loeb Classical Library 139. Cambridge, MA: Harvard University Press, 1924.

Laurens, Andre du. *A Discourse of the Preservation of the Sight: of Melancholike Diseases; of Rheumes, and of Old Age*. Translated by Richard Surphlet. London, 1599.

Leggatt, Alexander. *Ben Jonson: His Vision and His Art*. London: Methuen, 1981.

Lemley, John. "Masks and Self-Portraits in Jonson's Late Poetry." *English Literary History* 44, no. 2 (1977): 248–66.

Loewenstein, Joseph. "The Jonsonian Corpulence, or the Poet as Mouthpiece." *English Literary History* 53, no. 3 (1986): 491–518.

Marotti, Arthur. "All About Jonson's Poetry." *English Literary History* 39, no. 2 (1972): 208–37.

Martin, Christopher. *Constituting Old Age in Early Modern English Literature from Queen Elizabeth to King Lear*. Amherst: University of Massachusetts Press, 2012.

Maus, Katharine Eisaman. "Idol and Gift in Volpone." *English Literary Renaissance* 35, no. 3 (2004): 429–53.

Menninghaus, Winfried. *Disgust: Theory and History of a Strong Sensation*. Translated by Howard Eiland and Joel Golb. Albany: State University of New York Press, 2003.

Minois, George. *History of Old Age from Antiquity to the Renaissance*. Translated by Sarah Hanbury Tenison. Cambridge: Polity, 1998.

Nirenberg, David. *Anti-Judaism: The Western Tradition*. New York: Norton, 2013.

Paster, Gail Kern. *The Body Embarrassed: Drama and the Disciplines of Shame in Early Modern England*. Ithaca: Cornell University Press, 1993.

Prescott, Anne Lake. *Imagining Rabelais in Renaissance England*. New Haven: Yale University Press, 1998.

Preston, Claire. "Ekphrasis: Painting in Words." In *Renaissance Figures of Speech*, edited by Sylvia Adamson, Gavin Alexander, and Katrin Ettenhuber, 115–29. Cambridge: Cambridge University Press, 2007.

Rozin, Paul, Jonathan Haidt, and Clark R. McCauley. "Disgust." In *Handbook of Emotions*, 3rd ed., edited by M. Lewis, J.M. Haviland-Jones, and L.F. Barrett, 757–76. New York: Guilford Press, 2008.

Scodel, Joshua. "Making Literary History: Metrical Allusions and Distinctions in Ben Jonson's *Epigrams* and *Forest*." Draft circulated at the Renaissance Workshop of the University of Chicago. April 30, 2012.

Shakespeare, William. *Twelfth Night*. Edited by J.M. Lothian and T.W. Craik. The Arden Shakespeare. London: Thomson Learning, 1975.

Sidney, Philip. *The Countess of Pembroke's Arcadia*. Edited by Maurice Evans. London: Penguin Classics, 1977.

Skenazi, Cynthia. *Aging Gracefully in the Renaissance: Stories of Later Life from Petrarch to Montaigne*. Leiden: Brill, 2013.

Taunton, Nina. *Fictions of Old Age in Early Modern Literature and Culture*. New York: Routledge, 2007.

Thane, Pat. *Old Age in the English Past: Past Experiences, Present Issues*. Oxford: Oxford University Press, 2000.

Wall, Wendy. *Imprint of Gender: Authorship and Publication in the English Renaissance*. Ithaca: Cornell University Press, 1993.

10 "Rankly digested, doth those things out-spue"

John Donne, bodily fluids, and the metaphysical abject

Dan Mills

> The writer, fascinated by the abject, imagines its logic, projects himself into it, introjects it, and . . . perverts language-style and content . . . [A]s the sense of abjection is both the abject's judge and accomplice, this is also true of the literature that confronts it . . . crossing over . . . the dichotomous categories of Pure and Impure, Prohibition and Sin, Morality and Immorality.
>
> —*Julia Kristeva,* Powers of Horror

Nicholas Hilliard's 1591 engraved portrait of John Donne, the frontispiece for Donne's posthumously published *Poems* (1635), includes the Latin motto, "Antes muerto que mudado," which means, "Sooner dead than changed."[1] It seems to refer to Donne's decision to convert from Catholicism to the Church of England, but it also speaks to his preoccupation with death. Donne looked beyond the grave in his poetry, beyond corporeal life, and into the ethereal or the afterlife. The soul reigns for Donne, but the afterlife means the end of the corporeal life, as physical selves become corpses. This leads Donne to acknowledge all aspects of the body, beautiful or otherwise, and to incorporate imagery and commentary on the base, the ugly, and the filthy into his poetry. Donne experimented with the perverse, most particularly in his early poems, the *Satyres* and the *Elegies*, and his treatment of the ugly and the disgusting serves no less an important role in understanding Donne's entire body of work. The *Satyres*, focused more on Thanatos and Vulcan, and the *Elegies*, focused more on Eros and Venus, both engage with their generic conventions in a somewhat Dionysian register, and their use of disgusting imagery challenges cultural mores about taboo subjects and complicate Philip Sidney's Horatian dictum that poetry should "teach and delight."

Julia Kristeva would call Donne's treatment of the ugly and disgusting "abject." In *Powers of Horror*, she labels the abject,

> perverse because it neither gives up nor assumes a prohibition, a rule, or a law . . . It kills in the name of life . . . it lives at the behest of death . . . it establishes narcissistic power while pretending to reveal the abyss . . . Corruption is its most common, most obvious appearance.[2]

The abject refers to something cast out, and to abject in Kristeva's model means to push away from the maternal body. Kristeva's prohibition of rules and laws refers to Lacan's Symbolic Order, from his tripartite model of subjectivity that includes the Imaginary and the Real. For Lacan, the Symbolic Order represents the realm of language and the locus for normative subjectivity that begins at the point of initiation into language. Kristeva's abjection resides outside the Symbolic; she locates within abjection an ontological revolt focused on internal and external threats that originate from outside the "possible, the tolerable, the thinkable."[3] Revolt suggests the revolutionary or anti-authoritarian, but it also suggests revulsion and disgust with corporeal reality. In opposition to Hegel's strictly sensuous or sensible aesthetic model, Jacques Rancière claims that an artistic "aesthetic regime" seeks to retain "forms of rupture" and "iconoclastic gestures."[4]

Donne's poetry constitutes such a rupture, which challenges poetic, theological, and political tradition and authority. His use of disgusting and abject imagery employs an exclusion similar to Kristeva's abject: his disgusting poetics in the *Satyres* and *Elegies* exclude these poems from the more "delightful" poetry. Aesthetically, Donne's *Satyres* and *Elegies* anticipate Hegel's mandate for the sensuous appeal in art, but they also harken back to the medieval *memento mori*, the acknowledgement and acceptance of death. Further, they go beyond Hegelian aesthetics to foreshadow the ugly beauty sensibilities of modern and postmodern aesthetics. Reading Donne's *Satyres* and *Elegies* alongside Kristeva's notion of abjection and Hegelian and post-Hegelian aesthetics reveals Donne as innovative and forward thinking in ways for which his later, more traditionally studied poetry has become known. Examining Donne's use of abject and disgusting imagery also provides a glimpse into darker psychological territory than his religious poems.[5] Understanding Donne's *Satyres* and *Elegies* as manifestations of Kristeva's abject makes apparent Donne's conscious creation of a disgusted poetic persona for each of these poems, in addition to illuminating Donne's personal disgust with their subject matter.

Donne's use of abject imagery carries psychological, linguistic, and religious implications. Residing outside the Symbolic, Kristeva's abjection constitutes a symptom of a neurosis that prevents normal functioning.[6] Lacan partly bases his model of linguistic individuation on what he calls the "assurance of the subject in his encounter with filth."[7] This echoes Augustine's observation that if "the word filth is better than the thing it signifies, knowledge of the word would be preferable to knowledge of the thing."[8] Augustine's distinction between a word, a signifier, and that to which it refers foreshadows Lacan's linguistic paradigm of subjectivity, which he based on Saussure's theory of signification in his *Course in General Linguistics*. Filth for Augustine (and Donne) represents the disgusting object the subject must acknowledge, and for Augustine, Lacan, and Kristeva, the filthier the object, the more the subject wishes to turn away.

Kristeva's abject simultaneously complements and complicates the early modern rhetorical movement Debora Shuger has lucidly called the "Christian grand style," which sought to move emotions, both in the context of "harsher forensic impulses of pity and fear" and in the "numinous feelings of wonder and mystery."[9]

For Shuger, this rhetorical style, which yokes the harsh with the numinous, sought to elucidate early modern psychology instead of merely treating stylistic tropes as what she calls "formal decorations of meaning."[10] Donne's early poetry indeed does not merely "decorate" his topics, but instead litters them with imagery of waste, disgust, and the abject. More than merely performing poetic and rhetorical exercises of wit, Donne's use of abject and disgusting imagery intensifies Shuger's definition of the Christian grand style, and Donne frequently allows himself to contaminate religion with this disgusting imagery.[11]

Kristeva introduces what she calls a "metaphysician" of the abject, who follows the trauma of the abject into scatology.[12] In employing abject and disgusting imagery along with iconoclastic poetics Donne indeed becomes a metaphysician in Kristeva's sense, and his assumption of the role of metaphysician and not merely that of poet highlights the greater significance of Donne's body of work: attaining individuation at all costs, whether as a Catholic, ex-Catholic, lover, father, or priest. For Kristeva, "To each ego its object, to each superego its abject."[13] In other words, the ego, Freudian psychology's locus of the reality principle, falls under the control of the super-ego, the law-giving and regulative part of the unconscious that transforms the normal object into the threatening abject, which the subject must ultimately exclude and eliminate.

The *Satyres*

Donne's *Satyres* most immediately reflect influence from the Roman satirist Juvenal, whose sixteen extant satiric poems scornfully ridicule societal mores and customs. In this tradition, Donne's *Satyre I* ridicules the character of a scholar:[14]

> AWAY thou fondling motley humorist,
> Leave mee, and in this standing wooden chest,
> Consorted with these few bookes, let me lye
> In prison, and here be coffin'd, when I dye. (1–4)[15]

The pun on "humorist" and "humourist" to describe scholarly isolated bookishness suggests that Donne saw the humors as comedic as well as relevant and insightful for his own psyche. Gregory Kneidel has suggested that the "fondling motely humorist" refers to Donne's penis and that the poem engages with the "desire, ethics, and imagination" of English law.[16] Kneidel's phallic reading of the humorist resembles what Lacan calls the "Name-of-the-Father," his term for the law-giving father's function in the Symbolic Order. Lacan's phallus, the symbolic locus of this power and not the literal male reproductive organ, resides *in* the male and *with* the female. Donne's fondled penis/phallus signifies a site of transgression against both the literal body (his penis) and against the Symbolic Order (his phallus). This transgression resides in the Imaginary, the challenge to the Symbolic in Lacan's model, and in a poem about the isolated scholar it represents a kind of narcissistic alienation, which, according to Lacan, is "constitutive of the imaginary," the domain that challenges the Symbolic.[17]

Engaging with imagery of physical discomfort and nudity, the speaker in *Satyre I* mentions an itch that he likens to lustful desire, an image that much like "The Flea" makes the reader's skin crawl:

> Why should'st thou (that dost not onely approve,
> But in ranke itchie lust, desire, and love
> The nakednesse and barenesse to enjoy,
> Of thy plumpe muddy whore, or prostitute boy)
> Hate vertue, though shee be naked, and bare? (37–41)

The "ranke itchie lust, desire, and love" suggests a psychological conundrum about an unconscious itch that presumably needs scratching, which Donne equates to desire for a "plumpe muddy whore, or prostitute boy." Donne asks the scholar why he would "Hate vertue" although "shee be naked, and bare." *Satyre I* condemns the isolated bookish scholar for the hypocrisy of desiring a prostitute while simultaneously rejecting naked and bare virtue.

Exploring aesthetic development, *Satyre II* satirizes London society and foreign military threat with language of pestilence. The poem opens with the speaker declaring his hatred for "Perfectly all this towne," presumably referring to London, although he refers to "one state" in which "all ill things so excellently best / That hate, towards them, breeds pitty towards the rest" (1–4). Donne then likens poetry to a disease, but in comparison to the unnamed target of this *Satyre* this does not come off nearly as bad:

> Though Poetry indeed be such a sinne
> As I thinke that brings dearths, and Spaniards in,
> Though like the Pestilence and old fashion'd love. (5–7)

These lines associate poetry with the Spanish, whose armada the English defeated earlier in the decade, seemingly arguing that too much focus on poetry and creative endeavors led to the crisis with the Spanish. Donne also criticizes the legal profession, deriding a lawyer who, "like a wretch, which at Barre judg'd as dead, / Yet prompts him which stands next, and cannot reade" (11–13). The member of the "Barre" here showed up dead, and without the ability to read or interpret the law in spite of admittance to the profession. The inept London legal community, according to Donne, contrasts with the military prowess England exercised in the defeat of the Spanish Armada.

Satyre II also employs food-loathing and scatological imagery to rail against writers of lesser talent:

> And they who write, because all write, have still
> That excuse for writing, and for writing ill.
> But hee is worst, who (beggarly) doth chaw
> Others wits fruits, and in his ravenous maw
> Rankly digested, doth those things out-spue,

As his owne things'; and they are his owne, 'tis true,
For if one eate my meate, though it be knowne
The meate was mine, th'excrement is his owne.
But these do mee no harme, nor they which use
To out-doe Dildoes, and out-usure Jewes. (22–32)

"Rankly digested" in this poem signifies filth which results in vomit, a common motif throughout the *Satyres* that represents depraved morality. Although the meat-eater in lines 29–30 might suggest both control and ownership, the poem acknowledges that close proximity to others' bodies carries the possibility of death and decay.[18] The poem depicts lesser poets as victimized by the powerful signified in Coscus, but the speaker's confessions best prove the moral decay of an England that valued letter of the law over the spirit.[19] Eating the speaker's meat carries with it base sexual connotations, and Donne remarks that after symbolically eating his meat, the meat-eater will have only excrement to show for it.

Donne's use of excremental imagery serves to differentiate his poetic personae from both the subject's corporeal, bodily waste and from the conceptual, ego-defying waste product. Kristeva associates fecal matter with "decay, infection, disease, corpse" and claims that it signifies an exterior threat to subjectivity. The non-ego, external object threatens the ego. This represents an external threat to society in "life by death."[20] In the context of Puritan Christianity, the individual's religious subjectivity becomes threatened by both the literal, impure, excremental bodily waste and by the "non-ego, external object," which suggests Catholicism's mandate for ecclesiastical mediation between man and the divine.

Scatological imagery in this sense frequently appeared in early Reformation writings. Thomas More, for instance, wrote of William Tyndale's "shameless lies," which will "throw back into your paternity's shitty mouth, truly the shit-pool of all shit, all the muck and shit which your damnable rottenness has vomited up, and to empty out all the sewers and privies onto your crown."[21] Martin Luther, who struggled with constipation for much of his later life, wrote that if the Devil "keeps on nagging me and trots out my sins," he will respond by saying, "Write there also that I have shit in my breeches. Hang it around your neck and wipe your mouth on it."[22]

Slavoj Žižek frequently refers to Luther's belief that "man is like divine shit, he fell out of God's anus," and argues that Luther occupied a "violent debilitating superego cycle," because the more vehement his repentance and self-torture, the guiltier he felt. For Žižek, Luther's anal understanding of humanity suggests that Luther relied upon Protestantism's "excremental identity" of man to formulate Truth. Protestantism, according to Žižek, requires believing that the relationship between man and God transforms Christ into a God who "identified himself with his own shit, with the excremental Real that is man."[23] Žižek places the Protestant understanding of man in Lacan's Real, the unimaginable trauma that resists signification and resides completely outside both the Symbolic and the Imaginary. In order for God to make man in his own image, Žižek suggests, God needed a human manifestation of himself as the mediator between his own

sublime divinity and the inherent "fallen" state of man, as Protestantism elimi-
nated the Catholic stricture of communicating with God through the clergy and
the beatified. Luther could only understand himself and his fellow man as an
excremental graven image of Christ the man-god, which suggests that Protestantism can understand Christian love only as "love for the miserable excremental
entity called 'man.'"[24] In Žižek's reading of Protestantism, excrement resides
in the Real in a similar state as the abject, as both represent the unimaginable
and that which resists signification. Donne's use of excremental imagery at large
places aesthetics in the realm of the abject in addition to Donne's condemnation
of charlatan poets in *Satyre II*.

Abject excrement represents that which the subject must always separate from
his body in order to attain individuation, regardless of the heterogeneity of corporeal reality and death.[25] The body therefore must submit to this self-defilement to
"become clean and proper."[26] In *The History of Shit*, Dominique Laporte explains
that the pre-capitalist sovereign sought linguistic control through a fluency of language in an effort to perpetuate a populace inundated by accumulating waste.
Such a "compulsive purification," Laporte argues, in fact constituted a *"regres-
sion"* paralleling the early modern period's rediscovery of ancient and classical
thinking.[27] Laporte also reminds us that in the early modern period, alchemy and
the prevalence of scientific study of fecal matter contributed to a common belief
that fecal matter could sometimes signify the good.[28] Although immediately disgusting, excremental imagery in Donne's poetry signifies both a political and a
psychological transgression, and as with Lacan and Laporte, excremental transgression carries linguistic implications.

In addition to excremental imagery and bodily waste, *Satyre II* interrogates how
Time leads to the abject body in the context of decay, disease, and natural aging:
"Time (which rots all, and makes botches poxe, / And plodding on, must make a
calfe an oxe)" (41–2). Characteristic of Donne's preoccupation with death, this
Satyre indicts the noble, the beautiful, the valuable, and even mankind. As a result
of his hatred for London and incompetent lawyers, Donne uses abject imagery of
disease and death to underscore his disdain for the aspects of the post-conversion
religious beliefs he must dutifully accept.

Donne's departure from Catholicism similarly manifests as something he
must force himself to acknowledge. In *Satyre III*, he addresses religion and
questions how man can find the true God with so many different Protestant
sects. The poem opens by referring to a choking spleen, often considered the
source for anger in the early modern period: "KINDE pitty chokes my spleene;
brave scorn forbids / Those teares to issue which swell my eye-lids" (1–2).
This image serves to recollect individual human insufficiency and the fires of
hell promised to the religious sloth.[29] At the first new verse paragraph, Donne's
speaker mentions Mirreus, one of the gifts of the magi, but follows it with a very
unattractive image: "He loves her ragges so, as wee here obey / The statecloth
where the Prince sate yesterday" (47–8). Richard Strier argues that the "ragges"
in this context represent menstrual rags of "misplaced devotion to an imagined

Roman female" that unite Roman and English imagery devoted to the "lower body."[30] The path to spiritual enlightenment through the lower body does not come easily in this *Satyre*:

> Hard deeds, the bodies paines; hard knowledge too
> The minds indeavours reach, and mysteries
> Are like the Sunne, dazzling, yet plaine to'all eyes. (86–8)

The "paines" here may refer to the literal physical pain of Christ's passion, but they also suggest the difficulty faced with seeing a Truth "plaine to'all eyes," yet hidden in plain sight. Donne uses abject imagery in this *Satyre* to emphasize his physical revulsion toward the proliferation of Protestant sects.

Donne not only focuses on physical revulsion in his *Satyres*, however. In contrast to *Satyre I*'s physical itch, *Satyre IV* describes a mental one: "My minde, neither with prides itch, nor yet hath been / Poyson'd with love to see, or to bee seene" (5–6). The futile search for virtue at this point in the *Satyres* has become intellectual and psychological. The speaker ultimately scratches the itch "into smart" and uses a simile to compare the pain of scratching to "blunt iron ground / Into an edge" (88–9). "Crossing hurt mee" (91), Donne continues, referring to the Catholic genuflection Donne relinquished in his conversion, and in this case his mental or psychological "itch" to revert to his Catholic ways has become a very unpleasant urge.

Returning to legal satire, *Satyre V* presents a scatological image aimed at what David Colclough has labeled the "morass" of John Egerton's attempts at legal reform through obfuscation. Colclough concedes that the poem nevertheless lauds Egerton's aim to recognize and eliminate this transgression:[31]

> That which drownes them, run: These selfe reasons do
> Prove the world a man, in which, officers
> Are the devouring stomacke, and Suiters
> Th'excrements, which they voyd. All men are dust. (16–19)

Here Donne equates suitors and courtiers with the world's excrement. Like the "selfe reasons" that lead to understanding the world as a human subject, abject bodily waste and excrement represent that which life freely and easily opposes to locate the subject on the boundary of his ontological existence.[32]

Donne's imagery of corporeal decay and violence followed Catholic and Puritan precedents, as Catholic doctrine holds that the Eucharist actually becomes Christ's flesh and blood, while Puritans appropriated such imagery into the Calvinist conversion narrative in the context of the biblical model of death and rebirth.[33] The body must extricate itself from the boundary that separates subject from object through the exclusion or abjection of bodily waste, in order for it to transcend what Kristeva calls the "limit-*cadere*, cadaver."[34] Excrement represents the other side of that border, which, alongside death and the corpse, transcends it.

In a comparison that suggests Donne's wish to escape this transgression, *Satyre V* likens suitors to decaying flesh:

> How much worse are Suiters, who to mens lust
> Are made preyes? O worse then dust, or wormes meat,
> For they do'eate you now, whose selves wormes shall eate. (20–22)

In contrast to the meat-eating in *Satyre II*, Donne here debases suitors by making them worm meat, or buried corpses. Both the abject worship of corpses and abject consumption of bad meat signify transgressions resulting in "divine malediction." These transgressions represent carnal and moral biblical prohibitions.[35] Donne in other words specifically places the hated suitors in the realm of a prohibition and transgression, both corporeal and spiritual.

The *Elegies*

In the *Elegies*, Donne followed Ovid's *Amores* and Marlowe's translation by writing in English elegiacs (heroic couplets). But in examining the darker side of sexual desire, the *Elegies* may also suggest an elegiac (mournful) register. "Elegie I: Jealosie" compares jealousy to a woman who would wish her husband dead but who takes pleasure in the death-dealing and poisonous torment of his jealousy. The description of jealousy here becomes insightful as well as disgusting, as Donne's speaker relates jealousy to vomit, figuring the husband:

> Ready with loathsome vomiting to spue
> His Soule out of one hell, into a new,
> Made deafe with his poore kindreds howling cries,
> Begging with few feign'd teares great legacies,
> Thou would'st not weepe, but jolly,' and frolicke bee,
> As a slave, which to morrow should be free. (7–12)[36]

The food loathing presented here produces literal vomiting, but vomit results from eating something that paradoxically provides both nourishment and physical distress. Abject food loathing and the loathing of excrement provide therapeutic "spasms and vomiting" that allow turning away from the abject and the disgusting in an "elementary" and "archaic" type of abjection.[37] Like the meat-eater in *Satyre II*, this Elegie interjects a psychological paradox into the physical, abject realm of revulsion and disgust.

Sara Covington has argued that Donne's imagery of "bodily and spiritual brokenness" followed a theological tradition that viewed the Bible as both a "repository of resonant images" and a hermeneutical tradition associated with exegetical implications.[38] As an Anglican priest, Donne would have encountered exegetical and doctrinal controversy associated with the slow splintering of Puritanism in England. "Jealousy" describes Puritanism as deformed and monstrous:

> O give him many thanks, he's courteous,
> That in suspecting kindly warneth us.

We must not, as we used, flout openly,
In scoffing riddles, his deformity.
. . .

For better or worse take mee, or leave mee:
To take, and leave mee is adultery,
Oh monstrous, superstitious puritan. (15–18, 25–7)

Donne positions himself in direct opposition to Puritanism here, but paradoxically states that either option constitutes adultery. Again, his preoccupation with the complicated implications of Protestantism takes the form of disgusting imagery, and in these lines Puritanism becomes both deformed and monstrous.

Donne's negative depiction of Puritanism followed the common early modern understanding of deformity as a religious and natural condition. In his essay "Of the Monstrous Child," Michel de Montaigne argues that God does not see monstrous people as monsters because God "seeth the infinite of formes therein contained." Because he believes in God's wisdom, man assumes that God would not create anything other than the "good, common, regular, and orderly." Unlike God, however, men consider something "against nature" as tantamount to "against custome." Montaigne also implores that men should follow God's reason to "expell the astonishment which noveltie breedeth and strangenes causeth in us."[39] Montaigne's call to expel, or abject, the "astonishment" with the monstrous, therefore, brings man closer to God.

In "Of Deformity," Francis Bacon uses the term "nature" in place of God, but retains the same sense as Montaigne. Bacon places the physically deformed "even with nature" because "as nature hath done ill by them, so do they by nature," and he also argues that because deformed persons lack "natural affection," they seek "revenge of nature." Bacon also mandates considering deformity "as a cause, which seldom faileth of the effect." Anyone with an aversion for a deformed person, according to Bacon, "hath also a perpetual spur in himself, to rescue and deliver himself from scorn." Aversion to a deformed person amounts to an abject revulsion of the deformity, which Bacon claims signifies a self-loathing in the person with the revulsion. Deformity, according to Bacon, ultimately constitutes "an advantage to rising" for deformed persons because they must overcome their deformity by either "virtue or malice," and therefore it should come as no surprise that some deformed persons become "excellent."[40]

Modern aesthetics also sees a connection between the deformed and nature. Theodor Adorno, for instance, argues that ugliness relies upon man's "repressive" relationship with nature, "which perpetuates – rather than being perpetuated by – the repression of man."[41] Like Bacon, Adorno has replaced God's complicity with that of nature, in addition to blaming mankind for his own repression. Montaigne, Bacon, and Adorno all describe the paradoxical relationship between ugliness and beauty in a manner that suggests the abject, and Donne's notion of the deformity of Puritanism in this context implies Donne's aversion to the many Protestant sects.

Most of the *Elegies*, however, deal with more personal topics associated with love and desire. Using abject imagery in a paradoxical blazon, "Elegie II: The

Anagram" performs a juxtaposition similar to comparing jealousy with vomiting.
It begins with a series of lines containing praise followed by qualifications:

> MARRY, and love, thy *Flavia*, for, shee
> Hath all things, whereby others beautious bee,
> For, though her eyes be small, her mouth is great,
> Though they be Ivory, yet her teeth are jeat,
> Though they be dimme, yet she is light enough,
> And though her harsh haire fall, he skinne is rough;
> What though her cheeks be yellow, 'her haire is red,
> Give her thing, and she hath a maydenhead. (1–8)

The comparison of a woman's paradoxical ugly beauty with the titular anagram presents a considerably objective and non-judgmental view of physical beauty, which
he follows by noting no deformities: "Love built on beauty, soone as beauty, dies,
/ Chuse this face, chang'd by no deformities" (27–8). These two lines demonstrate
the rhetorical trope of the ugly beauty poetic tradition, as the love "built on beauty"
soon dies, and the face eventually becomes deformed.[42] Like an anagram, the same
components can form two different concepts that nevertheless share some kind of
inherent relationship; the sources of conventional beauty in this poem carry ugliness
but nevertheless the poem's sense of inner beauty survives the aging process.

In "The Instance of the Letter in the Unconscious, or Reason Since Freud,"
Lacan intriguingly uses an anagrammatical example to illustrate the prohibition
between any inherent, transcendent relationship between sign and signifier. He
rearranges the French word for tree, *arbre*, into *barre*, the French word for bar,
which signifies a conceptual "bar," the prohibition of such an inherent relationship between sign and signifier.[43] Lacan illustrates this prohibition with a picture
of a tree and the word "tree" separated by a literal bar on the page, symbolizing
the conceptual bar between sign and signified. In both Donne's poem and Lacan's
illustration contrasting images and concepts mediate between and among each
other. In "The Anagram," Donne uses the idea of an anagram to underscore the
complicated relationship between beauty and ugliness.

In "Elegie IV: The Perfume," Donne provides a similar example of ugly beauty
as in "The Anagram" in the context of losing beauty with age:

> Though he had wont to search with glazed eyes,
> As though he came to kill a Cockatrice,
> Though hee have oft sworne, that hee would remove
> Thy beauties beautie, and food of our love,
> Hope of his goods, if I with thee were seene,
> Yet close and secret, as our soules, we'have been. (7–12)

Although the woman addressed by the poem will lose her beauty, the speaker does
not care, even though love can also lead to physical disgust: "Base excrement of

earth, which dost confound / Sense, from distinguishing the sicke from sound"
(57–8). Love in these lines amounts to a loss of "sense," and a loss of distinction
between "sicke" and "sound," the ability to think clearly. The poem soon associates decomposition with his love's beauty:

> If you were good, your good doth soon decay;
> And you are rare, that takes the good away.
> All my perfumes, I give most willingly
> To'embalm thy father's corse; What? will he die? (69–72)

The ugly beauty trope here comes in the union of the "perfumes" that will presumably only mask the foul smell of the corpse. Throughout "The Perfume" Donne
engages with both physical and conceptual elements of the abject to interrogate
the nature of beauty.

As in the closing lines of "The Perfume," death and decay figure prominently
in the *Elegies*. "Elegie V: His Picture" explores fleeting youth, referring to his
"face and brest of hairecloth," suggesting Donne still wore a hair shirt, either
literal or psychological. The poem quickly becomes quite morbid, as the speaker
laments that his "body's a sack of bones, broken within, / And powders blew
staines scatter'd on my skinne" (9–10). The "sack" in this line suggests sackcloth
used to make hair shirts. The speaker eventually relates decay to his own fleeting prowess as a poet: "And thou shalt say, / Doe his hurts reach mee? doth my
worth decay? (13–14). "Elegie IX: The Autumnall" similarly ponders the decay
of youth, again referring to a hair shirt in line 38:

> If transitory things, which soone decay,
> Age must be lovelyest at the latest day.
> But name not Winter-faces, whose skin's slacke;
> Lanke as an unthrifts purse; but a soules sacke. (35–8)[44]

The "soules sacke" suggests that the true soul comes about from wearing a hair
shirt, which in essence imprisons the soul before death.

For Kristeva, an abject, decomposing body resides between the "inanimate and
the inorganic," and constitutes a "transitional swarming" and an "inseparable lining" of human life identical to the Symbolic because corpses represent "fundamental pollution." The hair shirt of this Elegie represents such an inseparable
lining, as it is worn by a devout person perpetually convinced of his own polluted
soul. The only escape for such a person, this Elegie suggests, is death and the
resulting corpse without a soul. Kristeva's soulless body becomes excluded from
both God's world and linguistic signification because a corpse no longer retains
the ability to engage in language.[45]

"Elegie XI: The Bracelet" employs a conceit that labels the French as a decaying body, literally lamenting the loss of "His Mistresses Chaine," but in the context of French coinage: "Were they buy Crownes of France, I cared not, / For most

of them their natural country rot" (23–4). Donne's patriotism continues a few lines
later with a comparison between body and geography:

> Which, as the soule quickens head, feet, and heart,
> As streames, like veines run through th'earths every part,
> Visit all countries, and have slily made
> Gorgeous *France* ruin'd, ragged, and decay'd. (36–40)

France here appears ragged and decayed geographically. In the context of Donne's
relatively recent Protestant conversion, it also appears ragged and decayed theologically, as France nearly avoided the Reformation altogether. Once gorgeous,
the ruined and decomposing France and its vein-like streams resemble Kristeva's
abject corpse, which signifies a "cesspool" that "upsets even more violently the
one who confronts it as fragile and fallacious chance."[46]

In another use of the ugly beauty motif, "Elegie VIII: The Comparison" engages
in a blazon of a woman by ironically praising her clearly disgusting attributes. The
poem describes "the sweet sweat of Roses in a Still," alliterating a paradoxical
pairing of "sweet and sweat" to refer to the sweat on his "Mistris breast" (1, 4).
The speaker continues by saying "on her necke her skin such lustre sets, / They
seeme no sweat drops, but pearl carcanets" (5–6). Carcanets refers to a chain to
which Donne compares sweat, but the speaker's mistress does not wear perspiration as jewelry: "Ranke sweaty froth thy Mistresse brow defiles, / Like sperma-
tique issue of ripe menstruous boiles" (7–8). The perspiration motif here has now
become considerably unpleasant.

For Kristeva, abject menstrual blood represents "danger" that resides in social
and/or sexual identity that endangers the coexistence of men and women in the
context of a "social aggregate" through which sexual identity exists merely as
a relationship of differences.[47] Abjection places such menstrual pollution and
maternal incest as the "symbolic equivalent of that conflict."[48] Donne's reference
to menstruation seems to go much further than merely combining Petrarchan and
anti-Petrarchan tropes, however, as he not only mentions menstruation but "menstruous boiles." Kristeva's male subject actually welcomes the menstrual "flow,
discharge, hemorrhage."[49] Erotic abjection, such as in this poem's engagement
with ugly physical attributes, attempts to stop the "hemorrhage," which represents
a hesitation preceding death.[50] Perhaps Donne suggests that menstruation amounts
to a little death as much as an orgasm. The poem quickly turns to the treatment of
French Protestants in Sancerre:

> Or like that skumme, which, by needs lawlesse law
> Enforc'd, Sanserra's starved men did draw
> From parboild shooes, and bootes, and all the rest
> Which were with any soveraigne fatnes blest,
> And like vile lying stones in saffrond tinne,
> Or warts, or wheales, they hang upon her skinne. (9–14)

The speaker here compares the starving men with the scum of the lawless French sovereign, whom he compares to motionless stones covered with wounds and warts. Donne's patriotic fervor in the poem leads him to describe the hated French in abject terms.

Born to Catholic parents in anti-Catholic Tudor England, Donne converted to Anglicanism and ultimately rose to prominence in the Church of England. Such a decision necessitated he psychologically negotiate one of the key parts of his religious conversion, the move from a belief in transubstantiation to a belief in consubstantiation. Protestant consubstantiation veers toward symbolism and metaphor, as the wine merely represents or symbolizes the blood of Christ, whereas in Catholicism the wine and bread actually become the blood and flesh of Christ.[51] Christ wound imagery shared equal importance with "the fluids – tears, blood, sweat, milk, semen" emanating from wounds that constitute "liquifatious expressions" of "bizarre and sometimes repulsive, religiosity."[52] Donne's preoccupation with bodily fluids signifies both change and exchange, "personal flux" and "interpersonal flux."[53]

Kristeva locates bodily fluids, including blood, within the arena of individuation, focusing on the Other's need to withstand the "misfire of identification with the mother" by creating a "devouring mother" signified by "urine, blood, sperm, excrement." The "staging of an abortion, of a self-giving birth ever miscarried" renders "the hope for rebirth" as "short-circuited by the very splitting: the advent of one's own identity demands a law that mutilates, whereas jouissance demands an abjection from which identity becomes absent."[54] Kristeva places jouissance, or pleasure, alongside the literal ejection of urine, blood, sperm, and excrement, and she links these fluids to the desire of the abject, as their appearance reaffirms an individual that lacks his "own and clean self."[55] The "flow" of the fluids becomes the object of sexual desire, "a true 'ab-ject,'" with which the subject transgresses the horrific bowels of the maternal figure to avoid the possibility of castration.[56]

Donne's preoccupation with what Mikhail Bakhtin calls the "bodily lower stratum" carries implications for Bakhtin's grotesque carnivalesque body, which includes "defecation and copulation" and the associated bodily waste products. Bakhtin also labels the grotesque body as "always satire."[57] The carnivalesque resides in a liminal space between the high and the low without ever entering either of them. Liminal space can also refer, however, to participation in initiation ritual, representing a space the participant can neither join nor leave.[58] Donne morphs the body into the grotesque, the costs of which come as "boredom, irony, and opportunistic agreement" which manifest in a tortured body.[59] Donne's tortured body and Bakhtin's carnival body both challenge authority, and both reside outside of the Symbolic Order.

Donne's early poetry reflects a young poet seeking his own aesthetic understanding of his craft. But it also hints at biographical elements of his life and career as they developed slowly and at times turbulently. This period in Donne's career as a poet is part of the development of Donne's poetic individuation, and the early poems contribute to such a perspective and greatly inform his better-known poetry. In much the same way as his poetry has created bibliographic and textual difficulties for editors since the seventeenth century, Donne's early development as a poet complicates the canonical value of his entire oeuvre. The speakers in these poems signify Donne's early attempts to create authentic, fully developed poetic personas he could ventriloquize to say dangerous and controversial things about sensitive topics. The individuation of these poetic personas mirrors that of a young poet, who used them to develop the poetic subjectivity that characterizes his later poems. Like Kristeva's abject, Donne's disgusting poetics separate him from the abject. Donne's *Satyres* and *Elegies* reflect his pursuit of an aesthetic ideal while simultaneously trying to construct himself as a unique poetic voice, both inside and outside poetic conventions.[60]

Notes

1　Colclough, "Donne, John."
2　Kristeva, *Powers*, 15–16.
3　Kristeva, *Powers*, 1.
4　Rancière, *Politics of Aesthetics*, 25, and passim.
5　Some critics have written about Kristeva and Donne in passing. Corthell examines Donne's poetry in the context of Kristeva's "work in progress" and her notion of approaching fetishism in *Desire in Poetic Language*. Corthell, *Ideology and Desire*, 132–3. For an intriguing reading of the complicated bibliographic implications of studying Donne's poetry through the idea of an "abjected" text, see Johnson, "Donne's Odious Comparsion."
6　For a lucid engagement with psychoanalysis and new historicism, see Corthell, *Ideology and Desire*, 11–22. For a thorough treatment of Donne's poetry and the theories of Jacques Lacan, see Saunders, *Desiring Donne*, 147–84.
7　Lacan, *Seminar Book XI*, 258.
8　Augustine, *Earlier Writings*, 89.
9　Shuger, *Sacred Rhetoric*, 6–7.
10　Shuger, *Sacred Rhetoric*, 194.
11　Whalen, *Poetry of Immanence*, 35.
12　Kristeva, *Powers*, 54.
13　Kristeva, *Powers*, 2.
14　Hester, *Kinde Pitty*, 12.
15　Here and throughout, citations to the *Satyres* refer to John Donne, *John Donne: The Satires, Epigrams, and Verse Letters*, ed. W. Milgate (Oxford: Clarendon Press, 1967), 3–25.
16　Kneidel, "Donne's *Satyre*."
17　Lacan, *Seminar Book III*, 146.
18　Cook, "Meate Was Mine," 126–7.
19　Hester, *Kinde Pitty*, 52.
20　Kristeva, *Powers*, 71.
21　More, *Responsio ad Lutherum*, 311–13.
22　Qtd. in Haile, *Luther*, 191.
23　Žižek, *Parallax View*, 187.
24　Žižek, *Parallax View*, 187.
25　Kristeva, *Powers*, 108.
26　Kristeva, *Powers*, 108.
27　Laporte, *History of Shit*, 14; emphasis added.

28 Laporte, *History of Shit*, 37.
29 Hester, *Kinde Pitty*, 66.
30 Strier, "Radical Donne," 293.
31 Colclough, "Donne, John."
32 Kristeva, *Powers*, 3.
33 Covington, *Wounds, Flesh*, 151.
34 Kristeva, *Powers*, 3.
35 Kristeva, *Powers*, 110.
36 All citations to the *Elegies* come from John Donne, *John Donne: The Elegies and the Songs and Sonnets*, ed. Helen Louise Gardner (Oxford: Clarendon Press, 1966), 1–28, but I have kept Grierson's numbering from John Donne, *The Poems of John Donne*, 2 vols, ed. Herbert John Clifford Grierson (Oxford: Clarendon Press, 1912), 79–144.
37 Kristeva, *Powers*, 2.
38 Covington, *Wounds, Flesh*, 147.
39 Montaigne, *Essayes*, 550.
40 Bacon, "Of Deformity."
41 Adorno, *Aesthetic Theory*, 47.
42 Dubrow, "Donne's Elegies," 59–70.
43 Lacan, "Instance of the Letter," 416.
44 Gardner does not include this poem in her collection of the *Elegies*.
45 Kristeva, *Powers*, 109.
46 Kristeva, *Powers*, 3.
47 Kristeva, *Powers*, 71.
48 Kristeva, *Powers*, 77.
49 Kristeva, *Powers*, 55.
50 Kristeva, *Powers*, 55.
51 According to Covington, "Blood, if shed toward the godly ends of martyrdom, could also be a badge not of sin but of divine election, not of debasement but salvation; blood, in other words, could redeem as well as condemn." Covington, *Wounds, Flesh*, 33.
52 Covington, *Wounds, Flesh*, 165.
53 Selleck, *Interpersonal Idiom*, 157, 163.
54 Kristeva, *Powers*, 54.
55 Kristeva, *Powers*, 53.
56 Kristeva, *Powers*, 53.
57 Bakhtin, *Rabelais*, 21, 306.
58 Douglas, *Purity and Danger*, passim.
59 Sullivan, *Rhetoric*, 10.
60 I would like to thank Barbara Correll for her insightful assistance in revising this essay.

References

Adorno, Theodor W. *Aesthetic Theory*. Translated by Robert Hullot-Kentor. Minneapolis: University of Minnesota Press, 1997.

Augustine. *Augustine: Earlier Writings*. Translated by J.H.S. Burleigh. Louisville, KY: Westminster Press, 1953.

Bacon, Francis. "Of Deformity." In *Francis Bacon: The Major Works*. Edited by Brian Vickers, 426–7. Oxford: Oxford University Press, 2002.

Bakhtin, Mikhail. *Rabelais and His World*. Translated by Helene Iswolsky. Bloomington: Indiana University Press, 1984.

Colclough, David. "Donne, John (1572–1631)." In *Oxford Dictionary of National Biography*. Oxford: Oxford University Press, 2004.

Cook, Trevor. " 'The Meate Was Mine': Donne's *Satyre II* and the Prehistory of Proprietary Authorship." *Studies in Philology* 109, no. 1 (2012): 103–31.

Corthell, Ronald J. *Ideology and Desire in Renaissance Poetry: The Subject of Donne.* Detroit: Wayne State University Press, 1997.

Cousins, A.D., and Damian Grace, eds. *Donne and the Resources of Kind.* London: Associated University Presses, 2002.

Covington, Sarah. *Wounds, Flesh, and Metaphor in Seventeenth-Century England.* New York: Palgrave Macmillan, 2009.

Donne, John. *John Donne: The Elegies and the Songs and Sonnets.* Edited by Helen Louise Gardner. Oxford: Clarendon Press, 1966.

Donne, John. *John Donne: The Satires, Epigrams, and Verse Letters.* Edited by W. Milgate. Oxford: Clarendon Press, 1967.

Donne, John. *The Poems of John Donne.* Edited by Herbert John Clifford Grierson. 2 vols. Oxford: Clarendon Press, 1912.

Douglas, Mary. *Purity and Danger: An Analysis of Concepts of Pollution and Taboo.* New York: Praeger, 1966.

Dubrow, Heather. "Donne's Elegies and the Ugly Beauty Tradition." In *Donne and the Resources of Kind*, edited by A.D. Cousins and Damian Grace, 59–70. London: Associated University Presses, 2002.

Haile, Harry Gerald. *Luther: An Experiment in Biography.* Garden City, NY: Doubleday, 1980.

Hester, M. Thomas. *Kinde Pitty and Brave Scorn: John Donne's Satyres.* Durham, NC: Duke University Press, 1982.

Johnson, Nate. "Donne's Odious Comparsion: Abjection, Text, and Canon." In *Discontinuities: New Essays on Renaissance Literature and Criticism*, edited by Viviana Comensoli, Paul Stevens, and Marta Straznicky, 139–58. Toronto: University of Toronto Press, 1998.

Kneidel, Gregory. "Donne's *Satyre I* and the Closure of the Law." *Renaissance and Reformation/Renaissance et Réforme* 28, no. 4 (2004): 83–103.

Kristeva, Julia. *Powers of Horror: An Essay on Abjection.* Translated by Leon S. Roudiez. New York: Columbia University Press, 1982.

Lacan, Jacques. "The Instance of the Letter in the Unconscious, or Reason Since Freud." In *Écrits: The First Complete Edition in English.* Translated by Bruce Fink, 412–41. New York: Norton, 2006.

———. *The Seminar of Jacques Lacan, Book III: The Psychoses.* Translated by Russell Grigg. New York: Norton, 1993.

———. *The Seminar of Jacques Lacan, Book XI: The Four Fundamentals of Psychoanalysis.* Translated by Alan Sheridan. New York: Norton, 1994.

Laporte, Dominique. *The History of Shit.* Translated by Nadia Benabid and Rodolphe el-Khoury. Cambridge, MA: MIT Press, 2000.

Montaigne, Michel de. *The Essayes.* Translated by John Florio. London: Grant Richards, 1908.

More, Thomas. *Responsio ad Lutherum. The Yale Edition of the Complete Works of St. Thomas More*, vol. 5. Edited by M. Headley. New Haven: Yale University Press, 1969.

Rancière, Jacques. *The Politics of Aesthetics: The Distribution of the Sensible.* Translated by Steven Corcoran. New York: Continuum, 2006.

Saunders, Ben. *Desiring Donne: Poetry, Sexuality, Interpretation.* Cambridge, MA: Harvard University Press, 2006.

Selleck, Nancy Gail. *The Interpersonal Idiom in Shakespeare, Donne, and Early Modern Culture*. New York: Palgrave Macmillan, 2008.

Shuger, Debora K. *Sacred Rhetoric: The Christian Grand Style in the English Renaissance*. Princeton: Princeton University Press, 1988.

Strier, Richard. "Radical Donne: 'Satire III'." *English Literary History* 60, no. 2 (1993): 283–322.

Sullivan, Ceri. *The Rhetoric of the Conscience in Donne, Herbert and Vaughan*. Oxford: Oxford University Press, 2008.

Whalen, Robert. *The Poetry of Immanence: Sacrament in Donne and Herbert*. Toronto: University of Toronto Press, 2002.

Žižek, Slavoj. *The Parallax View*. Cambridge, MA: MIT Press, 2006.

Afterword

The study of emotion and sensation has become an important force in early modern literary studies but, up until now, there has been little space for disgust in this new touchy feely Renaissance. This volume is one of the first to gather together essays on disgust, if not the first such collection, and it throws open a subject which intersects in multiple ways with all kinds of early modern obsessions. From disgust as a convention of early modern travel writing, through the manipulation of disgust to construct national, communal, and sexual identities, to disgust as the ground for exploring artifice, the power of language, or audience response, these essays reveal the rich potential in the subject of disgust.

Of course, each essay in this volume has its own distinct approach, ranging, for example, from the psychoanalytic thrust of Dan Mills' essay on Donne, to Colleen Kennedy's historicist analysis of the role played by disgust in the development of national myths and symbols. By setting broadly (although not exclusively) psychoanalytical approaches, like Mills' and Marcela Kostihová's, against broadly historicizing approaches, like Kennedy's, Ineke Murakami's, and Gitanjali Shahani's, the volume builds a conversation centered on the issue basic to the study of disgust: To what extent is there a shared experience of disgust? Is disgust a transhistorical phenomenon, or is it experienced in ways that are specific to a particular historical moment? One of the most fruitful implications of this volume is that the emotion of disgust, however visceral, is also irreducibly a rhetorical construction, and that, as Laura Kolb, Galena Hashhozheva, and Shahani each suggest, a shared experience of disgust is itself a rhetorical construction, so that the crucial question is not what is being described, but how is it being described. In analyzing the issue basic to disgust, each of the essays in the volume turns its attention to an important series of further questions: How can we access the experience of disgust? How did people articulate what we might recognize as feelings of disgust in the past, and what words did they use? What tools do we need to understand those words? What work can disgust be made to do? For Natalie Eschenbaum, Barbara Correll, and Murakami, disgust plays a role in canon formation and the creation of aesthetic value; for Emily King and Kostihová, disgust helps determine gender and sexual identities; for Kennedy and Shahani, it works to maintain community. In fact, the essays by Kennedy and Shahani lead me to wonder whether disgust is a reassuring emotion, just as the spectacle of the traitor's death was reassuring to early modern society. Do we feel disgust when confronted with something completely unfamiliar, or do we then feel bewilderment, rather than disgust? All the essays are united by their interest in articulating and analyzing those areas of experience that have been rejected and reviled. Their richness of approach and analysis suggests to me that disgust will be a fruitful focus for readings in other contexts. One obvious path for future research would be the interactions between religion and disgust. For instance, how does disgust work in religious polemic? Or how is disgust exploited and controlled by such Counter-Reformation imagery as the bleeding heart?

Reading these essays has prompted me to think much more carefully about the workings of disgust. At the same time, I noticed that, implicitly or explicitly, these essays have a conflicted relationship to the work of Norbert Elias, the sacred monster and, in many ways, progenitor of disgust studies. Eschenbaum and Correll acknowledge the importance of Elias in their introduction and Kostihová, to take one example, includes a considered, although brief, reflection on Elias, when setting out the theoretical context of her essay. In the rest of this Afterword, I want to take my cue from the volume and revisit Elias to give focus to the varied thoughts prompted by reading these rich and varied essays.

While literary critics may have shown little interest in the subject up until now, disgust became important to historians and anthropologists after the publication of Norbert Elias' *The Civilizing Process* in 1939, which argues that disgust is essential to the construction and maintenance of civilized society.[1] This new sociocultural formation starts to develop in the Renaissance and is characterized by the lowering of the threshold of disgust, with the result that more kinds of behavior come to be regarded as objectionable and are rejected as disgusting. Society moves from being one in which disgust plays a small role, to one in which disgust determines the internal processes and social interactions of those who subscribe to society's values. Before the advent of the civilizing process, behavior was controlled by issues of public honor and the need to preserve face. On the other hand, according to Elias, the civilizing process internalizes restraints, with the result that controls gradually come to be seen as natural and inborn.

The force of Elias' argument has, unintentionally, done disgust a disservice. Not only does Elias seem to have disgust sewn up, his privileging of pure disgust as fundamental to the workings of the civilized psycho-social formation makes any extension of the argument into areas which may interact with disgust appear either trivial or redundant. However, disgust does not dominate all other senses and emotions, nor does it exist in isolation. It always exists as part of a dynamic system of sensations, emotions, and ideas in which priorities change according to context. A particular ideology, for example, may momentarily subdue the power of disgust, as it does for Catherine of Siena, who famously drank the water and bodily matter she collected after bathing the suppurating breast of a fellow nun, not because she was a particularly disgusting medieval woman, but because her interpretation of Christian duty and her desire to control her body, led her to subdue her own bodily impulse to revulsion, by drinking the noxious concoction.[2] Elias is the towering figure in the study of disgust, and every subsequent researcher into the subject has to engage with his theories but, as these essays suggest, it is time to think more carefully about how disgust functions, both in texts and in the civilizing process.

The essays in this volume react to the prevalence of disgust in early modern literature, but does disgust become noticeable in this period solely as a result of the civilizing process? For example, to what degree does technology influence behavior and class distinction? Access to running water from a water pump, or from a tap leading from a tank, makes it easier to wash, and this might make those who can afford such luxuries more fastidious and more prone to notice the revolting incrustations under other people's fingernails. It is easier to feel disgust if one is clean and others are dirty. The office of The Groom of the Stool, which was once a great honor, may have gradually lost its luster, during the course of the seventeenth century, because of the gradual introduction of water closets into palaces and great houses. Closets take stools away from sight, and make them less familiar, a less obvious part of daily proceedings, and so more likely to provoke disgust. Elias' passionate analysis of the civilizing process deflects attention from other possible reasons for the prevalence of disgust in the early modern period, as the essays by Kennedy, Murakami, King, and Kolb suggest. These essays deal with texts influenced by city comedy or city forms, and implicitly raise the possibility that the prevalence of disgust in the early modern period is a symptom of urbanization. London, in particular, grew exponentially as people crammed into its confines, and its influence on early modern culture grew with its concentration of power, money, activity, and people.[3] In the plays of Ben Jonson, for example, or the prose of Thomas Nashe, the intensity of urban experience is reflected in the intensity of disgust, which articulates a sense of being in the city. Urban dwellers had to adjust their spatial awareness as they found themselves uncomfortably close to people in congested places, and disgust expresses the discomfort caused by the material, sensory, and mental pressures of the urban environment on urban dwellers, as people, smells, noises, multiple attitudes, and multiple activities pressed in on the crowded, frenetic urban space. Moreover, even if the civilizing process starts in the Renaissance, as Elias argues, disgust does not go unchallenged, and its limitations are exposed. Murakami touches on this in her essay on *Bartholomew Fair* where sensitivity to the disgusting, even good taste, can become another vice if allowed to run unchecked. So, too, Morose in Jonson's *Epicoene or the Silent Woman* is guilty of too much sensitivity, of an over-worked sense of civility, which makes him fastidious to a ridiculous degree. Morose is so sensitive to noise that he sets out to find a silent woman to be his wife. Not only is he completely incapable of living in a city, he is also incapable of living in a community, but his existence suggests that the civilizing process was not the smooth uncontested process it may appear to have been to our later vantage point.

It is tempting to treat disgust as a basic, generalized, human impulse, because it can involve such a powerful response. Yet, as Elias argues, even if sanctions like disgust have become so perfectly internalized, during the civilizing process, that they now appear to be inborn and natural, it was not always so. Such restraints may even be natural now, but only to an individual who is determined by, and helps determine, a particular cultural formation at a particular time. Each essay, in its way, points to problems in treating disgust as a fundamental constant in human nature. As Kostihová's essay on *Venus and Adonis* implies, we cannot assume that all readers found Venus' rampant sexuality disgusting, nor even that all readers now find it disgusting, even assuming that we understand more about our present than we do about the past. Nor can we assume that all readers who do find Venus disgusting do so for the same reasons. Disgust certainly does have an irreducible core of revulsion, but it is mediated, manipulated, and controlled by its context and its mode of representation. Consequently, disgust can access a much wider repertoire than we might at first imagine, and can, for example, be presented through the ironic, urbane lens of Herrick, through the more broadly comic strokes of Jonson in *Bartholomew Fair*, or it can be inserted into the evidence-based narratives of early modern travelogues, or larded with hyperbole to exaggerate its repulsive and distasteful elements. Our immediate visceral response to disgusting things in literature can homogenize disgust and swamp considerations of how disgusting things are put into words, how the presentation of disgust might succeed or fail in overcoming the linguistic barriers to the communication of emotion and sensation. It might simply obscure disgust's variety of nuance and function.

A disgusting object or scene, and the description of that disgusting object or scene, collapse the differences between reality and representation, the object and its description. For example, Eschenbaum turns our attention to Herrick's poem "Upon Reape" in which the object (sick eyes full of maggots) and its description provoke similar visceral reactions, at least in this reader. Rather than observing emotion, or imagining it, the audience experiences real disgust, or an intractable mixture of imagined and real emotion. The description of something disgusting is one of those occasions when text and reader, play world and real world, come closer together. For example, John Marston's play *Antonio and Mellida* includes a blistering attack on one of the cornerstones of Elizabethan politics: the identification of courtiership with courting. The Lady Rosaline demands slavish gestures of service from the male courtiers around her and this provokes Felice into an outburst that vividly conveys his disgust at such behavior:

> FELICE O that the stomach of this queasy age
> Digests or brooks such raw unseasoned gobs
> And vomits not them forth! O slavish sots!
> "Servant", quoth you? Foh! If a dog should crave
> And beg her service, he should have it straight.
> She'd give him favours, too, to lick her feet,
> Or fetch her fan, or some such drudgery—
> A good dog's office, which these amorists
> Triumph of. 'Tis rare! Well, give her more ass,
> More sot, as long as dropping of her nose
> Is sworn rich pearl by such low slaves as those. (2.1.92–102)[4]

Felice's attack on service to a lady, with its graphic evocation of vomit and pearls of mucus dropping from the lady's nose, attempts to provoke visceral revulsion and a powerful identification on the part of the audience with the disgust Felice feels. To the extent that this is successful, the audience converges with Felice and is no longer a detached observer, but equal with Felice, feeling disgust at the things that also disgust Felice, and feeling what Felice feels.

As the essays by King, Murakami, Kolb, Correll, and Eschenbaum argue, disgust appeals to early modern writers because it offers the chance to experiment with audience manipulation, to play with distance by drawing the audience in and then repelling them, in order to examine the limits of authorial control. It is precisely because the readers' or audience's responses are insistent and somatically underlined that disgust provokes reflection on the ways texts manipulate audiences. Aspects of experience, and particularly elements of a particular sensation or emotion, often remain beyond verbal communication, but in the case of disgust, the effect on the audience is much more immediate and vivid. At the very moment that disgust, at least temporarily, appears to overcome the barriers to verbal communication, it calls attention to the existence of such barriers to literary immediacy. Disgust is part of the Renaissance writer's armory of intensification, one of the rhetorical strategies that can be exploited to move the audience. Like other kinds of hyperbole, it encourages a self-conscious use of literary tactics on the part of the writer and produces a self-conscious response on the part of the audience. Its potential to collapse reality and representation means that it can serve as a metonymy for literary activity in general. Correll links disgust to the analysis of literary value, in an essay that focuses on one instance of disgust in romance: Guyon's destruction of the Bower of Bliss in *The Faerie Queene*. Disgust is a reaction to artificiality, to the painted forgeries of the Bower of Bliss that link painted women, cosmetic perversion, and corrupt art, through the character of Acrasia. As Correll notes, misogyny and Protestant iconoclasm notwithstanding, the episode still registers the appeal of the Bower of Bliss. Although the idea may at first appear very strange, disgust is an appropriate arena in which to analyze the nature of writing, because it echoes, in little, what literature attempts more generally. The vividness of the response it creates brings fictional and real worlds closer together and tests the differences between literal and figurative language. There are many reasons why Jonson might present himself as disgusting, some of which are discussed by Kolb, and why Herrick might intersperse epigrams on disgusting subjects among the jewel-like epigrams of the *Hesperides*, some of which are identified by Eschenbaum, but for writers who are interested in the consequences of literary self-reflection, disgust might have a particular appeal because it sets literal and figurative realms, subject, text, and audience, into intensified and unpredictable interaction.

By describing something so vividly that it produces disgust in the reader, a writer certainly brandishes their literary prowess but critics have often been suspicious of such sensationalistic flourishes. The apparent eagerness of early modern dramatists, in particular, to dabble in disgust is often seen as suspect. At best, it is interpreted as an example of self-conscious theatricality, which has little point beyond the celebration of playing; at worst, it is interpreted as a cynical, self-serving ploy to achieve commercial and cultural pre-eminence through notoriety.[5] However, disgust emphasizes the integration of experience. In the

Renaissance, moral failings and sinfulness are expressed in terms of things that are disgusting, decaying, and repulsive. Disgust is never morally neutral in this period. In Galen's theory of the humors, which was still influential in the Renaissance, the body and the senses have an inescapable moral function. The senses do not just perceive material things; they also judge behavior. Galen also predicates a balanced psyche on a balanced body. Good health is the product of a balance between the bodily humors. Bad health is the product of imbalance between the humors, and the predominance of a particular humor produces a particular vice, as well as a particular disease. An excess of black bile, for example, produces melancholy.

In John Marston's play *The Malcontent* the melancholic hero, Malevole, expresses his heightened moral sensitivity through intense expressions of disgust:

> MALEVOLE Think this—this earth is the only grave and Golgotha
> wherein all things that live must rot; 'tis but the draught
> wherein the heavenly bodies discharge their corruption;
> the very muck-hill on which the sublunary orbs cast
> their excrements. Man is the slime of this dung-pit, and
> princes are the governors of these men. (4.5.110–15)[6]

The passage associates vice with hideous physicality, discharges, pus, slime, decay, excrement, and organic matter that is rank, fulsome, and abhorrent. Typically, disgust is associated with mixed matter; either with liquids that are sticky, or so thick they approach solids; or with glutinous, squashy solids that are not completely solid or dry. These mixtures of solid and liquid attributes find their way from the inside of the body to the outside, and concentrate around bodily orifices, at thresholds where the body's seal is broken. Not only does disgust mark moral and aesthetic boundaries, it also marks the boundaries of the self and the boundaries of privy space. However, the nature of that privy space is ambivalent. On the one hand, the internal is the seat of the soul, of depth and sincerity, but to the extent that it produces excreta, like mucus, or excrement, that may find their way outside, it is polluting. Indeed, the disgust provoked by such matter, by Malevole's apprehension of the "muck-hill" of excrements, for instance, also conveys a degree of horror at our own potential to be disgusting.

Disgust may well confer a sense of superiority on those that experience it, because it defines the self against that which is low and objectionable. Malevole, for example, dismisses the disgusting conduct of his fellow courtiers as morally and socially contemptible: "How servile, is the rugged'st courtier's face!" he exclaims, with disdain (1.4.76). Nevertheless, that sense of superiority is destabilized by the intimations of common bodily experience, and the realization that "all things that live must rot" (4.5.111). This suggests that disgust plays a more complicated, even compromising, role in the civilizing process than might at first appear. It articulates order, but at the same time it compromises the civilizing veil drawn over rotten objects and morals. It reminds us of the body and its inconveniences and marks the irruption of strong feeling, rather than the control of emotion. There is an obtrusiveness about disgust, an irreducibility that cannot be swept away. In fact, as the essay by Shahani argues, the visceral power of the disgust provoked by early modern narratives of alien cultures serves as a kind of verification of the narrative and establishes its credibility. For Elias, the civilizing process is a gradual process of internalization and of individuation, because disgust gradually produces discreet subjects, in both senses of the word (discreet as individual and separate; and discreet as reserved, controlled and sensitive to convention). It patrols the thresholds where the body might invade its surroundings or be invaded by them. However, disgust also works to underline the body, to underline shared experience and establish community. Disdain and inclusiveness are competing components of disgust and the shifting balance between them is exploited in *Henry V* to define what Kennedy sees as a more inclusive form of national identity. Identity, just like the body, is difficult to contain, because it is constantly flowing outwards. Moreover, as several of the essays in this volume observe, disgusting things have a certain glamour, a mesmeric quality that can attract, as well as repel. Freud recognizes the function of disgust in structuring moral and cultural systems and classifies disgust as a reaction formation which, like shame, works to obscure desire and prevent its indulgence.[7] The implication of Freud's analysis is, of course, that the object or activity that arouses disgust is also actually desirable, mesmerizing, or erotic. It is simultaneously the object of revulsion and fascination. This is especially true of the kind of disgust that is suggested by early modern words such as "fulsome" and "rank," where overabundance and surfeit turn the enticing into the repulsive. This kind of disgust exposes the underbelly of consumption which, if left to run unchecked, will continue to consume, and will lead desire through satisfaction into excess. Murakami notes that Jonson finds materiality repugnant but indispensable. Other essays, including those by Shahani and Correll, explore the relationship between disgust, surfeit, and excess, and acknowledge disgust's role as a vehicle for the critique of consumer capitalism, and that special form of consumerism that is cultural consumerism.

In his essay on Donne, Mills notes that the mobilization of disgust often results in unexpected mixtures, and one of those unexpected couplings links body and mind. Malevole's observations on the "muck-hill" of the world merge a moral and physical response to sin. The thought of the world's moral corruption turns the virtuous person's stomach. Implicit in Marston's presentation of disgust is the realization that morality and cognition are facilitated by strong sensory responses, as well as by reason. They are not just affairs of the mind, but also affairs of the body. Disgust reminds us of our embodiment. It punctures pretension, by reminding us that we fart, snort, smell, exude, and rot. It engages with the nature of the human and this gives it moral potential. Malevole's words remind us that satire has an affinity for disgust. Both the word "disgust" and the word "satire" are related to matters of the mouth, food, and taste. As Eschenbaum and Correll note in their introduction, the term "disgust" derives from the Latin prefix of negation, "dis," and the Latin word for taste, "gustus." One possible root for the word satire is the Latin word "satura," which refers to a dish laden with a variety of fruits and sweets, brought on at the end of a meal. There is a competing Renaissance etymology for the word satire, which links it to the word "satyr," a being that is half human and half beast and a follower of Bacchus. This false etymology provides a sanction for satire to be both tasteless and bestial. Renaissance satire and disgust are gross, unrestrained, and tied to the animalistic.[8] Like satire, disgust unveils what politeness keeps hidden. It exposes things and refuses to accept decorum, euphemism, hypocrisy, or other forms of disguise. It lets things out that the civilizing process would cover and suppress. The irreducibility of the bodily effect of disgusting things, and disgusting descriptions, is an inescapable, if momentary, impediment to sublimation.

The early modern belief that sights and sounds could corrupt, and anxieties about artifice, contribute to Spenser's ambivalence toward the Bower of Bliss in Book 2 of *The Faerie Queene*, as Correll demonstrates, and to Jonson's ambivalence toward dramatic representation, as detailed by Murakami, to take two examples.[9] As something that can contaminate, as well as build order and morality, disgust offers a more manageable lens through which to explore the efficacy and morality of language, and literature's power to move its audience to good or ill. Do puppet shows, plays, and non-didactic texts pollute the mind? Does the description of a disgusting object or scene pollute the mind? The disgusting certainly can produce physical effects, and might therefore give credibility to fears about the power of words and images to contaminate.

The description of disgust challenges a writer's ability to move the audience and to create intense responses. The jaw-dropping, sensationalistic aspect of disgust leads Hashhozheva and Shahani to suggest that disgust has a place in romance, which prompts some rich discussion of disgust's relation to wonder in these two essays, in particular. The interest in disgust can be explained by the processes of Renaissance dialectic, where objects and ideas call up their opposites. In dialectic, considering what is contrary to a proposition is one of the strategies for devising arguments for the defense or refutation of an argument. Contrariety is typical of Renaissance accounts of natural, intellectual, and social phenomena, especially as they are influenced by Augustine. Augustine's vision of history is structured by antithesis, and the opposition between the *civitas dei* (city of God) and the *civitas terrena* (city of man).[10] The dialectical structure whereby beauty calls forth disgust, and vice versa, is reflected in the very structure of Herrick's lyric collection the *Hesperides*, a structure occluded by literary history, but recuperated by Eschenbaum, in which lyric calls up lyrics of disgust, and vice versa, in a play of comparison and juxtaposition that is also basic to satire. The disgusting is the flipside of beauty, and is implied by the intense recreation of beauty in lyric, just as beauty is implied by the intense recreation of disgust. The description of disgusting things is related to the blazon and to those inset passages of virtuosic description, in early modern writing, which modify the rhythm of the text. Inverted forms, like detailed descriptions of disgusting things, as opposed to beautiful things, or the paradoxical encomium, depend on the writer's precise identification of the component elements of forms such as the encomium or blazon. These elements are heightened and then manipulated to create an intense experience of something negative. The heightening of techniques, or the use of particular techniques in unexpected contexts, creates a critical perspective on those very techniques and encourages questions about the possible interrelationships between subject and form. Disgust seems to reject proportion and limit, but it actually depends on an acute awareness of proportion and limit. As King argues, in her essay on Thomas Nashe, degree, calibration, and even delicacy are essential to disgust, which develops out of the disruption of an acute sense of balance and limit.

The insertion of the disgusting epigrams into the *Hesperides* disrupts the rhythm of reading. Herrick reengages the readers by knocking them out of responses that are familiar or predictable. However, implicit in this attempt to reinvigorate writing is an acknowledgement of the weakness of the collection's more acceptable modes of representation. Indeed, all styles and literary novelties start to lose their edge once they become too familiar, and even disgust develops its own conventions. For Elias, disgust participates in historical development as it facilitates the civilizing process, but disgust may register the passage of time in other ways. It can acknowledge change and articulate a sense of periodicity. It can register a sense that certain literary styles and certain ways of understanding experience have become obsolete. For Kostihová, it is high courtly love discourse that is ridiculed by invoking disgust, just as Felice rejects Elizabethan styles of courtiership through disgust in *Antonio and Mellida*. For Eschenbaum, Herrick's interspersing of the disgust epigrams among the more conventional lyrics of the *Hesperides* punctures the lyrical atmosphere and highlights lyric's formal limitations. Disgust can express weaknesses in the dominant frames of reference, and can convey a sense that experience is over-mediated by conventions that have been overworked and have themselves become rank and fulsome. Early modern disgust may be the expression of a culture that is trying to come to terms with the dynamics of historical change. It may express the awareness that the political and cultural consensus is slowly disintegrating.

While the term "disgust" derives from the Latin for taste, it does not necessarily follow that taste is always the privileged medium for disgust. The disgusting may well provoke the desire to vomit, and things that are physically or morally disgusting are often associated with things that are foul tasting. Nevertheless, other senses can channel disgust, bringing it into the body and providing the images for its articulation. In Marston's play *Antonio's Revenge* Antonio disguises himself as a fool who blows both bubbles and farts (4.2.28).[11] The fool is full of different kinds of windiness, including the air that fills the passages of the body, the airiness of purely verbal invention, and the stinking breath of denigration and satire. Earlier in the play, elated by the fact that he has embarked on the course of revenge and murdered Julio, Antonio imagines that he has become all air and spirit: "Methinks I am all air and feel no weight / Of human dirt clog" (3.5.20–21). He imagines that he has become more than human and that he has risen above the physical, but the smell of farts hangs round his aspirations and introduces a sense of proportion which punctures any impulse, stoic or otherwise, to transcend the human. *The Malcontent* opens twice to bad smells. The Induction opens with references to "stool[s]," "stale suits" (l.7), and the fear of "hissing" (l.4), while Act

I opens in a room filled with such a foul noise and such a foul smell that it must be perfumed straight away. The noise, at least, emanates from Malevole's chamber, and the first thing he utters is "Yaugh" (1.2.5), a term of disgust, but the opening of Act I also raises the distinct possibility that the foul noise and foul smell emanate from the audience who fill the room into which the actors enter.[12] Malevole is not only sensitive to physical and moral stench; he enjoys the freedom of the fool. He is not only "as free as air" (1.3.2), but is equated with a fart. When Mendoza tells Malevole that the Duke hates him, Malevole replies, "As Irishmen do bum-cracks" (3.3.50). In these scenes, ears, noses, and eyes are the privileged channels of disgust, rather than the mouth.

All this farting is disgusting, but it also constitutes a wonderfully synesthetic experience, which speaks to the ears as well as the nose, as Balurdo says at the beginning of *Antonio and Mellida*, "O, I smell a sound" (1.1.44). However, farting does not only unite the senses, it also unites the senses to morality. Balurdo may identify one kind of sound-smell, but Felice immediately associates bad smells with sin: "Piero, stay! For I descry a fume / Creeping from out the bosom of the deep, / The breath of darkness" (1.1.45–6). Felice's status as a moralist and as a satirist depends on his ability to identify smells. In fact, for Marston smell unites the activities involved in the production of plays. The playwright, the actors, and the audience all smell, in the double sense of being able to detect smells, and being smelly themselves. When Rosaline comes on stage in the entourage of the Duke (*Antonio and Mellida*), her first words are a comment on the bad smell that hangs around the scene: "Foh, what a strong scent's here! Somebody useth to wear socks" (2.1.60–61). The stench may be the stench of corruption, the stench produced by muck-slinging satire, or the stench produced by actors and spectators who have not changed their socks for some time. A bad smell hangs around the theater, but rather than separating the playwright and his satiric mouthpieces, like Malevole, from the contemptible multitude and the contemptible players, smell serves to unite them. The etymology of disgust privileges taste as the sense through which it is felt and expressed, but in Marston disgust involves visual, tactile, auditory, and olfactory revulsion. It is unusual to taste things unless they have intentionally been introduced into the mouth, but objects can invade sight, noises can invade ears, smells can invade noses, as Kolb also makes clear in her essay on Ben Jonson, and things can accidentally brush against hands and skin. By shifting his focus from disgust as, primarily, a gustatory experience, Marston underlines its reactive, rather than assertive, nature. Since our senses can be invaded, we are not in total control of our bodies or ourselves, and the unsightly can unexpectedly thrust itself on us and stimulate disgust, mixed with the anxiety born from a loss of control.

With its ability to provoke a vivid, even physical reaction, disgust resists the abstract potential of language and any attempt to marginalize the body. It brings together authors, readers, and audiences in malodorous, cacophonous, revolting communities, and argues that there is an inescapable relationship between the internal and the external, between body and soul, and between materiality and abstraction. Physical, emotional, and moral experiences are interlinked. For Elias, disgust suppresses what is noxious to civility, but disgust is gross, and inescapably gross. If it suppresses, it does so imperfectly, and calls to mind the gross, lumpen bodies we all share. Rather than achieving containment, it acknowledges human vulnerability to invasion by external stimuli, and the external world's vulnerability to invasion by the human, as we sweat, snort, sneeze, and fart our way through life. Disgust is anything but Cartesian.

Georgia E. Brown

Notes

1 Elias, *Prozeß*.
2 Miller, *Anatomy*, 158–63. Miller discusses the role played by disgust in Catherine's type of devotion. He notes that Elias is blind to the ways religion might mould attitudes and societies, rather than passively reflect them, 170–71.
3 On the rise of London, see Finlay and Shearer, "Population Growth"; on London's potential to overwhelm inhabitants and visitors with uncontrolled and disturbing sensations, see Porter, *London*.
4 Marston, *Antonio and Mellida*. As the organ of smell, the nose plays a large role in disgust, particularly sexual disgust. Mucus, which Felice calls "dropping," was so disgusting that its production came to emblematize the Fall in medieval theology. Along with sweat, mucus was only produced as a consequence of original sin, and neither excretion existed in Eden. See Payer, *Bridling of Desire*, 29.
5 To take two critics of Marston as an example: on the one hand, Rick Bowers celebrates Marston because he is amoral and focuses his energy on creating immediate, powerful theatrical effects. Bowers, "John Marston." On the other hand, Samuel Schoenbaum is highly suspicious of Marston's exploitation of disgust, which he sees as evidence of perversion. Schoenbaum, "Precarious Balance."
6 Marston, *Malcontent*.
7 Freud, *Three Essays*, 7: 177.
8 Michael Seidel discusses the competing derivations of the term satire, and their consequences, in the first chapter of *Satiric Inheritance*.
9 Stephen Gosson's *Schoole of Abuse* is a classic attack on literary artifice. Words have physical effects, for Gosson, and can turn reasonable creatures into brutes. This is why, according to Gosson, Plato banished poets from the Republic.
10 For a succinct overview of the importance of antithesis in Renaissance thought, see Clark, "Meaning of Witchcraft."
11 Marston, *Antonio's Revenge*.
12 *The Malcontent* was written for the Blackfriars Theatre. *Antonio and Mellida* and *Antonio's Revenge* were written for Paul's Boys. See Gair, "John Marston."

References

Bowers, Rick. "John Marston at the 'mart of woe:' The 'Antonio' Plays." In *The Drama of John Marston: Critical Re-Visions*, edited by T.F. Wharton, 14–26. Cambridge: Cambridge University Press, 2000.

Clark, Stuart. "Inversion, Misrule and the Meaning of Witchcraft." *Past and Present* 24 (1980): 98–127.

Elias, Norbert. *Über den Prozeß der Zivilisation*. Basel: Verlag Haus zum Falken, 1939. Translated by Edmund Jephcott as *The Civilizing Process*. 2 vols. Vol. 1, New York: Urizen Books, 1978; Vol. 2, New York: Pantheon Books, 1982.

Finlay, Roger, and Beatrice Shearer. "Population Growth and Suburban Expansion." In *London, 1500–1700: The Making of the Metropolis*, edited by A.L. Beier and Roger Finlay, 37–59. London: Longman, 1986.

Freud, Sigmund. *Three Essays on the Theory of Sexuality*. 1905. Translated and reprinted in *The Standard Edition of the Complete Psychological Works of Sigmund Freud*. Edited by James Strachey. 24 vols. London: Hogarth Press, 1953–1974.

Gair, W. Reavely. "John Marston: A Theatrical Perspective." In *The Drama of John Marston: Critical Re-Visions*, edited by T.F. Wharton, 27–44. Cambridge: Cambridge University Press, 2000.

Gosson, Stephen. *The Schoole of Abuse*. London, 1579.

Marston, John. *Antonio and Mellida*. Edited by W. Reavley Gair. The Revels Plays. 1991. Manchester: Manchester University Press, 2004.

———. *Antonio's Revenge*. Edited by W. Reavley Gair. The Revels Plays. 1978. Manchester: Manchester University Press, 1999.

———. *The Malcontent*. Edited by George K. Hunter. The Revels Plays. 1975. Manchester: Manchester University Press, 1999.

Miller, William Ian. *The Anatomy of Disgust*. Cambridge, MA: Harvard University Press, 1997.

Payer, Pierre J. *The Bridling of Desire: Views of Sex in the Later Middle Ages*. Toronto: University of Toronto Press, 1993.

Porter, Roy. *London: A Social History*. London: Hamish Hamilton, 1994.

Schoenbaum, Samuel. "The Precarious Balance of John Marston." *PMLA* 67 (1952): 1069–78.

Seidel, Michael. *Satiric Inheritance: Rabelais to Sterne*. Princeton: Princeton University Press, 1979.

Index